Self-Disclosure

Changes From Within

Liara M. Covert, Ph.D.

Strategic Book Publishing
New York, New York

Strategic Book Publishing
An imprint of AEG Publishing Group
845 Third Avenue, 6th Floor — #6016
New York, NY 10022
www.StrategicBookPublishing.com

ISBN: 978-1-60693-859-1
SKU: 1-60693-859-2

Printed in the United States of America

*"There are two lasting bequests we can give our children.
One is roots. The other is wings."*

—Hodding Carter, Jr.

*"My visions are easily explained away through reason, but
the longer I live, the more limited I believe rationality to be."*

—Charles Lindbergh

Inspired in part by

Lao Tzu
Carlos Castenada
Edgar Cayce
Neale Donald Walsch
The 14th Dalai Lama
Sri Chinmoy
Alan Alda
Florence Scovel-Shin
Mark Victor Hansen
Pema Chodron
Joan Didion
Roy D. Philips
Omar Khayyam
Mother Theresa
Casey Stengel
Jean Vanier
Yoda
Anne Hutchinson
Sai Baba
Barbara Kingsolver
JoelOsteen
Wangari Maathai
Bill Gates
Andrea Dworkin
Erica Jong
Leonardo DaVinci
CS Lewis
Emma Thompson
Helen Keller

Paulo Coelho
Dale Carnegie
Grace Murray Hopper
Isabelle Holland
JK Rowling
Albert Einstein
Dottie Walters
Marianne Williamson
Eliphas Levi
Bhagavad Gita
James Redfield
Jan Denise
M. Scott Peck
Confucius
Pearl S. Buck
Eleanor Roosevelt
Mahatma Gandhi
Audrey Hepburn
John Ciardi
George Bernard Shaw
Kahlil Gibran
Janis Joplin
Henri Frederic Amiel
Katherine Hepburn
Deepak Chopra
Rabindrinath Tagore
Marcel Proust
Nastassja Kinski
Idi Amin Dada

Simone de Beauvoir

Dr. Rhinehold Niebuhr

Thomas Carlyle

Shirley MacLaine

Thomas Szasz

Mary Pickford

Norman Vincent Peale

Tim Burton

Alice Bailey

John Ruskin

Erma Bombeck

Buddha

Maya Anglou

David Letterman

Gail Sheehy

Ralph Waldow Emerson

Princess Diana of Wales

Ayn Rand

Melvana Rumi

Emily Dickinson

Wayne Dyer

Arthur C. Clarke

Basho

Ralph Waldow Emerson

Andrea Bocelli

Marilyn Vos Savant

Vince Lombardi

Daniel Boorstin

Laurel Thatcher Ullrich

Morihei Ueshiba

Jean Houston

Victor Borge

Barbara DeAngelis

James Van Praagh

Ludwig Wittgenstein

Joan of Arc

Douglas A. Adams

Bishop Robert South

Anne Jones

Uta Hagen

Arthur Schopenhauer

Grandma Moses

Ellen J. Langer

John Lennon

Byron Katie

Charles Dickens

Sarah Ban Breathnach

Susan Sontag

Janos Arany

Ross Bishop

Isak Dinesen

Thomas Moore

Reiho Masunaga

Walter Anderson

Carol Gilligan

Benjamin Spock

Helen Schucman

Leo Buscaglia

Helen Rowland

Helen Keller

St Francis de Sales

Ray Bradbury

Nina Berberova

Amy Bloom

Denis Waitley

Jane Roberts

Barbara Anne Brennan

Chin-Ning Chu

Galileo Galilei

Anthony de Mello

Robert Sternberg

Peter Drucker

George Santayana

Abigail Van Buren

Thomas Wolfe

Oscar Wilde

John Allen Paulos

Krishna

Elizabeth Kubler Ross

Esther Hicks

Paramahansa Yoganda

Don Miguel Ruiz

Morris Goodman

Dannion Brinkley

Contents

Introduction

"A good traveler has no fixed plans, and is not intent on arriving."

—Lao Tzu

"Only as a warrior can one withstand the path of knowledge. A warrior cannot complain or regret anything. His life is an endless challenge, and challenges cannot possibly be good or bad. Challenges are simply challenges."

—Carlos Castaneda

A tribal shaman is a healer who inspires high ideals. Traditionally, a tribe respects his advice. He grasps higher forces and universal laws. He discerns energy vibrations and has operational psychic abilities. The shaman may be misunderstood or not recognized by anyone with different degrees of awareness. As he expands his faculties, he interacts with the supernatural. As a medium he is believed to practice magic, demonstrated by his insight into the paths of his people. He offers guidance from his experiences in physical and spiritual worlds. He teaches about awareness of beliefs, feelings, and that the healing process involves personal or subjective recovery.

Modern shamans have diverse origins, but they all aim to guide you to your own creative and healing powers. These spiritual teachers urge you to take responsibility for your feelings and perceptions. As sages, they steer you to align with your intention. As you become more conscious and deliberate, you discover what you can do to cope better with life as you perceive and understand it. You begin to realize psychic development comes as you strengthen intuition. Learn to listen to your higher self. As you slowly dissolve your inner critic, you awaken dormant abilities you have always had. Without insight, you do not rediscover your true nature.

This book chronicles stages of my own expanding states of awareness and spiritual development. It offers perspectives to help you

1

sense differently and redefine your healing. You may ask when and how did this process begin for me, or how could it all begin for you? The reality is it is always unfolding, but you are unaware. You are slowly harnessing energy and insight. Each step will teach how love transforms you.

Choosing to listen more closely to intuition led me to take the romantic risk of my life. I traveled to twenty-five countries in three years, and married a kindred spirit. Through a curious process, this relationship has prompted me to open my senses in ways my prior life experience did not inspire. I consciously expand my spirit and attune to a deeper, healing nature.

Discomfort, anger, and resistance taught me to confront harsh realities within myself. I noticed skills I was initially not ready to accept or apply. As I moved to explore my psychic interests, I evolved to tap into profound inner power, find greater self-love and acceptance, and to sense what I had long disregarded. As I moved to grasp why I exist, I let go of assumptions. I realized if I was to feel I could exert control over my evolution, I would need to take steps to identify external influences, and learn to move beyond what I grew to view as distractions.

Every human being is on a quest for meaning. Throughout this process you are your own healer. You have the ability to rationalize, as well as to avoid and sense truth behind your thoughts and feelings. Each event has meaning beyond your impressions. Rather than presume what you see matters, consider exploring the less obvious. All thoughts you have created, all choices you have made, lead you to view yourself as you do right now. There is much more to you.

What began for me as a physical journey has progressively led me down a path that now enables me to view myself and the world very differently. I realized it is possible to expand my faculties, but I initially questioned the value of doing so. I wanted more than simply collect skills or information—I desired to put new ways of sensing into practical use. To do so, I had to slow down enough to realize I sense energy fields with emerging implications.

This book is for you if you:

1. Seek to discover deeper purpose in all areas of your life.
2. Aspire to better understand ordinary human awareness.
3. Hope to move beyond fearing or fighting what you perceive.
4. Desire to become a more deliberate creator of your experience.

Your thoughts are energy; they manifest physical experiences. You send and attract energy forms. When you are attentive, they teach you the nature of your vibrations. As you become aware of how you react to life situations, you learn about cause and effect. By reading this book, you are choosing to review your life story and to correlate your values, emotions, and experience. Each feeling resonates vibrations. As you learn why you do what you do, you can change you behavior.

FIVE STAGES OF GROWTH

In the next five chapters, I am going to take you through each of the five stages of growth. Each chapter will be dedicated to a stage. Here is a brief summary of what you'll discover in these pages.

Chapter 1: Recognize Why You Do What You Do

The first chapter reveals how I move from superficial awareness of my thoughts and feelings to a deeper understanding of myself. Distant romance led to a major geographical move, accompanied by unexpected work and financial challenges. Within this time I grow to realize I was using certain energy vibrations and frequencies that explained the state of my life. I learn whether emotions affect me or not is based on more than self-discipline. I decide to shift my sense of responsibility. I stop focusing on external influences and choose to listen to myself. Self-reflection allows me to change the quality of my energy. A mysterious guide seems to be my conscience.

Chapter 2: Understand Your Fear

The second chapter examines the basis for my fear of change. I grow to sense how negative feelings toward others evoke discomfort about my own choices. I had deliberately or unknowingly isolated myself from what I have always known. As I attune to how I feel where I am, I realize people I have met reflect how I have felt: lost, scared, confused, exploited, or abandoned by faith in oneself. I explore reasons why I do not permit all my feelings to flow. My revelations unfold more candidly with the guidance of a master.

Chapter 3: Reassess Your Evolution

The third chapter unfolds as I share experiences that have shaped dialogue between my rational and intuitive mind. As I acknowledge psychic events occur and involve me in some way, my attention is directed to the non-physical or soul plane. To experience things for myself redefines my sense of clarity and synchronization. I am guided to review choices made at turning points at different life stages. I recognize growing sensitivities within me. As I begin to discern energy differently, the underlying reasons take form to teach me, yet again.

Chapter 4: Raise Awareness of Perception

The fourth chapter continues to explore my growing insight into a holographic reality. Analogies help me to expand who and what I see. My guide inspires with insights into mind, body, emotions, and spirit. Our ongoing dialogue creates a clearer sense of universal direction and well-being. Each time I choose to broaden my perspective, I discover I am opening channels to help me differentiate energy movement, momentum, and thought patterns. My guide becomes more of a sounding board about my growing understanding of energy flow. I begin to sense connection to different realities. Everyone is invited to explore their senses.

Chapter 5: Attune to the Power of Love

The fifth chapter explores energy as a teacher in relationship interactions. I draw wisdom from my guide, from my experience, and from life stories to examine charged and uncharged energy exchanges in relationships. By exploring a series of relationship lessons, including who seems more or less important when and why, I invite you to identify energy connections to your feelings and behavior. This section outlines consequences of how and why you portray yourself to others, how you secretly think about others and about yourself.

As you identify the qualities and patterns of your relations, you can work to create what is desirable. Learn how love and fear both affect your energy fields.

Writing Exercises

Each chapter opens with lessons; each section ends with exercises for you to work through at your own pace. You are encouraged to journal your replies. The more honest you are, the better equipped you become and are less likely to misinterpret your thoughts and feelings.

A series of three questionnaires is included at the end. These will encourage you to explore deeper motives, values, and qualities of energy. Share how you perceive and/or evolve.

1

Recognize Why You Do What You Do

SEEKING SOLITUDE

> *"The monotony and solitude of a quiet life stimulates the creative mind."*
>
> —Edgar Cayce

> *"It'll become obvious we've really been working against ourselves."*
>
> —Neale Donald Walsch

LESSONS

1. Take responsibility for where you are and how you feel.
2. When you focus on something, you decide that it matters.
3. Find the courage to detach from what you do not need.

Back home, after attending yet another international convention, I discovered new meaning in solitude. I sensed I would not get where I wanted to go by continuing as I had been. I started to detach from my latest career plan. I realized I was both observer and participant in a life unlike what I had wanted, but that I once thought would make sense.

Increasingly, I reflected about the man I had met on a bus. After talking ten minutes en route to my seminar, and trusting positive vibes, I accepted his impulsive dinner invitation. Now, many miles apart, I wrote to him. I sensed mind bridged a deeper awareness, but why?

A highly-desirable process is unfolding. You feel energy. It teaches you truth. You create thoughts, yet underestimate the power within to live more effectively. As you begin to grasp who you have always been, you realize what you are doing, how you are influencing energy vibrating everywhere, and why. Your thoughts are yours.

Thinking back, my logical side was contemplating a long-distance romance with a man on the other side of the world. I questioned what would be fair to whom at 17, 324 kilometers?

The authentic you does not contemplate. As you follow your heart, you do not make assumptions or excuses. You do not simply admire or respect what you desire. You align with it. Impatient for a destination, you harness energy to create one.

You talk in riddles. I know my focus. I devote myself to it to improve my daily life.

"Better or worse" only exists in your mind. What you think you know shapes your perception. Ways of "seeing" are unlimited. You ask for exactly what you value.

Something tells me you would like me to open myself to unfamiliar encounters.

Encounters arise within you. They arise when you are ready to learn from the experiences. As you listen differently, you detect certain things you are ready to hear. Energy is conveying messages. As you choose to feel energy as love, you also sense this subject is becoming clearer. Still, you deny yourself more practical experience.

Admittedly, I was feeling more overwhelmed and disoriented by the second.

You desire this opportunity, but you also fear it is meant for you. Experiences you choose are those you decide matter. You suddenly realize visualizing something is not the same as living it. You always did want to skip steps, to start at the top.

To this point, I realized events had not unfolded for me to live as I had planned. I felt confused about how to take action so that they unfolded as I intended.

Your teacher knows the curriculum. As you found me, let us revert to basics.

What stands out is I constantly alter my sense of stability. Different kinds of study have earned me degrees and transferable skills, yet no permanent work situation. I have no partner. My feelings tell me I am meant for new experiences.

Your core consciousness is shifting. The questions you ask and how you phrase them reveal your level of self-understanding and what you will do next.

I thought I kept my senses alert? I remind myself different kinds of learning exist.

As you imagined a soul mate, you sensed that person was part of you, then with you. You chose to believe. You intend and give life to all your experiences. At this moment, you allow love to expand. This reminds you that you are never alone.

Right! I have read books all about that sort of fantasy. I used to conjure up dreams and write about fairy tales. Then, I stored them away in boxes. More recently, a strong pull urged me to write more of the words that inspire me. I did. I had clearly lost levels of self-control.

When you choose to act in spite of hesitating, you are learning to trust more. Stories you wrote and confined are waiting. Each breathes a life of its own. They are interconnected energy forms, cleansing, repairing and charging your energy field.

I realize words have power. Yet, timing is everything. Bills must be paid, a career forged. After preparing lectures, I emailed Australia and savored feelings arising inside me.

As you move beyond excuses, you apply your core knowledge and experience results. Part of you is quite prepared to believe experience itself is a worthy teacher.

Right! Anyway, a month later, I confirmed a vacation in Greece with my sister. I also planned to stop in Paris to visit my goddaughter. This led to things that caught me off-guard.

You knew what was coming. The universe responds to energy you send out. You experience effects of every one of your thoughts and feelings. Love is powerful.

Why would I hesitate with this example of unknown? I am at ease with uncertainty.

You move beyond simply learning new skills. This is about being willing to change your whole perspective on life. To feel connected to specific people is a step in the process. Your silent question, "why am I here?" prompts you to learn even more about yourself. Whenever you express how you truly feel, you discard what you do not need, and love more freely. You may recall you consented for me to read your mind.

Maybe I welcome your intrusion? I still ask myself why I do not sense what you do.

Impatience. You cannot grasp what is beyond you before you build solid foundations. Your mind has not yet accumulated the necessary experience.

Humbled, I thought back to when, out of the blue, he asked, "How would you like to meet for coffee in Paris?" I must have been sending and receiving some very intense energy!

You never experience anything unrequested.

Although part of me desired what I heard, my logical mind took over. I replied, "That is too far to travel when I am there three days." My ticket was unchangeable. He did not care.

It is all about gratitude. You are grateful to be found. Everything you had shared to that point was a pretext. This includes your letters. The hundreds you wrote and sent reinforced the direction of energy. Mental preparation had all led to this.

Within a short time he received more letters than I had ever written to anyone. I wrote story after story in cards and sealed them, and continued on the next card, working backwards. It was a puzzle. He mentioned my record was nine cards inside cards. I did not expect my communication would be so noticeable, even though I only had his office address.

As you choose to love and accept yourself more fully, you have more energy available to love others. Good feelings cultivate patience and understanding. Those envelopes you sent echo passion of soul. You realized something worth listening to.

I am not a drawer full of cards.

Before you really know what you are, you must realize what you are not.

Opportunities to learn through experience often evoke anticipation and fear. Separated partners create reasons to be cautious. Yet, they do not choose to take each other for granted.

You instinctively move further, yet make physical situations harder than they are. You are on a path to master yourself, to feel deeper joy. The moment will come when you understand a new spiritual phase is unfolding inside you.

As my mind pictured something I was not willing to risk creating, I dissuaded him from the trip. I was flattered, but it would have been too impulsive a move, even for me.

A self-delusion—you could not help yourself. The greater the risk, the greater the potential reward. Your newfound courage was causing you to ask, "what if?" As you let go of fear, you detached from the urge to lie to yourself and created a vision.

So you were not surprised that I received that peculiar phone call a few days later.

You know very well the universe responds to each request. What matters is you chose to connect with your feelings. Each thought came from the heart. You can never change or accept what you do not acknowledge. Everything you experience now results from your past choices. Your perceived future grows from present thoughts.

The airline booking glitch automatically cancelled my whole itinerary. I thought the timing was phenomenal, but I did not initially assume divine intervention.

When you do not take pleasure in what you do where you are, the universe is telling you this is not the place for you. As you act based on enthusiasm, you expand. You stop what is not working, change what does not serve you. This shifts your energy.

On impulse, I told the agent who phoned about the glitch about taking a train trip. She rebooked my return flight seven days later than my original ticket. Then, adventures really began.

You are not so naïve. That meant things were going according to plan. Living in a world of infinite possibility, you were beginning to realize the power you exert over your life. Your sense of elation was expanding beyond what you consciously accepted. You aligned energy to manifest what you desired most—new forms of love.

My instinct was to send him an e-mail. His immediate reply was, "Italy?"

I answered, "Need you ask?"

My ten day trip in Greece evolved to two days with my goddaughter in Paris, then a seven day train trip through France, Switzerland, and Italy. It was a memorable third date.

Not all of you is aware of or agrees with what the loving side of you chooses.

As it was, a girlfriend voiced concern. She suggested he may be an ax murderer. I thought gossip might ensue and said, "If it turns out to be true, I would jump off the train."

You only truly rise above gossip by deciding it does not matter.

My self-doubt did not last. I chose to believe I would not do this if I was not ready.

When you consistently align thought and feelings, you change your vibrational space.

To block incoming negative energy, I kept mainly to myself to savor the excitement. Part of me was also unsure where this thing was going or, even where I wanted it to go…

You always know where and why. Innocence guides you. You did not think you could be loved unconditionally unless you unlocked yourself to receive everything. Part of you yearned to separate from a false sense of security. To do so, you had to step outside what you knew, create perspective. You proved you are not afraid to love.

Even on the plane return from Europe, I met Australians—connections were emerging.

You discern the intensity of love energy. This enables you to play a more conscious role in the evolution of your life. Love blossoms everywhere all the time, but everyone does not choose to harness it. This uplifting feeling is teaching you to expand. If you do not know questions to ask, then you are unprepared for answers.

I hear you, and yet my mind is focused on something else. I left my new man friend in Paris to spend his last three days alone while I attended a wedding in Canada. Among two hundred guests, I was drawn to two women discussing the appeal of Australian hospitality. A Canadian was speaking about her sense of low respect and low pay in her hospitality field.

While on an energetic high, you identified sources of love that attracted you. This was teaching you to shift mental focus from what was not working in your life. Where revelations occur is irrelevant. When something is explained to you properly, you grasp it. Some experience requires no explanation. You accept inner knowing.

Turned out the woman who spoke of Australia and her husband were assigned to my dinner table. The couple had met in South Africa, yet married and had a son in Melbourne.

Coincidence does not exist. Whatever you think manifests in real experience.

The people I shared this with who also knew about my budding romance did not recognize connections in the kind of people I kept meeting. I was on another wavelength.

Synchrony is deep process that merges time and space. Each human is energy vibrating. You rarely anticipate how you will evolve. Yet, you do it to yourself.

Responsibility was distracting me; a post-doctoral fellowship contest was underway.

Romantic secrecy made your life seem more exciting to others, but you are continuing, even now, to decipher secrets hidden inside yourself. My reason for being is not to solve your problems, but to expand your understanding. You choose to reframe situations. You know where you are heading. You create your life.

As our romance unfolded, I turned on the Canadian radio to reports on poisonous spider clubs in Australia. The Discovery Channel showed Aussie documentaries. National Geographic was broadcasting about the Great Barrier Reef. I even stumbled on and read a book called, To Hell or Melbourne. It is about a historic ship built in my birth city of Saint John, New Brunswick, Canada. This vessel had carried its crew to a life-changing destiny.

As I lectured at the university, I awaited a verdict on a contract. What did I want?

The best way to get straight answers is to ask more direct questions. You create events that constantly evolve based on awareness. You devise your choices to test loyalty to your gut. Soul favors the choices that reinforce love inside your heart.

I felt unable to clarify destiny. Part of me believed I was beating my head against a wall.

You are never unable to do anything, only unwilling. That is fear. When conditions do not appease ego, this has been arranged. You get confused about lack of results and miss the point of the exercise. You have nothing new to learn. It is a question of learning to apply yourself differently, to view all results as what you need.

As I see it now, I felt torn between love and career. I was not realizing ambition from study or work. Part of me sensed I had to reorient, to explore opportunities for fulfillment.

Everything you learn, disregard, or change within yourself is your own choice. Part of the process is living with and adjusting to consequences. I offer views when asked, yet do not interfere. You are in process of developing strength and expanding. As you are guided to learn, it would be a setback if I relieved you of the responsibility.

Researching opportunities abroad made sense. I believed that would bring me legitimacy.

Anything you do is legitimate. Not succeeding is useful. You rarely want what you think. You were doing things you did not wish to do and getting results you did not desire. Lately, you realize you attract conditions, resist change, and favor drama.

Oh, really? I surprised myself with Australia. Certainly, people wondered about my job choice and decision to move so far. They were not convinced the new business roles would satisfy me. I had lectured, been a policy analyst, a consultant and held other positions.

The nature of your choices never matters. How you feel does. People judge you based on how they view themselves, on what they fear or accept, not on who you are. It is not approval or disapproval that matters, but how you think after sensing it.

All this reminds you that you filter energy vibrations. You absorb or exude by choice.

Initially, when I moved Down Under, I chose to travel with my partner, to help him with his work and to write. Yet, I was restless and decided to set up job interviews for myself.

The meaning of your restlessness surpassed what you consciously understood. You told yourself to learn the value of calming down, to just be, but you resisted that.

At that stage, I had no job related to my developed expertise. Based on my conditioning at that stage, I felt unfulfilled.

Rejection is a wise teacher. You mistakenly assumed you were unworthy. To realize you are not meant for certain jobs shifts your attention to other things. Your authentic self got you this far. You opened doors you were not initially ready to enter. You are in the process of learning to fully understand what it is you intend to do.

Part of what you say makes sense to me, but I hesitate to believe everything I feel.

The refusal to accept your true self leads you to the "why." That is the point.

Since you seem to know so much, from your vantage point, what is it that I want?

You want what you already have. I guide you back to where you belong. You are eager to produce results in life, and you feel certain choices will better you, but you overlook the why. Absorbing knowledge is not the same as knowing how to modify what you learn or knowing how to adapt or apply it. That comes in practice.

Love unfolds as I attune to it. After two months in Australia, my partner surprised me with a ten day trip to Bali, Indonesia. It was my first trip there. I sensed a very spiritual place.

Exploring love shows you second-hand insight is no substitute for personal experience. Part of you mistakenly assumes you are to experience what people say to expect. The spiritual side is in control of who you are. It senses your growing awareness.

After three months of researching job options, I was impatient to justify returning to Australia after visiting my family over holidays. In my mind, a relationship was not enough.

At a given moment, where you are and how you feel are always sufficient.

At that stage for me, love was of secondary importance to independence.

Conditioning. You feared love as reason to move—it was, but you resisted. Many people build a façade to fulfill external rather than soul-level requirements.

When a work visa came through, this signaled to me to go the next step to explore my growing insight into love. I wanted both, not love at the expense of the self-sufficiency.

All fear is illusion. True love is a frequency. It is not sexual, romantic, or passionate. It is light energy. To misunderstand your core motivation brings challenges.

Imagine how I felt arriving in a distant country, work visa granted by a company that agreed to sponsor me for four years at a set salary. My partner was a director. Yet soon after arrival, the co-director (who agreed to sponsor me in December) told us the tax department had clamped down on company accounts and credit cards because he had not paid back taxes.

You will not raise your own energy vibration if you view yourself as a victim.

I told myself this was not happening. Yet I would make the best of a difficult situation.

For all intents and purposes, this was a new kind of wake-up call. The significance is absorbed gradually, as part of your inner developmental process.

I wondered why key documents had been supposedly sent to my partner's old address. Certain things did not jive. Yet, a tax re-payment plan had been set up, and a part-time book keeper worked, so I agreed to postpone being paid till later that year, rather than lose my visa.

If work was your motive, then you would not have stayed without being paid. You consciously believed you were abroad for work while financial conditions revealed the truth. You loved and felt loved. That drew much needed attention to soul.

Admittedly, being paid very little forced me to face my pride and sense of entitlement.

As you begin to acknowledge your true motivation, you begin to widen your perspective. You also learn non-physical thoughts have noticeable physical effects.

My partner experienced his own setbacks. Shared hardship brought us closer together. We made do with less. I chose to reframe discomfort, to ask why I attracted that to me.

Why does any human being attract hardship? You attract conditions that evoke opposite feelings to those you desire. This is required to attract what you want. As you detach and disregard feelings you do not want, you realize what you do.

My conscious reasoning was changing. I felt ready to accept new challenges in exchange for ability to balance my life.

You have always had the ability. What you require is the will or, a shift in mindset. As you outgrow your beliefs, you are shifting to align with different energy.

Circumstances force me to reassess my choices.

Nobody, other than yourself, ever imposes or forces anything on you.

That is humbling. Well, I benefited from observing office staff and management. People did not share my sense of accountability. I raised issues, but was repeatedly ignored.

Human beings are unaware of what they do. In the absence of awareness, they do not ascertain effects of conditioning. To judge anyone reveals you reject parts of yourself. You constantly draw attention to what you have not been able to see in you.

I noted my work ethic was incompatible with that office. I recognized it as transition.

Some people convince themselves they must work one job in order to afford to focus energy on what they really desire to do. Other people believe when they listen to their hearts and focus on what they love, they will attract the means to continue. You sense the truth behind why you act or do not act. You learn some choices are self-destructive while others will favor uplifting energy and continuous inspiration.

During this turbulent office period, I read hundreds of books. They encouraged me.

No matter what books you study, they do not provide the practical experience required to stretch you. You are invited to recognize the answer when it is given.

So I do not know what I am doing, but I do have the best of intentions? That figures!

A vision of completeness sets your mind in motion. Your combined thoughts and feelings manifest this reality or chip away at it. When you explore reasons for fear or pain, this influences healing. It is not about one area of your life, but all of it.

Well, even with my positive thinking, office energy stagnated. My partner and I entered into side ventures that boosted our morale. We listened to motivational CDs and reframed our conditions. Nevertheless, we were unable to influence habits or beliefs of office peers.

You do not change people. You are only able to change how you view them.

I recall a passing remark made by the co-director's mom during an office visit. Not knowing we had not really been paid, she noted my partner and I were too scrawny and I should learn to cook. She was unaware her son had bullied and threatened to deport me.

Life is a jigsaw puzzle. Every piece offers you a facet of truth you do not see. As you transcend your emotion, you hear soul speak in silence.

By September, when my partner's co-director initiated questions about a buy-out deal, this seemed a welcome option. Yet, by October when consulting a good lawyer, we discovered the business partner was unqualified to offer us the tax liability. He also assumed that for a minimal sum, my partner would shift from role as co-director to contracted "on-call" employee. As my partner's software built efficiency in the company, and he wrote it during his own time when he was not paid, the buy-out conditions seemed inappropriate.

Suspicion of foul-play distracts you from what you ignore about yourself. This situation emerged to prompt you to review your beliefs about love and commitment. You still believe pleasure is earned. You are meant to bless injustice with love.

I think I see where you are going with this, but the curve balls! When do they end?

Everything is a blessing. You must realize this to rediscover your true path.

When the business co-director suddenly denied any knowledge of my work visa, he tried to shift liability for my unpaid salary as debt to my partner. Both directors faced a government fine if treatment of my visa situation was deemed unacceptable. By this point, I held a replacement visa. Yet, each time I felt I had overcome an obstacle, another presented.

At any given moment, grief reflects a sense of loss that is misplaced. What seems to matter does not. Reactions reveal your esteem and self-worth. To grasp unconditional love is to learn not to condemn. You choose to send love instead.

You imply that my focus on hardship means other invisible things bother me.

The loss of salary was less important than how your love was threatened by the prospect of being deported. You learn to detach from what you do not control. You were learning to shift conscious focus from the physical world to your inner self.

Solitude gives me far too much time to think. It does not always help me step back. Yet, crossword puzzles and mental exercises like meditation strengthen my mindfulness.

Your focus is shifting away from physical conditions. Events encourage you to receive and transmit energy differently, to accept everything as it is.

I am not sure about that. When I was revising my view of stability, I met a man at a public meeting. This retired technician was studying for a psychology degree. He had cleaned hospitals and held other jobs in the United Kingdom before he met his would-be wife on an over-land bus trip from London to Nepal and Egypt. He later became a forensic lab tech in Australia, worked in a lab in Libya, then bought into a lab business in Australia, which he later sold. His story reminded me each person creates the life that makes sense to him.

Choices are not right or wrong. Good feelings tell you what works for you.

Why does this seem to echo, "You already know this?"

I echo what you believe when your energies are aligned. You have different levels of awareness. When part of you wants distractions, you create them.

How many levels of awareness do I have and how many distractions? That evasive purpose drives me nuts! I accept I am not doing "something." But, how do I get there?

You decide what is meaningful for different parts of you and when. You adopt lessons based on unfulfilled needs you discern. You seek confirmation that not giving up on yourself is right, but you already know soul exists. Your choices reveal that.

Unwavering faith still eludes me. I was taught "purpose" is an enduring sensation. Some people express an overwhelming sense of connection to one thing. I never have.

Only you ever question your own commitment. Doubt distracts you.

I do know the meaning of commitment. Knowing when to turn that off is the issue.

Parts of you still ask how long discomfort will last before you adopt another person's view of stability. Self-acceptance is a state of mind you can create anywhere.

Part of me sensed it was not the answer to give up on myself or my partner.

Challenges stretch you. You are meant to accept everything you do not like. Nonetheless, you resist believing that even your own senses deceive you.

People were after him for debts he never knew about due to his co-director. Part of me asked why "I hung in there." I just felt it was the right thing to do.

If you are willing to identify reasons for discomfort, then you alleviate them. You are always where you are to expand. Nobody can teach you to tell the difference between what feels good and what does not. This comes through living and learning.

When I would run or walk alone, I started to think and listen to myself differently. Perhaps I was quietly preparing for unforeseen hardship? I wondered if I deserved this.

Punishment is never warranted. Creative energy uplifts destructive thoughts. You begin to see the world as it as you you sense your own misunderstandings. As you realize you mistake the nature of others, you realize you have also mistaken your own nature and motivations.

My options seemed limited.

You avoid what you fear until you explore the basis for beliefs. By taking steps to raise your awareness, you attune to parts of self you were not ready to see.

In declining the buy-out offer, my partner scrutinized financials and opened his eyes. His co-director had revoked responsibilities from the bookkeeper and took tasks on himself.

You only acknowledge what you are ready to accept about your imperfections.

That co-director secretly opened bank accounts. He had done this before until they were discovered and closed by a previous book-keeper who later resigned. This co-director was mixing accounts and hiding money where my partner had no access. Review of sales from embedded software tracked money based on select client orders. This did not track missing cash, but did find a big discrepancy. Four hundred thousand dollars emerged, which the co-director "had stored." He refused to provide bank transactions, records of his and his wife's personal credit cards. To avoid providing key data, the co-director declared the company insolvent. He still withheld the books.

As you unravel this mystery of indiscretions, you also unravel your own. You have been overlooking other signs in all this. Dishonesty takes many forms. Each feeling you sense around you draws your attention to vibrations within you.

Although details had been requested from the accountant and co-director by lawyers and my partner directly, the accountant stalled, blaming the co-director for missing details. Inaccurate financials led to the accountant being reported for misconduct. Nothing came of that. Rather than provide data, the co-director declared the company insolvent based on existing payment arrangements. This enabled him to continue withholding the books and not pay me.

Discomfort serves you. The energy of your living and working space affects your energy field. You create and enter spaces to gain wisdom. You shift away from spaces as you grow to recognize they represent parts of you that need attention. Discomfort serves you.

Well, my intuition told me that former space did not permit me to express who I am.

Through lawyers my partner and his co-director continued negotiating. Key figures were still missing. Next, the co-director cut off my partner's company gas card, other cards, and mobile phone, and reported his freeway toll pass stolen. He also changed office locks, incurred new company debts without discussion, and stopped paying office rent when the guarantor was my partner. The rent company then came after us for unpaid backdated rent.

Suffering ceases to bother you when you find blessings in it. You create experiences to raise awareness about yourself, your perception, and ignorance.

If my awareness was not expanding as it is, I might lose my mind over this.

From the moment you changed your attitude about what you thought was a tense situation, you realized you were in control of how you reacted. You became grateful for everything. Do not discount things or assume they are unimportant.

How do you know me so well?

Every human being has ability to become more than he or she feels s/he is.

I refused to accept I would not get paid for work I had done. It seemed like a sham. Urgency led my partner to withdraw eight thousand from a company account for holiday pay and backdated company expenses for which he had not been reimbursed. Although only paid a small sum that year, his co-director sent a legal letter to "stop stealing" and cut off my partner's bank access. This co-director continued flying lessons, yet no authority would act.

The more a situation seems to spiral out of control, the more you benefit from telling yourself you do not need to trust others as much as relearn to trust yourself.

I remind myself how Mother Theresa said, "God would never put me in a situation he didn't think I could handle…sometimes I just wish he didn't trust me so much!"

No person knows you as well as you know yourself. You endure discomfort for your own reasons; part stays loyal to hidden truth inside until you evolve to accept it.

I do not know why you reawaken the past. I felt I was over this.

What you really mean is you are not yet willing to accept what I represent. You always get what you need. I actually awaken your dormant, creative process.

A revised buy-out deal came, including offer to pay my 2006 salary within two years. I refused. The co-director had spent more than the amount owed in the previous three months.

Reality is what each being believes and perceives it to be. You resist letting go of anger and forgiving. Emotions distract you from why you made particular choices.

Realizing the company had not paid my salary, taxes or superannuation, I decided I had no choice but to sue the company in The Magistrate's Court. This was an effort to regain self-respect and prevent myself from being made liable for additional financial issues later.

Some people only begin to listen to their inner voice as they detach from outer influence. You felt helpless not because of having little control over unfolding external conditions, but because all your soul really wanted was to shift mindset and life focus.

Recent circumstances prompt me to rethink the idea of "slow learner."

You learn at your pace. Solutions always appear as you create problems. Positive exists when you perceive the negative. Rejection is struggle for self-esteem.

As if I would just drop the case and ignore this exploitation. I had to set limits.

Discomfort about anything signals you do not like how you treat your true self.

This co-director's lawyer saw a solvency expert and billed it as a company expense.

When you focus on what you do not control, you avoid what you really want.

This specialist generated a solvency report, based on inaccurate financials my partner had not seen, yet had been requested through his lawyer for over six months. That was an attempt to avoid all creditors, and to escape investigation into questionable transactions and debts.

Notice how talk of negativity spirals. You can contribute to this, choose to feel alienated, or find new meaning in the energy vibration. Every event teaches you why you do or do not trust yourself. You attract situations to reorient your focus within.

My initial thought is I must miss the point entirely. The situation refuses to disappear.

Experience enables you to evolve. What you dream is real. Every feeling you generate is a step to making more fulfilling choices. They are always available to you.

Imagine as you work for free, assuming your partner's company is near bankruptcy, you learn your partner's business partner engages in questionable dealings for which both directors are liable. Imagine you discover your salary was "reallocated" to your partner's co-director and his wife, whose salary had been secretly increased 33% going back two years.

As you move from blaming to self-judgment, you feel emotions under that.

I was told to believe I would be paid at a later date that never came. When I began to doubt, my assertiveness was ineffective. At some point I realized part of me had to grow up.

Human beings feel what it means to lose everything before they truly gain everything. Each moment is a chance to love the self fully and let all feelings flow.

I must have a ways to go, or this dialogue would be pointless. Granted, I become more aware of what I am not. Seems I confront different energy levels in dishonest choices.

People lie so long without consequences, they become blind to harm it does inside themselves. Discern how perception and ego personality cloud judgment. It is not just other people's either. Each person imagines and lies in their separate reality.

Okay, so it is vital to say what we mean and mean what we say.

Getting too wrapped up in the powers of the mind does not serve you. To detach from events enables you to refocus on what they reveal about yourself. As you let go of desire to control out-comes, you rediscover energy and what to do with it.

Speaking of energy, I recall when an office co-worker accused me of discrimination behind my back. My boss threatened to fire me and deport me. It was more negative energy.

Every perceived scenario adds enormous value and richness to your life.

Anyway, I referred to employment law and asked my boss to provide me with detail. The incident was not proven, and was later disregarded. I learned people choose to deny or ignore reasons for negative energy. This brought my attention to fear and accountability.

Negative energy hijacks your true focus. To acknowledge negativity in passing can be useful. If it becomes a habit, then it is not cathartic. To be aware of negative energy can be part of a positive intent to heal, to recreate balance, and shift energy.

You have a point, there. I am listening.

As you feel drawn to certain people or activities, your feelings about them offer clues to something you are ready to visualize and release. What you want is mirrored by the fear you sense and desire to avoid. It is how energy communicates.

Then, the evasive truth reveals itself in sensations, in what I do and what I do not do.

You foresee things that may happen, compare them to what you would like to see happen, to what you sense is destiny. As you develop courage and self-confidence, you learn to see through conditions. You must remove all labels you have adopted.

Unemployed does not mean "useless." I grow to ignore such mistaken assumptions.

You are learning to read yourself and your core energies more consciously. Compassion and understanding heal you and send healing vibrations to others.

When I am alone I reflect on what I have done and what I would choose to do differently next time. I learn to become more aware of my choices and to realize they have implications. I sense clearer how I was, but not who I am right at this moment—or will be.

Each decision brings you that much closer to remembering who you are.

I tell myself to reframe the discovery—a co-director did not pay his business partner's retirement savings, but rather, chose to overpay his own. This is a test of forgiveness.

Human beings evolve based on views of "good" and "bad." What someone did or did not do does not control your thought-process, your feelings, or perspective. Human beings often make excuses for their behavior. Yet, each person is responsible for his own action or inaction and the consequences. To accept everything about yourself means you accept your degree of responsibility in all situations.

I recognize I am clearing and healing emotional baggage. Certain people say life is not meant to be easy. At the same time, I believe the fundamental motivation is love or joy.

You are always "somewhere." Even nowhere is meaningful. Knowing what something is not is a step closer to mastering it. In solitude, you rediscover inner power. You clarify meaning in all reactions. You slow down, and focus on present.

What about the time constraints imposed from outside myself?

Time and constraints are limits you impose. As you evolve to enjoy all that happens in all seasons, you sense every experience is not meant to seem like a renewal of who you were. You take initiatives as a way to attune to energy in feelings.

Come on! I do not see change as a problem to endure so I finally begin to enjoy life.

Each experience invites you to identify your self-judgments and their effects.

In the midst of office turmoil, the owner of a house my partner and I rented suddenly opted to sell. We were asked to vacate. I sorted through what we had and gave away what we no longer needed. This reminded me that when a door closes, the consequential new experiences are right for me. That is a lesson.

Human beings can use solitude as a tool to shift their thought process. You sense positive meaning in situations that themselves are tests of your abilities.

My recent experiences have enabled me to grasp better how thoughts and feelings influence each other. I find I more readily shift focus away from reason for negative feelings.

To sense meaning in what happens is one thing. To detach fully is another.

Admittedly, my self-awareness is changing. I believe I attract people with parallel energy into my life. The awkward office experience taught me it is essential to draw the line somewhere. I was dwelling on my emotional reactions, not the underlying reasons for them.

Before guides empower you, you must be willing to help yourself. Scenarios may unfold several times with different people and places until you understand why.

With each personal drama, I begin to see stress is not necessary. This wastes my time.

Effort is never wasted. Recognize each situation is a teacher. You learn when intervention is appropriate and when it serves no meaningful purpose. You generate and release energy to find balance. Your view of this world is your experience.

What I mean is some choices do not raise my awareness as high as others could.

This is not a race. You do not skip levels of awareness. As you gain a deeper sense of what it means to be on the level you are right now, your consciousness shifts. Without that, you have no sense of movement in a timeless, immeasurable place.

Well, recent events teach me gratitude as I take responsibility for my negative energy. Unreasonable people actually help me. I sense them as teachers who unconsciously interrupt their own periods of growth to help me. That is a generous side of them I overlooked.

Life is a full-time awareness and experience process. To live what you learn requires that you also commit yourself to follow though and apply what you know. This means you choose to listen to all of you, learn to read your physical body's signs.

But wait! Just when I think I get the gist of some situations, my perspective changes. It disorients me and causes me to lose faith in my perception. What if I miss the point?

Your inner self is always a worthy guide. Your discernment becomes more accurate as it expands with each experience. As you let go of negative energy, you transcend it. Heightened beings are unaffected by fear or anger—they only see love.

That is a tall order. You imply emotions prevent me from knowing myself. Each job and role teaches me new things, granted, but I do not feel like a stranger to my own soul.

Human beings redefine motivation in everything. As you grow you sense when what you do appeases your authentic self, rebels against, or chooses to ignore it.

I sense whatever is happening will be deep, meaningful and life-transforming.

To evolve is to realize everything happens now. Nothing "will." It just is.

That has to be why the mystery is so cryptic. It is like a novel you cannot put down.

Nothing about your life is cryptic to your true self. You conscious side simply decides when to work through certain fears that obscure your core understanding.

At different stages of my life, I may lean truth of where I am at that moment, but what about confirmation? Recent life events teach me I do not know myself as well as I thought.

To be happy, reflects you have learned what you need at a given moment. If you do not sustain consistent, positive energy, then you re-awaken in meditation.

Solitude: End of Section Exercises

1. Which lessons do you retain from this section? How may you apply them in your life?
   - In your relationships?
   - In your work?
   - In your spiritual pursuits?
   - In other ways?

2. Describe memorable risks you have taken. What kinds of risks do you avoid? Why?

3. What do you believe would enable you to feel more content?

4. Describe some of your dreams.

5. What prevents you from achieving these dreams?

6. If you could do anything, what would it be?

7. Describe a spiritual experience you have had or would like to have. Why?

8. When was the last time you took time out for yourself? What did you do and where? How did it affect how you feel about different areas of your life?

9. What would you like to do the next time you are alone? How will it help you?

10. List the five things that evoke good feelings and five things that bother you. What do you recognize among things that boost energy and/or drain you?

11. Write down benefits of each of the five things that bother you.

MEDITATION

> *"Sleep is the best meditation."*
>
> —The 14th Dalai Lama

> *"If we know the divine art of concentration, if we know the divine art of meditation, if we know the divine art of contemplation, easily and consciously we can unite the inner world and the outer world."*
>
> —Sri Chinmoy

My heart tells me I need to be more aware and attune more to things happening around me. As I shift my energy focus, what I viewed as problems before no longer exist.

Perceived hardships encourage you to attune to how life runs its course. What you choose to sense in a given situation is for you alone. You can evolve beyond that to discern how perception of suffering is not what you assume. It is part of your process to discover nothing is meant to trouble you.

I admit I do not always sleep soundly when areas of my life are in turmoil. I change my focus, but ideas keep the wheels in my head spinning. My mind is busy; it resists idleness.

At every moment, your journey to heightened inner peace evolves. You learn value in introspection. You identify what inspires you. Revelations are triggered, not sought. You begin to discover everything about life is a kind of trance or meditation.

Part of me realizes I am always learning about energy flow. I shut discomfort out of my conscious mind by using mental training. And yet permitting any reaction reveals I falter.

Precisely! You function on levels you have yet to discover or understand. As you learn to empty your mind and focus on the present, you confront what limits you. Meditation develops calmness. You discern that emotion interferes with core nature.

I took steps to move beyond my old mindset. After ten months and almost no wages, I stopped going to the office. The co-director did not write anything to state I no longer worked there. Although he signed my tax forms and knew I worked, it was like I dreamt it all.

You did dream it. Not that it matters so much as what you retain as a result.

When a person seeks closure, that person aims to forget an experience. Meditation is one approach that helps empty the mind of undesirable emotions. Yet how to dispel anger?

Truth cannot be attacked. As you meditate, the urge to attack dissipates. Do not just believe what others tell you. Discover the truth through mental discipline.

Gracious! Could it be possible to fear one's own energy and extent of creative force?

As you practice meditation, your thoughts flow more clearly and deter your mind from destructive thinking. Perception of time is a human invention. This is the fourth dimension, alongside height, width, and depth. The first three reinforce your sense of connection to harmony in the physical world. Meditation helps you link dimensions.

While my former office situation was up in the air, I went to Sydney to volunteer for a cause. During the travel, I met a young man who described how he was building confidence as a musician and performer. He nurtured his creativity. For him, composing music is a love meditation. As he brainstorms lyrics and melodies, he listens attentively to his reactions and instincts, and notices more about his principles. He admits he is inspired by sidewalk artists. They taught him to block out everything, focus only on sources of creativity that inspire him.

At this point, you view purpose as if you were a movie spectator. You are partly engaged, but you are an outsider in the life you lead. You are struggling by choice.

I do not feel like that musician, but I sense growing energy in my creative process.

Meditation takes different forms. It enables you to immerse yourself in things and stop creating emotional distance from your truth. You become more attuned to new levels of experience. You evolve to stop withholding or hiding from who you are.

Who says I withhold anything?

You have been catching errors in your own thinking. My meditation experience develops increasing depth.

Well, my meditation develops depth. I am drawn to jungles, rainforests and mountains. I reflect on being above clouds at observatories in Chili, Brazil, Greece, and Kazakhstan. As I feel light-headed, it is more than altitude. I float away from old thinking.

You rationalize when things are not working and you justify your old patterns.

I am drawn to spiritual places. They profoundly affect me, as if to open my soul and whisper secrets. I get in touch with energy vibration in nature. I grow to value wherever I am.

Certain events stun you briefly as part of spiritual development. It is only through confronting ego that you arrive consciously where you have always been.

Maybe I should not oversimplify, but for me meditation is like riding a bike.

Whatever you think you already know, this is only the beginning.

Pieces of what I need to recall come back to me when my focus is in the right place.

Meditation may be one of the most vital rediscoveries in your quest to regain or unleash parts of yourself that you had "put away."

Put away? Now you have stumped me. I thought I was becoming an open book?

The more you expose parts of yourself within your own mind, the more you realize you have nothing to fear by sharing your core sense of your truth with people. Human beings relate to trials on some level even if their own differ from yours. Reasons why you evoke your emotions are personal, but experience itself is universal.

From what I gather, people exist in part to learn what it means to live through trials. Mediation is a means to separate yourself from emotions you generate to postpone healing. I think of so many occasions where I permitted emotion to guide me. I permitted it to be my logic, my reason to rationalize, my truth. And yet, something about that is not right.

Your "inner mechanism" to create functions without fail. How you use it changes based on your chosen focus. Emotion does not always serve you. Yet, everything you think and feel reverberates into the universe as energy and bounces back. Your life unfolds not only directly, but also indirectly from your thoughts.

I suppose you are urging me to rethink where I apply patience and discipline?

Where you choose to take action is less important than choosing to do so.

Something tells me what you are saying to me in all this is being heard elsewhere simultaneously. I initially thought you were my conscience. I fooled myself yet again!

Life is a meditation. You choose which images or thoughts enter your mind. You choose what voices you hear, which energy levels you deny, emit, or penetrate.

You know, there was a time when I assumed that meditation was a practice restricted to practitioners of certain religions. I explored some religions to sense what they were like.

Your life has been built on a foundation of misunderstandings. It requires a change of heart and courage to turn inward and shatter your own myths.

When I proceed to enter meditation, I enter a silent period. I do not time this or exert effort to define it. I sense nothing. How do I know whether I pass through it to a new level?

Detail more of your observations. Learn to read your senses.

I slowly move away from scattered thoughts and voices to where I sense things of significance in the nothingness. I sense valuable things are achieved. They defy description.

Meditation: End of Section Exercises:

1. Which lessons do you retain from this section? How would you apply them?
   - In your relationships?
   - In your work?
   - In your spiritual (or religious) pursuits?
   - In other ways?
2. What subjects or activities focus your mind on peaceful feelings?
3. Describe a creative activity you have tried or plan to explore. Why?

4. List some examples of how you judge yourself and external influences.

5. Have you ever engaged in meditation? Why/ why not?

6. How might meditation help you in different areas of your life? Take initiatives to investigate approaches that would suit you or not. Brainstorm your thoughts.

7. How does your current awareness of emotions and behaviors orient your purpose?

8. If you block out what is around you, or separate from your general awareness, how would you "just be" without sensing, thinking, or feeling?

9. Describe a quiet place where you could rest alone and reflect on your life purpose. Include details that would use all your senses (smell, taste, touch, sight, sounds).

10. As you reflect, what kinds of environments seem to influence your choices?

11. How do you view coincidence? What have you learn from it in your life?

DEVELOPING INTUITION

> *"You have to leave the city of your comfort and go into the wilderness of your intuition. What you'll discover will be wonderful. What you'll discover is yourself."*
>
> —Alan Alda

> *"Intuition is a spiritual faculty and does not explain, but simply points the way."*
>
> —Florence Scovel Shinn

Each time I emerge from solitude, I reframe the idea of 'risk.' I am more apt to follow intuition and imagine things other than what I think I have known. At times, I sense that I develop courage without exerting effort. I build confidence and gain insight into faith. At earlier stages of life, I let myself feel intimidated. That shaped my self-image and job choices.

Holding a series of positions is not meant to show you the world will evolve to suit you, or that you must struggle to evolve so as to suit the world. Rather, each experience you choose is meant to help you better understand which choices work or do not work for you. As you sharpen your intuition you empower yourself, but...

But what?

To move beyond who you are not, you have to be willing to dissolve all your negative energy; thoughts of revenge, anger, ill-will, and discontent. They undermine your true self and also keep you where you are. All situations arise as stepping stones.

Oh, I get it. Just turn energy off, like a tap. That seems rather overly-simplistic.

Life is as hard or as easy as you choose.

Giving me that degree of freedom is an opportunity to reinjure myself. I have known people to fall out of unfulfilling relationships or situations and attribute blame. I have known yo-yo dieters who scorn ineffective diets. I have known addicts who gave up a habit, but caved in and lashed out at rehab programs. Rigid views appear to be the underlying problem.

When you compare yourself to others, you relentlessly judge, but do not see.

As a non-conformist, I resist categories. My life is as it is because of resistance.

Your behavior reveals you still seek outside yourself for answers. Intuition only truly starts to evolve as you become accountable for your thoughts and beliefs.

The nature of this dialogue is causing me to question whether I know "the truth." I have been sharing facts as I see them—a sense of injustice, ignorance, and comedy of errors.

You explain as an effort to master what you have taught yourself, to feel less threatened. Reality still escapes you. As you begin to build your current perspective, the truth of this moment becomes easier to clarify. To detach from your own emotion shows you that you do not have to be controlled by it. At your pace, you shift energy and begin to recognize an expansive world lies within you and beyond your senses.

I assure you that I do not consciously create routines, feel unfocused, or disconnected from the physical world. I may falter briefly when I seek a meaningful direction, but that does not last. My intuition tells me conflict does not last either.

Conflict does not exist. You invent it. To what end, is also up to you

I do not dwell on past lessons.

Really?

Part of me believes I am beyond it. To reassure myself, I meditate on gratitude.

Refocus. Listen to your senses. You review your life to become more aware of the real reasons behind your thoughts and behavior. You remove layers of illusion.

Certainly I empathize with pain and discomfort experienced by others. In that regard, I have learned the value of the transference of negative feelings in order to sort through them.

Higher laws tell us every human has to accept and manage results of actions. Every move you make or do not make directly affects your personal energy vibration. As you sharpen intuition you begin to grasp principles that explain forces at work.

Western society conditions people to listen to elders, study hard, land a well-paying job, get financially independent, and commit to a mortgage and life of debt. If you resist this image, well, you hit obstacles. In order to apply for credit, home and car loans, to make investments, you are required to give proof of solid financial history. Now if conditions are such that you do not fit this profile, or you lose everything, then you start to believe you lack what is desirable.

As you sharpen your intuition, you grow to transcend narrow-minded thinking.

Intuition tells me to think differently from other people yet, somehow live the same.

To misjudge your experience shifts focus away from taking responsibility. Options exist beyond what you assume. The non-physical part of you believes that.

My awareness is shifting. The agent who sold the unit I rented found a replacement.

You intended it to happen, and it did. You always create your own situations.

Okay, so we did not have money available to buy the property we had lived in. We looked into loans, but it did not feel right. It did not phase us because conditions did not fit.

Your chose to expand your comfort zone and you stretched differently.

Moving was an undesired expense, yet part of us had outgrown where we were. Intuition told me that neighborhood served a purpose for us while we lived there. The unit is perfect for the young couple starting out. It felt right for us to leave, before we were asked.

Intuition highlights the bright side. As you listen you align to energy flow. Nothing matters except learning not to consciously direct your thoughts. As you allow your mind to go, forces lay the groundwork for you to prove things to yourself.

I may not have focused on energy flow, but I read signs that that unit was not in my future. I learned starter home loans are available with no down payments, so long as you have proof of regular salary. That ruled me out. Home loans are complicated if you have no consistent work history, if you work for yourself or, have no five year business history with profits. If you have inconsistent financials, lack assets or a guarantor, required down payments are high.

Your intuition has come a long way. All perceived realities are accurate as far as you believe them. You share experience. This is a stage to learning to turn it off.

Do you mean to say that my situation reveals I am not meant to live as others?

The mind assumes the form of whatever it thinks. Every thought brings you closer to what you desire, but you are unwilling to consciously accept it. Part of you feels lost. Each experience teaches about love and fear, humanity and inhumanity.

I actually dreamed of living in a lighthouse and other unconventional places.

You see value in possession and ownership, or realize that both are illusory.

My sense of needs is certainly changing. If I invoke the presence of a mentor at any time, I can also invoke desirable qualities inside to assist or effectively reframe any situation.

Some would attribute this to the law of cause and effect.

I am increasing realizing that what I think I learn is fundamentally imposed beliefs.

Deep within you exists a knowledge you have always had before any of that. Intuition is how you teach yourself to reconnect with what lies beneath the surface. Strengthening your senses equips you to rebuild and reopen your memory bank.

Are you suggesting I need to have a particular set of memories about my origin?

Human beings imagine needs at every stage of their lives. To uncover what you have buried inside yourself about your spiritual origin will assist you to develop and apply your intuition more effectively.

I realize I have a degree of freedom with choices in this game of life. What is less obvious is how to clarify rules or parameters. Intuition does not come boxed with a rulebook.

Imagine rules do not exist except universal laws. The point of life experience would then be to create obstacles for yourself, or imag-

ine they are set up for you, for the sole purpose of exercising your acquired knowledge and skill. The quest for understanding brings purpose. Your attitude and intuition determine your choices.

The game board has not been encouraging me to keep my questions simple.

The more you practice at anything, the better you will become. Any effort to apply intuition is already raising your energy vibration, even if you are as yet unconvinced. Feeling teaches you to shift awareness.

Developing Intuition: End of Section Exercises

1. Which lessons do you retain from this section? How would you apply them?
   - In your relationships?
   - In your work?
   - In your spiritual pursuits?
   - In other ways?

2. What does the concept of intuition mean to you? When do you/ have you used it?

3. List specific character traits and convictions that help to define who you are.

4. Which initiatives have you taken or do you feel you will take to sharpen a focus?

5. Brainstorm ways you believe developing intuition would enrich your own life.

6. Describe a situation where you chose to follow your intuition. What were the results? If you do not follow your intuition, have you learned to trust yourself? Why or why not?

7. How does this section cause you to reconsider risk-taking and thoughts of change?

8. Describe a situation where you witnessed someone else struggle with life changes. Describe them: personal, professional, others. How did this make you feel?

9. Recall three major changes you experienced during your childhood. Did you anticipate any of these life changes? Describe the signs you felt before the changes. How did such experiences affect your faith in intuition then and now?

10. Recall three major changes you have experienced during adulthood. Did you anticipate any of these life changes? How you feel

about each one? Did one change affect another? What did they teach you about intuition?

SHARPENING THE FOCUS

"What you think about comes about. By recording your goals on paper, you set in motion the process of becoming the person you most want to be."

—Mark Victor Hansen

"We work on ourselves in order to help others, but also we help others in order to work on ourselves."

—Pema Chodron

As I interact, I realize I have been closing myself off to natural skills and abilities.

To decide you must conform alters how you view yourself.

I would imagine that changes a relationship between the mind, perception and focus.

Sensitive beings instinctively retain early skills and resist distractions. As skills resurface, you reconnect and develop as initially intended before you forgot.

Okay, I detect new insight. Each situation reveals sides to me that I had overlooked.

You can awaken gifts anywhere. Contemplation does not mean not knowing where to start. You are simply discerning what it means to start "in the right place."

So, I determine what suits me based on recognizing what does not, what I outgrow, and when I feel unfulfilled. Yet, people stir a kind of lingering restlessness inside me.

Nobody does anything you do not want them to do. You choose your energy vibration and the energy frequencies you align with or not. Judgment, like self-acceptance, begins and ends within. Doubt is lack of faith in all that you are and do.

Some days I think I focus on what I am, then I abruptly discover it is what I am not.

Never allow doubt to paralyze you. Your choices are guided by your free will. If you dwell on anything else, you are not channeling energy wisely.

As I take time alone, sometimes I think about how my conditions are hurting me.

Nothing hurts you but ego that creates fear and misunderstanding of what you perceive. Part of you only knows or accepts things after experiencing the opposite.

Some people work hard to create a sense of security where they are. They want jobs and paychecks that provide food and shelter. Yet, not everyone who works hard feels secure.

Security means freedom from harm. When you imagine harm, you make it up. Lack of self-confidence uncovers beliefs of inadequacy and lies you tell yourself.

I see myself working hard to create freedom. Who likes to face their sense of lack?

You are listening to yourself. If things do not feel right, then they are not. Choosing conditions is a step. Approval and acceptance are found inside yourself.

Sometimes action is not a good thing. I think back to when I sought approval in primary school. At times I went out of my way to be liked. In grade five, once, during recess, I accepted a dare to jump out a window. Cool kids locked the window behind me and tattled. As I sat outside the principal's office, I reflected on peer acceptance. I realized how approval had to begin in me. Why would I choose to forget a lesson that I learned ages ago?

What you learn during experience is never forgotten, only stored for future reference. You grow to realize why the mind would override your own understanding and former lessons. You are blind to what serves you, but you do it nonetheless.

Self-sabotage? That reminds me of vicious circles when people do not learn a lesson. Then, the universe brings new opportunities to learn the same thing again until a person "gets it." Why would I do that to myself? After all, if I already got it, why not move on?

Growth that truly matters is imperceptible. The next step is to discern this.

Are we not on the same plane, you and I?

That depends on your perspective. Imagine I fly a helicopter and you are skiing. I can land on the snow near where you are, but only briefly. From my heightened vantage point, I see more than you, but I have trained to get where I am. At your level, you discern when you engage fully in life and when you retreat.

As life unfolds, I face inconveniences, irritations, and accidents beyond my control. Dealing with grievances distracts me from my focus. Why permit them to distract my peace of mind? Well, I aim to accept what I cannot change. Impatience I have yet to master.

Any sense of struggle empowers you to detect unfinished inner work on you.

I detect echoes about intermittent stages of my process of growth. Am I losing it?

Self-doubt emerges when you fail to realize every reaction is an act of faith.

Well, I have learned comments from strangers can be constructive. To encounter negative people prompts me to reexamine reasons behind my feelings. I used to avoid them.

You still evade the key issue. You recognize how you think and feel have not been working, but you refuse to tackle why you feel inadequate and unsatisfied.

Let me get this straight: you say I do not focus as well as I could in areas of my life because I appear deeply unsatisfied? Frankly, my own view is I am happy where I am.

Your thoughts, behavior, and environments you create indicate the contrary.

So, if I am not reading myself accurately, then I am likely missing other subtle nuances.

It is not just likely, you are. If you permit jealousy to disturb your focus or, peace of mind, you alienate yourself from the source of your greatest potential. Progress is when you no longer blame others for your naiveté, ignorance or inaction.

I thought a conscience worked in parallel with the conscious mind or, on the same wavelength. Your perspective evokes discomfort in me as if you wish for me to be unhappy.

I have been here from the beginning of time as you know it. My vantage point offers an outlook that comes from being able to see beyond what you are willing to see right now. You already know what steps you will take to clarify your destiny.

Since you see beyond what I do, why am I encountering such difficulties getting there?

Your abilities have always been suited to how you would excel. Anything you do leads you to greater wisdom so long as you listen to your soul. Uncover what already is. Difficulty is a mindset. Other people do not define your abilities. Your mindset does. As you rediscover self-discipline and inner expansion, you will shift focus from giving emotion control to doing what you have come here to do.

I know it is up to me to identify when to embrace changes, but which ones and when?

To switch away from the physical, you need to learn to stop effort to control.

I have been employee, contractor, and other roles. I often reformu-late the skills and experience I offer. My optimistic mind senses I need different energy.

You are in process of a reality shift. Judgment blocks your potential. Move beyond old patterns. Explore the fringes. Rethink security. Assume you have it and never lose it. Tap into time's memory. Recall life when you were something else.

Hold on! When I was something else?

You create snags by perceiving with fear rather than lessons open to you.

Okay. To experience life with little money taught me that I create "how" I live and "why."

Learning to live without physical luxuries teaches you of self-importance and ego-based decisions. It is part of a process of reviewing needs and desires. The truth is experienced. You do not think you send negative vibes until you feel the echo. You are learning that you must stop judging others to fully accept yourself.

That reminds me: when my partner was told by his co-director that I would be paid out as part of a new buy-out-deal, our spirits lifted. Then ego interfered and the deal vanished.

That is how energy works. Negative thoughts bring undesirable energy shifts.

Later, when this person repeatedly came after us with legal pro-ceedings threatening bankruptcy if we did not pay more money, it just seemed a bit too much, like a bad dream.

In his Four Agreements book, Miguel Ruiz reminds you troubles are rooted in assumptions and taking things personally. Be clear in your intentions. Ego-based motives are always exposed. Every thought form has moving vibrations you can feel.

I realize uncomfortable situations recur when lessons remain to be learned. I only wish I could heighten awareness faster. People know experience has more than one purpose, even if they do not say so. It is 'not knowing' that prevents me from learning to stop pretending.

As you alter perspectives, your thoughts reorient. For me to share my process with you would not help if you had not reached a certain stage in development. You cannot force your mind to go blank anymore than you can force yourself to grow before you are ready. You have reached a new stage where you distance from what you know.

Looking back I did not feel good about the suit against my partner and his co-director.

Feelings never lie. People only choose whether to listen or disregard them.

Part of my issue was learning to interpret feelings in ways that serve me and everyone.

The urge to interpret obscures truth. Sense energy as it is, simple and pure.

My job situation became a catch-22. I had no job and in order to obtain one, I believed I needed a recommendation from a previous local employer. When I found "a no-win no fee" law firm to take my case to sue for unpaid wages, it was a godsend. I only had thirty dollars.

The answer is always compassion. Any other view is an illusion. You desire for events to evolve, but in order for this to be so, you must evolve inside to forgive.

When I come to a crossroads in life, turning to solitude always enables me to find focus.

As you struggle to control outcomes, you realize it is not your job. The mystery you are really after will linger until you accept it and integrate it in your life.

As it happened, the company was liquidated. This nullified my court case.

You know no other future if you do not release what keeps you as you are.

The former co-director registered a new business name. As the liquidated company was under administration, he put his wife in charge as director. All former employees were rehired except for me. As a foreigner, I was ineligible to receive compensation for lost wages. My partner had been a director of the troubled company, but disassociated from his former co-director and was never paid for lost salary. We chose to feel a sense of a new beginning.

You were reminded you have skills to offer that you were ignoring. Efforts to put it out of mind were ineffective. Negative energy dissipates when you are at peace with yourself. You create issues to draw your conscious attention to something else.

If each person plays mind games, how do you get a definitive answer of what is right?

If you assume a single right answer to your situation, you will seek it like a recipe and dismiss options that teach you. As you explore your deeper thoughts, you can learn to mentally view and work though energy blocks. Step back from yourself and your conditions. Learn to detach and re-assess them more objectively.

Sharpening my focus has come to mean that if I want to make a positive difference, then I must be willing to adapt to situations that challenge what I know. What about limits?

Limits are mental. You define where a lesson begins and ends, and which steps you are prepared to take to evolve. Everything comes from energy you do not grasp.

Must I be accountable for absolutely everything?

Of course not!

Phew!

You are only responsible for your reactions to absolutely everything.

Is that level of accountability supposed to be consolation?

As you create your own sense of trouble, then it is only reasonable to accept it.

I guess you would say this version of reasonable focus is the only version that matters?

Now you begin to recognize the power of your ESP.

That is quite a mouthful. It is also a bit of a shocker to think you take responsibility for your life only to realize you are not really doing that at all. It is like restarting at ground zero.

Ego is stubborn when things do not go its way. Your learning is a permanent cycle with no start and no end. You are invited to sense meaning in each moment.

Sharpening the Focus: End of Section Exercises

1. Which lessons do you retain from this section? How would you apply them?
   - In your relationships?
   - In your work?
   - In your spiritual pursuits?
   - In other ways?
2. Describe your role models. How do they prompt you to think about yourself?
3. Describe a situation where you have nurtured faith in yourself. How did this affect your behavior? If you have had little or lost faith in yourself, why do you think this is? How would you propose to you build self-confidence?
4. Describe an experience where you went out of your way to seek approval. How did this make you think about your desire for self-acceptance?

5. List personal traits that bother you. What are some advantages of this awareness?

6. What do you do when you feel bad about things you have or have not done? Describe lessons learned. How can you behave differently to move ahead?

7. List specific goals you wish to achieve. Why?

8. If you feel restless, guilty, or worried about goals, then how do you read yourself?

9. Isolate five subjects or activities that motivate or inspire you. How do they influence your choices about security and life priorities?

10. What elements of short-term goals are within your control? Out of your control?

11. What patterns do you see in how you express yourself and interact with others?

EVALUATING SELF-WORTH

> *"To have that sense of one's intrinsic worth which constitutes self-respect is potentially to have everything."*
>
> —Joan Didion

> *"We often give to others advice we need ourselves."*
>
> —Roy D. Philips

At times I honestly wonder where this dialogue is leading.

You initiated it. It goes as long as you require and takes you where you like.

I do not readily accept all you say. It suggests people are often wrong or misdirected.

Self-worth is a decision, a vital part of your evolution. How you grow to know and love yourself relates to how you view identity. You readily mirror how others treat or describe you. If you deny your core feelings, then others will not value or respect the real you. If you tolerate rejection inside yourself or, take opinion personally, then you miss a key issue. You do not care about yourself enough to stop denying who you are.

You echo that I do not value myself. I have been ostracized before, but not for that.

As you let go of inflated self-importance, you no longer feel a need to prove anything. You will begin to focus on what really matters, that part of you that hides.

Okay, for example, by not making a fuss earlier in a former job, I conditioned office management not to care whether I was paid. I did this in another work setting before as well. Since I was grateful to be in these settings, I accepted situations and did not see beyond them.

You succumb to distraction when you resist being true to yourself. If you feel negative or vulnerable, then there is always deeper significance. Whatever you choose to ignore makes you a prisoner of what you refuse to see. Your morale is battered each time you fail to meet your misdirected expectations. Beneath it all, you do not meet your own criteria for self-acceptance.

That sounds rather harsh. I do not believe it is completely true.

As you live to take risks to be yourself is the most common human fear.

I take risks. I realize I am not perfect. But I would say that I do savor every moment.

Whenever you do not fit your own ideal, then you fall into the trap of inadequacy.

I find the courage to shift my mindset. Feeling unappreciated energizes me to clarify why I under-appreciate myself. People around me remind me I desire to better understand myself. It seems I conjure up harsh scenarios so to stop acting based on erroneous thinking.

Exploring your soul at a deeper level enables you to heal self-defeating behavior. All your feelings and responses are valuable. Destructive situations exist to train you to see new meaning in your reactions. You already sense the appropriate course of action. You desire to reconnect with your core energy or reason for being.

As for self-value, everyone I encounter does not perceive or value me the same way. Does this imply I attract unhealthy energy?

Your self-view begins and ends in you. Outside views tell you what you are not. If you do not value yourself, then you will not attune to your true calling. What you bury beneath temporary experiences is the key to your own personal freedom.

What I get out of that is, do not focus on other people's issues. Should I ignore them?

You raise your awareness and energy vibration as you learn to see people for who they are. They mirror parts of yourself that you accept or reject. Your reactions are clues to your destiny. Read the mood. It reflects energy. You develop deeper awareness of what you are at your core. You are creating a personal dream.

So, when I focus on something, this is not what I really believe. If I question skills or conditions I do not have rather than value those I do, then I do not use my abilities wisely.

Wisdom is subjective. Your sense of this is constantly changing. To condemn your behavior or undervalue your potential weakens your energy field. This leaves less energy to develop and attract teachers. The state of your self-worth is a sign.

The more I reflect, the more self-worth seems grounded in love. That emits energy.

Many people admire love yet, do not create their own. If you give into the voice that says you cannot rather than believe that anything is possible, then you overlook that the mind is fertile. You are always ready to receive the seeds of love.

Solitude enables my thoughts to flow more freely. I recognize all choices I make are part of me. This leads to revelations, provided I do not hold back. How do I know if I do?

You need not ask. You sense it. Trust yourself more.

Facing hardship deepens my ability to decipher what I'm thinking and feeling. I have done work that motivated me initially, only to be reprimanded for enthusiasm and efficiency.

Notice your assumptions and comparisons. Judging others disconnects you from the truth. Release people from the spell of your tunnel vision.

I believe I write under the spell of words. I realize spells can be broken, but not how.

Re-interpret your conditions and align with energy. It always guides you.

I sense that a deeper connection to myself is what I need. This is not taught in school.

You are a perpetual student in the school of life that has no walls, no borders.

What I overlook affects me more than I initially realized.

You become the vision you create. As you learn to stop thinking and feeling in ways that do not serve you, reality only seems to transform. It is really you evolving. Reality does not change.

As it happens, I have asked myself what is "safe" to say to whom, regardless of what is on my mind. I have met people who evolve to withhold feelings and ideas rather than to freely share them. After repressing feelings, people then expect to have their minds read.

Minds can be read, but only when sender and receiver are on same frequency.

Telepathy is an intriguing concept, but not every human being believes in it.

Not everyone has to believe, just the sender and receiver with parallel intent. I am reading your mind right now, and you are responding quite favorably.

Excuse me? You are already in my head, so you would read my mind like a book.

More than one can read the same mind. Oh, I neither exist nor cease to exist. Through my astral presence, you feel my spiritual energy. We will explore invisibility more later.

I fear one of us is getting off topic.

Fear requires separate discussion. As you shift awareness you notice me. How and why you notice me evolves. Your reaction tells me you believe perception depends on your conditions. Your beliefs determine what you see in me and how you form your thoughts.

If I did not believe in you, I would not continue the dialogue. That does not mean I know your game. You offer a lot to take on-board. I sense you have more than one agenda.

With practice, nothing is beyond mastery. Even suspicion can be dissolved.

I have learned I have different motives for my choices, including views on self-worth, though many motives I do not recognize consciously. For me, sharing details of hardship is limited by my own discomfort and disbelief. As I detach from opinion, I regain more power.

You accept self-created limits in areas of your life in order to excel in others. To develop courage enables you to sharpen perception and redefine "normal." You open your mind wider and suddenly sense in new ways that seem like second nature.

And I would gather this is another side of the mystery about me which is unfolding?

Listening to intuition enables you to read energy more consciously. To be aware of how you feel and to listen to energy flow re-orients your evolution.

Evaluating Self-Worth: End of Section Exercises

1. Which lessons do you retain from this section? How would you apply them?
   - In your relationships?
   - In your work?

- In your spiritual pursuits?
- In other ways?

2. On a scale of one to ten, how would you rate your self-worth? On what do you base your perceptions? How does your self-worth affect different areas of your life?

3. Describe three experiences that have shifted your sense of personal value.

4. Describe three experiences that have diminished your sense of self-worth.

5. What have you learned about yourself as the result of these experiences?

6. When have your jobs related to external influence? How did this make you feel?

7. What does your behavior indicate about your desire or ability to take risks?

8. Describe a situation where you felt you were taken advantage of or exploited.

9. How did you deal? In what ways did this experience shape your overall character?

10. Describe experiences that lower your esteem. How can you boost your morale?

11. Describe a situation where your thoughts about the success of others had a negative effect on how you viewed yourself. How could you strengthen your self-confidence?

12. When have you been a thinker, talker, or doer?

13. What prevents you from taking different initiatives? What would you like to do?

CARING AND DEVOTION

"The thoughtful soul to solitude retires."

—Omar Khayyam

"Love begins by taking care of the closest ones—the ones at home."

—Mother Theresa

Something about solitude facilitates revelations. I see caring and devotion differently.

You redefine existence as you become more caring and devoted to your own transformation. If you get complacent or discouraged when situations do not turn out a certain way, then you are not consciously expanding your sense of who you are.

I know people who choose not to care about their health and well-being. Admittedly, I have wondered what this says about me. I like to think I make choices to help not hinder me.

Human beings are at different levels of awareness. People will not always see the world as you do. All choices have value for the person who makes them. Many people are not aware of what health and happiness feel like. They only relate to other people's opinions. If you are not vigilant, you adopt thoughts and behaviors of others.

I remove myself from destructive environments. I see and dedicate myself to growth. While this noticeably raises my energy level, I still feel confused by judgment and injustice.

Discernment allows you to sense what is useful and why.

Parts of me sometimes feel very discouraged. I fall back into the, "if I had only…"

Rediscover the meaning of every kind of energy. Devote yourself to pursuits that strengthen you. Be persistent. As your mindset evolves, more challenges and obstacles mark your learning. When you sense events do not go as you wish, tell yourself to believe they are meaningful. Embrace all you are rediscovering.

I do believe in myself. If I did not, what sort of example would it set for others? I do sense that serving others is part of my responsibility. It is a common thread in all my choices.

People you meet gently remind you what feels right or not . Your destiny will not always seem cryptic. As you notice behavior in other people that you did not notice before, you are moving beyond this inside yourself. You are expanding beyond previous awareness and previous habits. Before long, you will recognize implications.

I think of an analogy: disciplined athletes train hard to prepare for competitions. All athletes do not win their races in the eyes of spectators, but they always seek to better themselves and redefine their own standards. I learn from my own perceived races.

Competition is an illusion. You only ever truly compete against yourself.

Caring & Devotion: End of Section Exercises

1. Which lessons do you retain from this section? How would you apply them?

- In your relationships?
- In your work?
- In your spiritual pursuits?
- In other ways?

2. Write down three things in each category that you care deeply about and why.

3. Explain how each item listed above could contribute to more meaningful life pursuits.

4. How does the above list inspire you or make you feel good about yourself?

5. How does reflecting on your feelings assist you to clarify your life purpose?

6. What is becoming more obvious to you now that you did not notice before?)

7. What kinds of affirmations could you write to encourage yourself along your journey? List five encouraging phrases to motivate you. How will you apply them?

8. Imagine where you foresee desirable results from your efforts. What happens?

9. Which of your recent experiences suggest you could benefit from self-growth?

10. Describe an experience where feeling discouraged meant you didn't pursue certain goals. How could you reframe your perception so that you recognize positive sides?

11. Describe a goal you had that other people told you was not possible. Did you realize this goal? Why or why not? How are you inspired to work on goals differently?

12. Who are your inspirations for self-care? What did they teach you?

GROWING AND SUSTAINING TIME

"The trick is growing up without growing old."

—Casey Stengel

"Growth begins when we begin to accept our own weakness."

—Jean Vanier

My sense of progress is gradual, yet constant. I realize I do not grasp everything now.

That is unnecessary, even undesirable. You see, if you knew all you needed to know, then you would miss out on resources provided by intuitive guidance.

Why do I revisit the issue of belonging or not belonging? Why encounter monumental obstacles if a new business is going well? This disrupts my evolving energy alignment.

Obstacles are your strategy to avoid the debilitating nature of complacency. Routines signal you are meant to see new meaning in idleness and resistance.

I guess I am not consciously aware of learning as much when things are going well as I am when troubles arise.

Precisely! You invite all circumstances into your life for your own benefit, like a reward, but you do not always choose to be aware of that or the growth that ensues.

If I get where you are coming from, then reasons exist why I meet honest or dishonest people. I would not go so far as to say discomfort feels like a "reward" for previous efforts, but I can see where certain situations enable me to develop useful skills and gain insight.

Confusion is a feeling that invites you to take initiatives and grow. Apathy does not bring clarity. Change how you respond to conditions that evoke discomfort.

Growth is something I associate with the physical world, with things I touch and see.

You are also unconsciously growing as you work on energy in unseen worlds.

Well, learning about myself has revealed more than a few surprises already. I feel forces like wind, electricity and sound without always seeing them. It requires mental steps to move beyond that.

Imagine ivy climbing a wall. Its roots stretch to reach water. The vine endures dry and rainy days. Growth occurs as it clings to rock, finds its rightful place. Weather challenges the vine. If one season is shorter, longer, warmer or colder, then the vine evolves to adapt. Like a vine, you sense sources of light and energy.

Well, this definitely drives a point home. I think of how I meet people who resist being or expressing what they feel. Their inhibition prompts me to reflect on my own. Pessimism is grounded in self-defeating thinking. I did not think that sentiment defined me?

As you raise awareness, you discover why you think as you do. If you were saved from hardships, then you would not become resourceful, wise, and resilient. Whenever you ignore core abilities and reality, they find ways to get your attention.

I notice I am increasingly drawn to mystics for what experiences they have to offer.

Only you magically deliver yourself from difficulties. It is up to you to create tools, build strength, to find courage to examine or resolve your beliefs and situations. As you view each one, you begin to be inspired to excel in new and meaningful ways. Until you view a situation as a problem, you will not feel urges to change yourself.

My selective hearing is noticing more unusual places. I recently visited an enchanted garden filled with fantastic carvings. This experience led me to sense other magical places.

Like attracts like. You believe in magic and it grows through you. To sense beings, find them, you recognize your faith in what other people deny or disbelieve.

Part of me thinks my confidence grows from being my own boss at work. If I had not experienced hardship, I would not be defining new frontiers. I would not have pushed myself to create a business. My most previous work did not stimulate joy or renew my core energy.

It is one thing to recognize potential. It is quite another to initiate changes within your power. You always understand things at levels you have yet to grasp.

I sense hardship in different forms all around me. I do not have to adopt or absorb it. I used to ask why people go mountain climbing, do triathlons, and initiatives I viewed as risky. Then I evolved into a thrill-seeker, without understanding why impulsiveness felt right.

Challenges are a state of mind. You invite everything you experience to learn. Human beings have diverse sources of motivation. You decide what serves you or not. All experience is worth something, even if you cannot measure physical results. Some people feel progress is measured by stronger muscles. There is more to it.

Maybe this is like some kind of verification of self-awareness? As a runner I am motivated to push myself longer distances.

It is not the length of time or distance of a challenge that matters, but how your mind and body evolve to respond to physical signals. How you feel tells you what appears to exist. The next step is to work through the nature of your illusion.

I learn to build stamina and to struggle as part of the process.

You may not be aware of exact experiences you will have, who you will meet, and what they teach you. Yet you can decide to see significance at each stage of your life, to learn from all, and to recognize your future in your reaction to what happens.

Yet, in the midst of suffering itself, it can be much harder to view events as constructive and worthwhile. Part of me wants the growth to happen so I can move on.

Impatience explains why things seem to take longer. Rest assured, if you continue to struggle with aspects of your identity, you are not lost.

Funny you mention that. When people say 'I have lost it," I reply, "How do you know you ever had it?" It is a play on words, which reminds me people do not question many of their assumptions.

The mystery of temporary purpose baffles human beings. How and why each individual arrives at a certain time and where, is not meant to be understood in human terms. To fear not knowing what you might have known, what you might have had the power to change, is irrelevant. What matters is your mind continues to play games with you to distract you from your higher truth. Growth happens in stages.

From the way you are talking, I might begin to think that my whole life has been a distraction or charade. A person needs a reference. What am I supposed to concentrate on?

The focus of your attention right now is leading you to your answer.

You use brainteasers. Why not be straight with me?

Negative feelings cloud your sense of direction and faith in your gut feelings. You have a sense of duty to illusion and external pressures you imagine. Acknowledging your feelings helps you discover why you have hidden the answer from yourself.

Much to my dismay, not everyone develops a conscience to value the lives of others and the world around them. I guess this is a kind of diversion from a focus on what is good.

That is it!

What?

To sense a conscience connects you more to your spiritual side or inner voice. Each person forms and adopts value systems. Ideally, they are based on "healthy" habits and beliefs that promote increasing growth. Yet, some people develop beliefs that justify violence and rationalize choices and behaviors that do not serve them.

In terms of people I have known, not everyone has a conscience. Some people choose to live by their rules. I gradually step back and observe. It is disconcerting, mind-blowing.

Monitor your reactions. Other people mirror aspects of you. Whenever you judge others, you are distracted from the truth beneath negative emotions they evoke in you. You are redefining endurance now through how you exert yourself and feel.

Growing Time and Sustaining Time: End of Section Exercises

1. Which lessons do you retain from this section? How would you apply them?
   - In your relationships?
   - In your work?
   - In your spiritual pursuits?
   - In other ways?
2. List five things that discourage you. Why?
3. What could you do about these things to feel more in control of your life direction?
4. What do you learn from taking time to reflect? How will you use the wisdom?
5. What does your life experience teach you about your strengths and weaknesses?
6. Where do you sense your own resistance to people and situations? How could you adapt to overcome your resistance to change?
7. How does your faith in a higher authority shape your beliefs?
8. What does a higher power mean to you? How does this assist your growth?
9. When do you refer to forces beyond you? What are your feelings?
10. What can you do in your life to feel more joy? List options and experiment.

LEAVING FOOTPRINTS

> *"The Force will be with you, always."*
>
> —Yoda (Star Wars Trilogy)

> *"But now having seen him which is invisible I fear not what man can do unto me."*
>
> —Anne Hutchinson

If I am honest, I have been avoiding what I want. Admitting discomfort does me a favor. My feelings actually prompt me to shift focus and take control of my destiny.

Whether or not you realize, your choices leave invisible foot-prints that define your evolution. Other people learn from your path. You also learn from their paths.

That makes sense. My perception is expanding to show me invisible footprints.

Retrace the prints. You are beginning to understand experiences are teachers. Suddenly you choose to be a more active creator. You expand how and what you see.

Although I still remain somewhat in the dark about the significance of all this, I do sense inner voices are getting louder. They are unconcerned with jobs or relationships, geographical change or anything physical. Instead, they bring me back to how I feel.

Your identity is not defined by what you do or the relationships you choose. Each choice you make opens your senses wider to the truth. You discover what it means to change your priorities, to surpass your previous view of energy or power.

I am entitled to feel restlessness about uncertainty. That is what "humans" do.

A sense of entitlement is not helpful. As you explore faith and trust, you learn how your views change or not. Invisible footprints are soul prints. This records your choices in energy form. How you think and react is a blueprint you can evolve to see.

But, when is the right time? Why not now? I feel ready!

If this were the case, then you would see.

Is there not any way to pinpoint where I am with respect to "the final destination"?

Thoughts of start and finish are distinctly human. As part of your journey, you follow invisible energy footprints. This is based on instinct and faith in intuition.

If they are invisible now, I would like to evolve and see them. Would surgery help?

Energy vibration is not invisible to everyone at this moment. You perceive and believe what makes sense for you. Your abilities exist, but you do not always choose to sense them. People took this path before. Others follow. Awareness grows in you.

Leaving Footprints: End of Section Exercises

1. Which lessons do you retain from this section? How would you apply them?
   - In your relationships?

- In your work?
- In your spiritual pursuits?
- In other ways?

2. Describe those things in your life that contribute to your overall sense of purpose.
3. What kind of legacy would you like to leave for people you know? Or don't know?
4. In what ways do you think you lose power or momentum in a quest to define purpose?
5. In what ways do you think you build power or momentum toward a clearer purpose?
6. How will your life change as you learn to be content in and adjust to any situation?
7. How do your emotional states shape your sense of happiness and progress in life?
8. What have you learned about your own energy vibrations and awareness?
9. As you attune more to how you feel around certain people and in certain places, what do you notice? Have you experienced repeated situations that work for you or not?
10. Brainstorm ideas that surface in your mind about footprints. What do you believe you understand? What would you like to explore in more detail?

SECRETS TO INNER PEACE

"Man is lost and is wandering in a jungle where real values have no meaning. Real values can have meaning to man only when he steps on to the spiritual path, a path where negative emotions have no use."

—Sai Baba

"The very least you can do in your life is to figure out what you hope for. And the most you can do is live inside that hope."

—Barbara Kingsolver

"Success should be measured by the yardstick of happiness;
by your ability to remain peaceful and in harmony with
cosmic laws."

—Paramahansa Yoganda

I believe the secret to inner peace includes things like a good night's sleep and a clear conscience, a willingness to be observant, to be honest with myself, and to feel more open.

Examine your choices. They teach you what you desire, what inspires you, and what nurtures your soul. The root cause of your unhappiness is you.

If I knew what I avoided, then I would channel energy differently.

To acknowledge energy in ways you did not sense before is a step to creating peace. When you deny discomfort, you postpone creating a more fulfilling life. If you permit yourself to feel bitter, or regret, then phases of spiritual testing are extended. You create a flexible, invisible timeline with every thought, word, and deed.

Okay, already! I did not realize I ignored pain of inner situations. I was unaware aspects of my life are a form of delusion. Who likes to believe that? I do not view myself as being dishonest when part of me has knowledge that other parts deny. At least I am beginning to realize dishonesty has different facets. Selective ignorance is one.

If you are not open to recognize your needs, or do, but do not act to satisfy them, then you are dishonest. If you do not choose to figure out why, and you hide from revelations, inner peace will escape you.

I did not think I was hiding from knowledge I already have. I know people who delude themselves into believing their behavior is good for them when from my vantage point, it is not. People with addictions, for example, will say another drink or fix is okay. I sense this is self-destructive. If dishonest people mirror some level of dishonesty in me, then I begin to realize I must attune to my personal experience differently to appreciate it.

Choosing to accept all of you can become a conscious choice. In the physical world, you do not consciously register all knowledge at your disposal at once from your subconscious. You evolve in stages so not to startle yourself. What you view as subjective becomes objective, and vice versa. You move beyond where you were.

Where is this "beyond"? I sense no guarantees exist. Inner peace is not assured by acknowledging challenges. I see how avoiding them postpones that peace.

Peace is a feeling born within by the choice to greet experiences without prejudice, resistance, insecurity, or fear. Learn to forgive enemies, to eliminate the idea of enemy. Destructive feelings are signs to shift attention. Any challenges you perceive are not threats, but rather, invitations to learn meaningful lessons, to grow, and make different choices next time. For there will always be another next time.

That sounds foreboding.

Only if you decide that it is. Why not envision perpetual rebirth or chances?

You like putting me in the driver's seat.

I do not put you anywhere. I simply remind you where you are.

It would really be nice to expand my perception to "see" how you "see." I imagine my life would be very different—more peaceful and infinitely enriching.

The grass is never greener elsewhere.

Throughout time people have gained wisdom from learning more about inner peace. What is it about people who profoundly inspire the world? They glow hope and compassion. Something about energy that surrounds them touches me. I sense inner peace there.

People who have deep understanding of inner peace have all been deeply challenged, threatened, and tested. They choose to adapt to and transcend issues.

I relate. Every human can relate to challenges. Not everyone perceives or faces them.

Human beings behave based on awareness. You can decide not to be affected by conditions. People who change the world become changes they wish to experience.

Truly peaceful people often make their homes in slums, alleys and even prisons. Some choose to exist amidst oppression, poverty, violence and deprivation. Is it necessary?

You decide what makes sense. To become someone else is not your destiny.

Discomfort is meant to be welcomed then.

You create your path your way. Peace is relative. You move away from the familiar. It stifles your dreams. The secret to inner peace is not to fight anything.

How do I know what it is that I am really fighting?

As you attune to yourself, to frequencies beyond superficial perception, you know. You have a "light body." It is stabilized by electromagnetic energy that causes changes in your thinking and behavior. Your feelings gauge your conscious mind. When you feel good, you choose to "go with the flow," to experience inner peace.

This is big, really big. Please clarify "go with the flow."

Going with the flow is evolving to accept yourself fully for all that you are. That means no more judgment and choosing only sentiments on path with pure love.

I used to think I had insight pure love, but now I am not so sure.

Your mental states and experience reveal love originates in the heart, soul and mind. Otherwise it would not endure. Your soul endures for the sheer joy of living. You serve yourself out of love. You serve others as well. It is a journey to remember.

And I thought I was giving myself and you my undivided attention?

Human beings who value quiet time suddenly experience "eureka" moments. This is when you are doing something on one level of awareness, like washing the dog or cooking a meal, and another level of awareness kicks in. That is, you suddenly think of a solution to a situation you did not know how to handle earlier that day or even days before. You send out vibrations and receive an answer when it comes. You tune out or dissociate from one level of awareness in order to tune into another. Initially, it is a matter of priorities. Your mind is like a symphony. Different instruments represent different levels of awareness. Each one gradually begins to play and align to create harmony.

Secrets to inner peace then include not trying so hard.

While you may seek advice from outside yourself, it is up to you to determine whether to receive or act on the advice that is given. Solitude enables reflection.

Secrets to Inner Peace: End of Section Exercises

1. Which lessons do you retain from this section? How would you apply them?
   - In your relationships?
   - In your work?
   - In your spiritual pursuits?
   - In other ways?
2. What kinds of things do you do to nurture and reduce your sense of inner peace?
3. List as many negative feelings and emotions you can think of. When have you experienced them?
4. Which situations in your life evoke negative energy?
5. What evokes peace within you? What is it about this that affects you?

6. List who hold you back from or disrupt your inner peace. How do they do this?

7. Compare sources of inspiration and gloom in your life. Consider how you spend your time. How do your attitude/focus affect your potential for inner changes?

8. What has this section led you to wish to change about yourself?

9. Which efforts can you make to calm your own troubled heart?

10. Which thoughts, feelings and actions drain your energy and seem counter- productive?

11. What are some of the words you use most often? Ask a friend to listen and help. Notice feelings you evoke by using each of these words; positive or negative energy?

SHADES OF SPIRITUALITY

> *"You've got to speak it out. Your words have creative power. One of the primary ways we release our faith is through our words."*
>
> —Joel Osteen

> *"Higher Forces represent the spirit that unites all life on this planet."*
>
> —Wangari Maathai

Energy and spirituality seem to have a lot in common.

Spirituality is concerned with sacred or mysterious inspiration. It is an idea that empowers you to seek new kinds of truth, to feel devoted or, to nurture faith.

I do sense feeling connected to something greater than me. It also has healing power.

Spirit heals, and yet, the source of spiritual power and consciousness eludes all physical inquiry. How you view life has potential to enhance your mental, physical, and emotional health and well-being. Spirituality offers coping mechanisms.

Who would not like to reframe adversity? How does spirituality work, exactly?

As you deepen concern for areas of the spirit, you awaken your inner power. You already choose to express yourself in ways you had not acknowledged before or, ways you did not consciously admit as meaningful. As you reach out for guidance to help clarify your reason for being, you rediscover love and let service drive you.

And I suppose you are going to tell me the trail I am following is not visible "per se."

You are onto something there!

Strangely, I am hearing more voices. Now, these are uplifting and positive ones.

As you develop your spiritual side, you strengthen intuition. It is the voice that helps you become more aware of your own nature and what cries out for expression.

The secret to deeper satisfaction then must involve connecting with a spiritual side in ways I have not done. Is this where it would make sense to mention I am not religious?

Religion is a human invention based on interpretation and imposed beliefs. Spirituality is soul-based. It is in everyone, regardless of religion. Spirit does not encode your purpose or magically enable you to absorb all you hope to learn now.

If you put it that way, spirituality seems more like a tool, a means to progress my way.

It does not make anyone feel balanced who does not choose to feel that way. It is not a potion you take to heal illness, to chase away depression, or to enable you to rise above suffering. Spirituality does not control faith or skepticism. You do.

I have found it is easier to realize what purpose is not than to clarify what it means

At soul level, human beings always know what they are. This is the spiritual perspective. Other sides consciously choose distractions. You learn as faith falters.

So spirituality is like a friendly reminder that suffering is fine as long as you choose to learn something? That is not so intimidating. Lots of people assume it is something else.

You never change anything, only the experience of everything. Each experience is your own. It is not moral or immoral. It is what you are ready to take on.

I have this increasingly reassuring feeling inside that fills me with joy. I reflect on situations and I am stunned at how I exaggerate the nature of their influence on who I am.

To be consciously unaware of the purpose of writing does not matter. To permit yourself to experience emotions and to reflect on choices, you do not have to be sure of how chapters of your life will unfold.

So, spirituality is not only a gizmo or label, it is also like a catalyst for deeper reflection.

Each part of your life has its own rhythm. Spirituality invites you to rise above defenses. This voice within you enables you to reconnect with your choices in duality (right or wrong; good or bad; etc). You live on spiritual, mental, physical, and other levels. The only way you change your physical life is to first change your inner life (the mental understanding of the spiritual and the universal laws that make it work).

All the while, society urges me to seek results. This requires action. Messages around me tell me purpose eludes me. I want to experience a more far-reaching sense of purpose.

Purpose never eludes you. This is a misunderstanding. Reality eludes people who forget who they are. What you have been taught clouds the truth. Learning about spirituality gives you new choices to revise your conscious sense of reality. Awareness of who you are has nothing to do with being focused on a specific physical activity or, being in a particular place. You exist to create and to evolve self-understanding.

I sense happiness is a state of mind. Spirituality seems to be teaching me that I distract myself from how I see and what I truly desire to see. Why?

You benefit from attuning differently. Much of your thinking and feeling dwells on other people. Their ways of thinking and doing became your conditioning. Spirituality invites you to work through the programming that disorients you.

Spiritual concepts urge me to detach from what grounds me. Will prayer or faith help?

Prayer is an exercise of the spirit. It does not alter universal laws like cause and effect. Prayer redirects energy from destructive feelings and whatever holds you back on Earth to focus your energy in positive directions. To nurture belief in possibility and higher forces attracts and manifests those things that strengthen you.

This is more than enough to teach me a lesson.

You are your own life preserver. You draw energy from everything. You can use this power to dissolve illusions you have created. At a given moment, you believe you need all and none of what you experience. You always pick, choose and discard.

Come on, in the physical world, people relate based on perceived time. You will not keep a job long if you decide to come and go as you please. Relationships suffer and disintegrate if you decide not to keep your word or you regularly let people down.

Every belief you create becomes what you think and perceive.

Are you trying to tell me that if I come and go as I choose, I will keep any job and strengthen all my relationships? Are you implying that people will appreciate my behavior?

As you step back, you recognize you do not share this mindset. You have moved to see beyond it. If you do not relate to a particular view, way of doing, seeing or feeling, then this is not wrong. Right and wrong are illusions. You consciously move away from environments and immerse yourself in those more suited to you.

Wow! Spirituality is teaching me about energy through my own choices. Imagine that?

You already have. That is why your awareness is where it is at this moment. As you realize how much energy you channel and in which directions, and that how you think and feel is always within your control, feeling happier "here and now" becomes your experience. By attuning yourself to your inner voice, you may experience a spiritual flow that enables you to feel interconnected to things.

Meditation is only part of it then. I did not realize the depth and reach of spirituality.

You get closer to inner peace as you learn what it is not. You can rise above and beyond the ideas that do not serve you. Each message you have ever heard about spirituality influences how you think about the concept right now. Deepening spiritual awareness is a way to replace destructive thoughts with more meaningful ones.

I would be grateful if you would expand on that idea of transcendence.

It is the process of moving your consciousness into the soul.

That sounds deep, like something unattainable or unverifiable. I am becoming more aware of things that were hidden by my conscious self. This tells me solitude is very useful.

You verify everything with faith. Learn to be true to yourself, not only who you believe you are, but who you grow to know you are. Your awareness grows to levels beyond thought. To attain soul awareness, work through temporal distractions. They shape self-image, emotions, and mind, but do not fulfill or grow you spiritually.

So, this kind of transcendence is always present and available?

You do whatever you choose, anytime, anywhere.

Excuse me if what you say sounds too easy. I mean why is everyone not doing it?

Move beyond the urge to compare. When you choose, you will open your conscience wider. Focus your conscious mind on affir-

mations, pure positive communication and the power of your intuition. Strengthen ties to all things. Begin the process of becoming more aware about how and why people and situations disturb you. As you stand back to reframe them, you already see beyond them.

Okay, what about when I lose touch with this omnipresent source of support? I begin to connect my negative feelings with how I invite negative people and situations into my life. And yet, is spirituality supposed to become the light that dissolves it all away?

Every circumstance in your life results from when you create an illusion and allow it to grow. If you doubt yourself, judge your self-image or abilities, these thoughts become real. Some illusions you create include; feeling you are too busy to change your thoughts or circumstances. This is never the case. When it comes to reprimand, if you judge yourself, you fail to recognize lessons you choose to learn.

You are telling me I want to know what different kinds of discomfort really feel like?

I do not have to tell you what you know. Nothing other people do is because of you. Their behavior is because of themselves. How you react tells you about you. Any obstacle or sense of lacking is always explained through self-reflection.

Fear is a big topic. It "phases" me. I work through it, and yet it daunts.

Human beings are all evolving toward fearlessness. This is an unspoken goal for the human mind. In some ways, this includes you.

Hold on there! Do you mean to say that in some ways I am not "human"? The last time I pinched myself, I felt it, but to pass the threshold required a certain degree of pressure.

Your sense of humanity is deeply rooted in something magical. The more you interrogate yourself, the more you will remind yourself why you chose to forget who you are. What I echo is not a secret. It is simply energy reformed in a way you are willing to hear. You read energy in vibrations and signals every moment. Not only your awareness is changing, but what you choose to do with this wisdom is changing.

As I sense my energy vibration, I sense pre-set patterns that require further revisions.

Timing of your requests is always perfect. Do not expect anyone to tell you the truth. Trust your feelings. The only way to permanently change is to shift thinking. You nurture and perpetuate patterns when you do not know what you do or why.

Shades of Spirituality: End of Section Exercises

1. Which lessons do you retain from this section? How would you apply them?
   - In your relationships?
   - At work?
   - In your spiritual pursuits?
   - The other ways?

2. What does spirituality mean to you? List words/associations. Check dictionary.

3. When have you been honest about your true feelings? What would you say if they echo part of your spiritual truth?

4. If you don't believe you are spiritual, what experiences have influenced this view?

5. Which new realizations would cause you to rethink how you view spirituality?

6. How do events beyond you (things you are unable to explain to your satisfaction) influence your sense of progress? Explain how events evoke certain feelings.

7. What conflicts can you begin to work through right now? How would this help you develop your inner peace and to focus more on what you desire out of life?

8. What kind of inspirational reading material have you read or heard about? How does this influence your understanding for faith and trust in relation to goals?

9. Think of a life experience you had where you didn't anticipate how it turned out. What did you recognize about events beyond your control? How did you grow?

10. If you feel disoriented, what would you do differently in your current pursuits to feel more centered? What holds you back? What would it take you to change?

11. What does it take for you to reevaluate your priorities, get more focused? How you do one thing reveals how you do everything; mindset, effort, attitude.

12. Examine your habits. What could spiritual understanding to enhance your focus? How might your mindset be preventing you from where you really desire to be?

2

Understand Your Fear

ADMITTING YOUR FEARS

"People always fear change. There will always be ignorance,
and ignorance leads to fear."

—*Bill Gates*

"We live in it, we inhale it, exhale it, and most of the time we
do not even notice it. Instead of 'I am afraid,' we say, 'I don't
want to,' or 'I don't know how,' or 'I can't.'"

—*Andrea Dworkin*

LESSONS

1. The dividends from your efforts arise later than you think.
2. Places of emptiness bring us closer to grasp the imperceptible.
3. To better understand yourself, listen closer to your words.

My journey in solitude uncovers fears. They threaten my desires, hopes and plans.

Growing awareness means you begin to see obstacles you cre-
ate to keep you where you are. Fear hinders a sense of "progress."
To explore why you imagine fear permits you to face self-created

61

limitations. Admitting discomfort helps you determine underlying causes. You see anything that postpones accepting who and what you are.

It has been said the greater the perceived risks, the greater the imagined fear. In life, when I listen to my heart, I do not sense fear. Is it illusion or, a kind of procrastination?

You convince the mind of absolutely anything.

What you seem to say is that the greater the fear, the more meaningful the lesson. You also imply I favor self-destructed thinking and do not trust myself. That disturbs me. I do not view myself in a negative light. Are you exaggerating?

Every moment, you distort a vision of your abilities. This fuels your ego and generates fear. You guard against wounds that have never healed. Discomfort is a sign to shift your attention to different energy.

Okay, like many people, I may not totally understand all reasons why I fear certain things. When I think I put them out of my mind, then events unfold as if to provoke me.

To work through your fear, admit each time you sense it and learn its causes. Everything is conditioning. You gain a sense of what you want by understanding what you do not. You get closer to who you are by experiencing who you are not. Whenever you fear aspects of the unknown, soul prompts you to address this.

My heart, mind and soul are not always aligned. You do not make this easy, do you?

Nothing imposes anything on you but yourself. Your evolution is perpetual.

Understand Your Fears: End of Section Exercises

1. Which lessons do you retain from this section? How would you apply them?
   - In your relationships?
   - At work?
   - On a spiritual level?
   - In other ways?
2. What scared you as a child? How do you explain your fear of these things now?
3. How did you deal with fear as a child? If you did not, what prevent you?
4. List five major fears you have had (or still have) as an adult.

5. Why do you believe you fear each of these things?

6. What people, situations, and experiences used to scare you as an adult, but scare you no longer? What triggered the change in you to face certain fear?

7. What advice would you offer to people who grapple with their fears?

RELEASING THE PAST

> *"I have not ceased being fearful, but I have ceased to let fear control me."*
>
> —Erica Jong

> *"Obstacles cannot crush me. Every obstacle yields to stern resolve. He who is fixed to a star does not change his mind."*
>
> —Leonardo da Vinci

I struggle to forge a clearer path. Certain life choices do not jive, but where to next? Which country? Which relationship? Which conditions? The infinite choices disorient me.

Discomfort urges you to identify the source and let go of the reasons for it. Remaining closed to why things are not working does not serve meaningful purpose.

Which behavior serves a meaningful purpose? Is one more helpful than another?

During any quest, mystery invites you to be humble, it urges you assume nothing.

That means "walk in the dark."

As you become more deliberate with your intention to learn, you do. In order to heal the body, you must free the soul. You awaken to why you create barriers like attitudes, why you choose experiences or relationships that hinder expression of your spirit. To release what does not serve you shifts your energy to create more joy.

You make it sound like I help others while I attune to myself. Am I always healing?

You are. As you realize destructive emotions do not help, you release them. You let go of fear and doubt and speak of a situation in a detached way. To postpone facing sources of anxiety only magnifies them and does not expand your soul. Well, when I focus on alternatives, obstacles do arise, yet, they work themselves out.

This means you reach a level of evolution that activates the law of attraction.

To recall when I was going to travel to my sister's wedding, I was so rushed. I went to the airport without my ticket. I had had so many electronic tickets before that a part of me assumed electronic ticket again. My lack of awareness almost led me to miss the event.

But, you did not.

No. I remained calm and felt higher forces intervened. I sensed the ticket sales agent truly loved the challenge of rebooking my series of boarding passes. His colleagues thought he was nuts. Yet the bigger the challenge seemed, the more focused and eager he became.

Look beyond the surface. All experiences offer lessons about love and fear. The progress you have made is demonstrated in how you applied power of intention.

To release uncomfortable memories then, I need to see the point or benefit of them?

Sometimes you follow a path because you disbelieve its possible and do so to convince yourself anything is. You evolve to shift your views about "the impossible."

So the struggle I felt inside led me to choose a dishonest employer? That was a trial.

You let those feelings prevent you from taking more personal responsibility.

This reminds me how I went from feeling insecure to feeling my goals are worthy of me. I learned while you hold onto the pain and dwell on conditions causing it, the mind fixes on what you cannot change. I disciplined my mind.

Discipline is often misunderstood by human beings.

Is this where I should add that I feel self-discipline is highly overrated?

Discipline is not about learning to control "you" based on what other people expect. It is about disciplining the mind differently at varied levels of awareness.

Well, I continually gain deeper insight into what was not working at that life juncture. As I wonder what went wrong at given moments, I forget I serve myself with every action.

Human beings are deeply connected to what is going on behind all this.

You mean I am not supposed to analyze to better understand myself? You lost me.

By refusing to accept what you know, you also learn about cause and effect. Spirit has a far-reaching view. Dwelling on past hurts disconnects you from soul.

So it takes longer for me to learn certain lessons. You said everyone has a pace.

You cannot gauge spiritual progress with physical measurement. If you focus on frustration, you detach from reasons for it and what lies beyond that. Why is it so hard to let go? To tap into what you know means you will rise above whatever holds you back. You discover more energy for present work, relationships and priorities.

I am becoming an expert in avoiding, and then overcoming rejection. I have had such diverse roles which I assumed were preparing me for paths that were not to be.

Your reaction to rejection reveals you misread your energy vibration. Inadequacy is an illusion born from fear. You spirit remains unrecognized. It might be necessary to remind you that humans exaggerate their sense of unworthiness.

Before I decided how to react to my employment crisis in Australia, I reviewed my feelings and options. Underneath it all, I was afraid of losing what I felt was desirable.

That feeling is inaccurate. You never lose anything. Everything is desirable.

By doing nothing I was giving into fear. I was allowing a dishonest person to threaten me. I was accepting my own lack of assertiveness and judging behavior around me. By denying myself what I thought I needed, I was denying my self-respect.

Closure is attained as you heighten your awareness of reasons behind it.

I evolved to rethink reasons for detaching from my uncomfortable conditions.

You realized you had to become aware of what you were ignoring about yourself before you could shift energy to explore how to develop it.

One of my biggest difficulties in taking steps to release the prickly emotions from this incident was that I did not feel I could discuss it. I thought talking built more negative energy.

When you hesitate to disregard emotions completely, they do not dissipate.

Okay, so I sought environments where I could discuss a "hypothetical situation" with professionals I assumed would understand. I did not believe this was rationalizing.

No human being ever does anything they feel inappropriate, based on their self-view, interest, or limited world model. The very things you fear are what you create to get over it. The route you take to a personal solution is a universal process.

How can it be okay to feel mistreated and okay for anyone to hold a limited vision?

You will not agree with everyone. As you learn to perceive through the eyes of others, you lessen self-importance and stop imposing your view of what is acceptable.

It is curious how different I view that experience without emotion, ego, and motive.

To deny things happen in life that hurt, damage, and restrain you would be to deny you are human. This would also deny infinite possibilities of love, enthusiasm, giving, sharing. You constantly learn more about imbalance or misdirected vibration.

I thought I nurtured passion. I did not realize my choices drain my own energy.

You do not boost your energy or inner power from seeking to control yourself in a similar way to how someone else has tried and failed. You desire another way.

While I aim to release the past, I do not always see what I need to see in myself.

All assumptions are wise teachers.

How true! I suppose shattering myths underlying assumptions helps release the past.

You got it. You come to believe people around you assume negative things about you, like weakness, lack of will-power, lack of motivation or skill. Yet you actually project your own fears and insecurity in forms that teach you the most.

So, a lack of self-confidence in one area of my life attracts unacceptable treatment in another seemingly unrelated area. How do I sense what to turn toward instead?

Nothing is unrelated. Everything you do attunes you to energy. No matter what you fear, you are empowered the instant you stop repressing part of you to fit in.

Fit in?

As you take responsibility for what you feel, you raise awareness of a mystery. You initiate a journey to re-energize in what appear new places. You become less self-conscious, learn to accept more of you. Reframe everything as "progress." After all, if you had not lived as you have, you would not be the person you are right now.

As I look back on my life, I can decide I feel a sense of failure because of not realizing goals or, I can see all outcomes as blessings. I become aware of new choices.

Choices are what many people decide they cannot bear. As you make a new choice, you teach yourself the limits of illusion and the extent of your creative power.

Life has taught me people who reject often feel rejected for other reasons, and have often never learned the meaning behind their fear of rejection. In my early years I developed self-image issues. Over time I worked through them. Apparently, I did not learn enough?

Whatever you do is enough. The source of fear already happened. Release it.

By overcoming a fear of not succeeding, I build a bridge to completely unanticipated sorts of dreams. It is like I die small, imagined deaths to truly appreciate the life I am living.

As you realize what is happening is not a dream, you redefine "awakening." It only requires you to be willing to shatter your myths. To release the past you learn a process to examine levels of fear. Each level has energy and affects deeper processes.

If a person needs the right beliefs in order to make headway, what are they?

Right beliefs are positive thoughts that encourage and motivate you. When they are repeated, they are reinforced. Thoughts become habits and manifest visions.

Releasing the Past: End of Section Exercises

1. Which lessons do you retain from this section? How would you apply them?
   - In your relationships?
   - At work?
   - On a spiritual level?
   - In other ways?
2. How would you benefit from a process of letting go?
3. Which behaviors, attitudes or situations do you cling to? Why? What made you aware?
4. Reflect on three situations where you wish to learn to let go and move on. Brainstorm feelings, reasons you have to feel pain, confusion, hurt and/or regret. What's next?
5. How do you know if you have moved on from a painful or difficult situation?
6. What do you imagine will happen when you make positive changes?

7. How can your past challenges offer you a helpful perspective on current ones?

8. Where can you simplify your life by ending unfulfilling relationships and unproductive endeavors? How do you plan to channel this energy instead?

9. How do your body, mind and spirit enable you to become aware of discomfort?

   - Physical signs?
   - Emotional signs?
   - Spiritual signs?
   - Other signs?

GRIEF AND LOSS

> *"No one ever told me that grief felt so like fear."*
>
> —C.S. Lewis

> *"If you've got to my age, you've probably had your heart broken many times. So it's not that difficult to unpack a bit of grief from some little corner of your heart and cry."*
>
> —Emma Thompson

I feel happy my circumstances are changing. I am starting to understand that change unfolds from my regular, unconscious initiatives. Sensing loss really means I gain things.

In the process of admitting any loss, you also need to allow yourself to grieve.

What if I believe a given "loss" is good? I do not choose to dwell on what is over.

Loss may relate to the death of a loved one, the unexpected or desired end of a life phase. Often, people remain in situations that are wrong for them, be it a job, a relationship, a contract, a friendship or a mindset. When you sense the loss of something that once felt vital, treat it as the means to an end. A period of grief or renewal gives you closure and relief. This is not the same as denial of pain.

I get it! You mean take responsibility for the role I played in a loss. To deny the truth means choosing not to be aware.

No person benefits from carrying unresolved feelings to new circumstances. To harbor negative feelings is to ignore the most valuable part of past experiences, that is, those repressed parts of yourself to which your attention is drawn.

As I take responsibility for my own actions, it is a way of releasing myself, and recognizing what is happening is not about me alone. I did not have as much control over the outcome as I believed I would have. People bring their own personalities.

As you discern who you are and who you are not, this shapes your personality.

Learning lessons includes freeing myself from conditions. This also frees people to go about their lives as they choose without me focusing energy on them or being drained.

You already channel energy differently. This reinforces your personal power.

Accepting loss means rethinking forgiveness. I do not punish myself for all errors.

To desire punishment prevents you from setting your soul free. As you liberate parts of yourself that you have outgrown, you build strength, dignity, power. The past served you because you focus on what precipitated your sense of a crisis.

Is this energy what it feels like when a part of your soul is being resuscitated?

As you choose to gain wisdom from past relationships, you are willing to learn about yourself. Discomfort has different meanings. If you are closed to recognizing root causes of loss, then you are unwilling to heal, grow and change.

When certain relationships end, I realize new ones evolve to replace them.

Your attitude is affected by each person you meet.

If I cannot trust my sense of what is worth doing and my perception is changing, when will I truly know myself? When would anyone get to that stage of knowing?

The process to move beyond the past is accessible to all. You truly know who you are when you no longer attribute, blame, deny your delusions, or attract people or conditions that evoke discomfort. The more you love, the more you evolve.

On the topic of grief and loss, it is curious how societies tell people which kinds of killing and grief are acceptable or worse than others. Many people adopt external opinions.

Some societies are built by human beings who have forgotten why they exist.

If a military soldier commits suicide with a gun even when over-whelmed emotionally, this is dishonorable. The surviving family will not get a military pension. Yet if a person kills himself with alcohol, tobacco, lust, or obesity, families do not lose insurance benefits. In many cases, if a physician helps with a mercy killing, manslaughter charges ensue. Fate is cruel.

You are beginning to realize this is not about you.

Pardon me, but what am I supposed to do with my life now? You seem a wise guru.

Your life force emits energy vibrations. You decode them. You are gradually elevating your frequency. Your next revelation may unfold anytime.

But you seem to say my path has nothing to do with the physical situations I create.

Mirrors are everywhere. When you permit fear to control you, your spirit disconnects until you choose to love yourself again. Unconditional love changes you.

This may just help explain the squiggly energy lines I see pulsating when I squint.

Whenever human beings choose to rethink assumptions, they are learning new ways to heal. Many choices drain your energy. Many ways also exist to replenish it. As you understand emotions you create, you detach from them and create new ones.

Grief and Loss: End of Section Exercises

1. Which lessons do you retain from this section? How would you apply them?
   - In your relationships?
   - At work?
   - On a spiritual level?
   - In other ways?
2. Describe experiences in your life for which you grieved and felt regret.
3. Is feeling or expressing sadness openly acceptable to you? Why or why not?
4. What has learning to feel sad taught you about yourself?
5. Which approaches to dealing with grief and loss appeal to you?
6. Explain how you think learning about grief can assist you to clarify your purpose.

7. Detail a situation where you lost someone you cared about. How did you grieve?

8. If you did not, what held you back? How can unresolved feelings hurt a purpose?

9. Describe a situation where you punished yourself for not doing what you wished you had.

10. You can't change the past. What can you do to get over fear, regret and move on?

DISAPPOINTMENT

> *"All the world is full of suffering. It is also full of overcoming."*
>
> —Helen Keller

> *"Many times in our lives we see our dreams shattered and our desires frustrated, but we have to continue dreaming. If we don't, our soul dies. . ."*
>
> —Paulo Coelho, The Pilgrimage

The more I think about it, the more I sense disappointment is an unnecessary detour.

If you have not yet understood and moved on from previous relationships or sets of disappointing circumstances, then each new experience may re-introduce a sense of failure. It is useful to learn to attract all kinds of conditions. You can teach yourself to grasp why you attract them, why you react, and if there are patterns.

Great! My crises have less to do with a given situation than unresolved issues from my past I supposedly ignore. I grow to realize I feel fear on varied levels and intensities.

Any force you feel stems only from internal influence. Ask yourself why.

I get the sense that this is a kind of vicious circle. How will I know as I transcend it?

As you explore the nature of disappointment, it triggers revelations about a lack of fulfillment. You ask why you feel bad or ignorant. Part of you refuses to raise awareness about what motivates and discourages you. Learn to decipher why you overwork or overcompensate, under-nourish or overindulge. You distract your mind.

I observe negative effects of incompatible or judgmental people.

You do not understand what your senses tell you. Experience shapes you. To think and talk as if you move on from a bad experience, but to retain bitterness of harmful feelings, reveals you have not yet released the disappointment. Repressed discontentment prevents you from truly devoting yourself to your destiny.

I do not believe I consciously dwell on disappointment.

You are not mindful of why you create that feeling. Human beings can accept each other as they are without interacting or agreeing with everyone. Disappointment stems from expectations and vibrations outside your conscious range of perception.

To avoid a focus on disappointment, the universe is nudging me in a more suitable direction. I need to teach myself to stop resisting. What happens around me reinforces this.

As you see roots of disappointments, your awareness and sensitivities grow.

When criticized, I used to be disappointed when I did nothing or became defensive. Now, I am likely to view criticism as an effort to provoke me, and I choose calmness instead.

Unless you become less rigid, you limit your perceptions to old habits or fears. Identify your patterns. Although you are free to alter your thoughts, many of your decisions reinforce the past until you go further inside yourself to move beyond them.

If I am honest, historically I have had faith in people who repeatedly let me down. I give them the benefit of the doubt. Are you implying I consciously let myself down here?

It is not about others. The nature of your patience determines whether you believe you have reason to change. The root cause of your disappointment in others reveals hidden disappointment inside. You only ever have reason to feel self-love.

How long must I be willing to wait to know certainty?

The only certainty is impermanence. To grasp disappointment requires you grow to understand what triggers your emotions. Then you anticipate and react differently. This is a lesson in self-discipline.

To deny things happen in life that hurt and constrain me would be to deny that I have a heart and soul. I believe disappointment teaches me I dwell on things I cannot change.

Character evolves as you focus on changing what you can, that is your energy vibration and efforts to show kindness and compassion. This dissolves discomfort.

You echo it is "human" to judge. Since this is so, you suggest I become less human?

Introspection is required to move beyond disappointment, to move transcend the limits of your humanity. Accepting disappointment begins with admitting why you create illusions. How do they benefit you? Maybe you forget why you summoned me.

Whoa there! Summoned? You are beginning to sound a bit "spooky."

I pass through you to draw your attention to the nature of your perspective.

Okay. I thought this life was not meant to bring instant results and gratification?

You have been working toward heightened awareness longer than you realize.

Not getting what I want has taught me the world does not revolve around me. As a child I was conditioned to develop expectations. Now I choose to trust what I do not see.

Like me.

One moment, you suggest we do not think alike. Then you infer the opposite.

Interpretation sidetracks human beings. Your starting point does not change. Whether you choose to view me with love or fear is what changes everything. It is common to assume both sides of this dialogue arise in your mind. Maybe they do not.

I will not go "there." Consider how certain schools condition students to learn and regurgitate information. The students who do well in this system and complete school may be surprised if a well-paying job is not simply waiting for them. Professional and trade schools often have placements where students go directly from training to internships and full-time work. Many students develop fear because they feel they must struggle wherever they are.

The perception of the work force is different depending on where you are.

Rejection seems harder to take if directly related to perceived survival. It can also be tough to nurture lasting relationships in cut-throat environments.

As you choose to go with the energy flow, you leave fearful feelings behind. Whenever you suppress your true self and your intuition, the lies evoke discomfort.

I was conditioned to expect measurable experience and education would be perceived by people and prospective employers as valuable. I evolved to think no matter what I did, it was not acceptable. I was conditioned to want to do more for myself and others. Shifting my mindset taught me working for myself is preferable. And yet, this self-perception obliges me.

You sense awareness will help set you free. Yet, you are always free.

I suddenly have a vision of a genie in a lamp. Is my process freeing you or others, too?

You learn fast.

What if I do not want to set you free? I do not even know what you are. Is it safe?

It is for you to determine how to bring this experience to others.

I am not sure what you are getting at now.

I reveal a process to guide you to re-experience when you had no beliefs, no expectations, and no assumptions. This blank slate reminds you of what is invisible.

Who says I would like to learn more about the invisible?

You are conscious of physical limitations. Yet you are filled with humility and detect faculties you have forgotten. Given time, you will drop pretenses and truly see.

Then this whole discussion is an exercise in exploring what is real and what is not.

What filters through your human feelings is part of a much larger exercise.

Disappointment: End of Section Exercises

1. Which lessons do you retain from this section? How would you apply them?
   - In your relationships?
   - At work?
   - On a spiritual level?
   - In other ways?

2. List five significant disappointments in your life. What do they teach you about yourself?

3. Reflect on a situation where you are unhappy with you were treated. How did you react?

4. How can your attitude permit you to reframe and grow stronger from disappointments?

5. What might you have done differently in the past to better deal with disappointments?

6. How might you assist others to see positive sides to their own disappointments?

7. Do you think this may influence the way you interact with people in the future? How does this relate to your sense of evolving purpose?

8. Reflect on a relationship disappointment. How did this shape the person you are now?

9. Reflect on reasons for your confusion or disappointment with a work associate.

10. How did you deal with this situation? If it remains unresolved, what else can you do?

11. Describe a situation which caused you to be disappointed in yourself. How did you react?

12. How has experiencing disappointment changed ways you perceive yourself and others?

13. In what ways has your views of happiness and fulfillment changed as a result?

14. Describe a disappointment in your life which led, or can lead, to positive life changes.

FORGIVENESS

"When dealing with people, remember you are not dealing with creatures of logic, but creatures of emotion."

—Dale Carnegie

"It is easier to ask forgiveness than to gain permission."

—Grace Murray Hopper

This seems a bit far out. To grasp my emotions is one thing, but to explore magic...

Nothing comes from nothing. If you cling to situations, then your learning is not complete. When you work through issues thoroughly, they do not arise again.

Tell that to any person who has had their heart broken or who has lost yet another job.

Forgive yourself and everyone else involved. You do not only forgive for others. You forgive to set your soul free, and other souls. You let some people into your life and keep others out. You stand in your own strength, dignity, and power.

So learning to trust my intuition requires discipline and attentiveness.

You trigger revelations you are not even aware of yet. Why not loosen up? Learn why you resist the unknown. When you let go of a hurtful situation, you create a vacuum. This becomes a space for opportunity, a place for you to fill with love and gratitude. Shattered dreams or false hopes are only misdirected perception. Negative vibes are like views of black magic. You assume something outside you controls you.

Pardon me—I do not see cauldrons. I distance from anything hokey like black magic.

Neglect and abuse are different forms of black magic. Human beings cast spells with their words, malicious intent, and other unconscious gestures.

Then items like powders, charms, elixirs, and spell books are only secondary tools?

Black magic is not always obvious or conscious. It is related to suffering. People blame themselves for failure, for being imperfect, less than their ideal. If you mistreat your physical body, mind, or spirit, then what are you really doing? Each situation is preparing you to learn the healing power of forgiveness.

I know intuitively what is happening, not what has happened or, what happens next. Black magic is not what I assumed.

Learning to forgive yourself for actions you now see as misunderstandings is as important as learning to forgive others for their past behavior. You are evolving.

This conversation is redefining the idea of unexpected twists and turns. You remind me love is always worthwhile. When it is given freely, it comes back to me on its own terms.

You sense love, but you do not grasp it. An awakened soul is not indifferent. You learn more and more about the powers you have and the ways you can do good. Still, your understanding of reality is incomplete.

Forgiveness: End of Section Exercises

1. Which lessons do you retain from this section? How would you apply them?
   - In your relationships?
   - At work?
   - On a spiritual level?
   - In other ways?

2. Describe three examples in your life where you have forgiven people. Did you find this difficult? If so, then why? How did people involved react to your gestures?

3. Explain three situations where you have found it hard to forgive. What causes you to hold grudges? How could hard feelings affect the state of higher energy vibration?

4. What can you do to overcome a fear of not being able to forgive and forget?

5. How does forgiveness contribute to your greater happiness?

6. How can your increased happiness and well-being help satisfy the needs of others?

7. How might forgiving others and you be connected to a more meaningful life?

8. How would you feel if someone refused to forgive you? (Recall a story)

9. How do you describe your self-image? How could forgiveness affect self-acceptance?

10. What external influences may have contributed to your perception?

11. How have you abused your physical body? Pushed it over limits or deprived it? How do you feel about the behavior? In what ways can you grow to re-orient your direction?

LETTING GO

> *"Guilt is the price we pay willingly for doing what we're going to do anyway."*
>
> —Isabelle Holland

> *"If the time should come when you have to make a choice between what is right and what is easy, remember what happened to a boy who was good, and kind, and brave."*
>
> —Albus Dumbledore, *Harry Potter and the Goblet of Fire*

I feel like events occur so I will recognize and correct my self-defeating behavior.

To eliminate the instinct to control outcomes is an exercise in self-mastery.

What if I am already there? I realize I choose to blame, victimize, or empty the mind.

That is ego. Learning to let go involves physical, emotional, mental, spiritual, and other levels. Negative thoughts affect energy vibration. Until you let go of what holds you back, you stifle energy flow and cloud levels of vision before you.

It is possible for me to rebound.

You are always rebounding from something. The state of your awareness shapes your view of guilt and sanity. You feel guilty for what you feel was wrong. If you do not forgive yourself, you will not overcome the guilt. Most humans have felt guilty. Some people feel guilt often. Other people do not choose to acknowledge guilt.

As I become more immersed in spiritual practice, will negative energy go away?

To heighten perception, you work through emotions in your physical world. Your awareness is closely connected to conditioning until you make another choice.

On the emotional level, if I nurture hopes about something that is not meant to be, then I sense I limit myself. Do I block tangible things in ways that prevent the exchange of energy?

Some human beings experience guilt when they see others happy. If you focus on the external world, rather than develop yourself, you reinforce emptiness. Each situation invites you to let go of debilitating energy so you gain new insight.

On a mental level, when I cling to things, I permit myself to get anxious. At times, I have found myself going in circles, and not resolving problems. I want to let go, but do not.

As you hang onto situations that do not satisfy your need for certain kinds of energy, your mind remains stuck in situations or, on people you cannot change. You expend energy on what could have been, rather than on expending it differently. You are constantly glimpsing possibilities in energy form. These are not always related to your own life. You are evolving to sense prayers have been answered before you ask.

At the end of relationships where I have felt an intimate connection or bond, part of me initially used to sense misdirected energy. I see value everywhere now. Gaining insight is a blessing, but it does not permit me to transcend new difficult situations that arise.

You are not meant to transcend everything at once. Lessons lead you back to your true path. The magic is always there, taking different forms, expanding quietly.

You mean when I transcend all my issues, then I will experience magic differently?

Actually, parts of you leave this world regularly. The physical part is dense.

Okay, I am letting go of all previous misconceptions. That will enable me to "see"?

It does not work that way. As you feel your life is evolving in ways to enable you to become master of your game, events unfold to shake the foundations of your perception. This not only humbles you, but reveals inner powers you are not using.

I suppose not letting go of negative feelings means I weaken or lose a sense of connectedness with myself. Yet, when things seem to be going well, I do not want to change.

Resistance does not ward off fear.

Is that what you think my game is?

To be born implies you have accepted your fate to reach new levels of wisdom. Yet you distance yourself not only from your spirit, but also from instincts you stifle. Reliving wounds cuts off your inner voice and prevents you from opening your mind. Whenever you focus on fear, you become spiritually detached and isolated.

Perhaps everything that is occurring here is a figment of my imagination?

The more you listen and respond, the more you realize it is not.

Since childhood I have heard voices and felt connected to angels. At age twelve, I also had a bloody bike accident in a residential area that was curiously deserted. I shattered my nose. Two Mexicans arrived out of nowhere, drove me to hospital where I had surgery, then disappeared like on the TV show, *Highway to Heaven*. Later in life while driving during a snowstorm, I hit black ice and careened toward three oncoming cars and truck only to jolt out of the way. It appeared an external force took control. At each stage, I sense I was helped by loving beings. They showed me where I believe I am is beside the point. They appeared from nowhere and returned to nowhere, as if to draw my attention to what I have not been willing to see.

You go to lengths to knock sense into yourself and grow to sense harmony and peace differently. If you did not love yourself, you would not react as you have done.

Letting Go: End of Section Exercises

1. Which lessons do you retain from this section? How would you apply them?
   - In your relationships?
   - At work?
   - On a spiritual level?
   - The other ways?

2. Which of your life experiences would benefit from beginning a process of letting go?

3. Why did you refuse to feel the pain, or sort through the confusion, hurt, or regret?

4. What do you gain from hiding or repressing embarrassing or negative feelings?

5. How does "letting go" shape your growth and enable you to reevaluate your life?

6. Describe a situation where you or someone else has felt guilt or held a grudge.

7. How has harboring guilt negatively affected your relationships and life? How could you learn to let go and forgive yourself on physical and emotional levels?

8. Describe a situation where communication issues made it difficult for you to let go.

9. Describe a situation where making efforts to dialogue helped you let go.

KNOWING SETBACKS

> *"In the middle of difficulty lies opportunity."*
>
> —Albert Einstein

> *"Failure? Never knew it. All I ever met were temporary setbacks."*
>
> —Dottie Walters

Everything that is happening tells me I crave exercise for the spirit. You imply awareness of my potential is not based on traditional training. What do you mean?

You raise awareness of essentials in every area, and of your life. This redefines what matters now. Setbacks are what stands in the way of getting what you want. You forget how you exert energy brings you closer or alienates you from joy. Step back from your ego. See it for what it is. Discover how wise you are.

That is a tall order.

How you think is ingrained. Obstacles are imagined. As you see through them, you learn to read energy. When you do not fail soul, you realize it never fails you.

So, people ultimately create their own setbacks. They refuse to accept accountability.

What you believe is possible or not is part of the process of uncovering. You do not follow your path as if you are others, because you are not them.

Doing things differently does not permit me to push a square peg into a round hole.

To let energy flow naturally, you sense how to love naturally and realize anything else is unnatural. If you view yourself as "pegged," then you judge. People impose their views of "normal" based on their conditioned experience. Learn to look beyond opinions. Instead, feel energy inside that vibrates here and now.

As much as I would like to open my senses to new realities faster, it is humbling to reframe experiences to begin to sense why I create my own setbacks.

To identify sources of fear reminds you that you are a messenger of light.

If I get it, then each of my relationships brings me back to love and what I do with it. It is like I identify a target for my thoughts and decide how to react to it. Love is the baseline.

What you hope you eventually believe. What you believe, you eventually think you know. What you think you know, you will create and experience and evolve to become. Your experiences unfold in parallel dimensions that you do not imagine. All experiences exist simultaneously, but are not always seen with human eyes.

This reminds me evolution goes beyond the physical body. I strengthen in ways I do not see. Where I am matters less than what I learn from setbacks, how I anticipate next time.

Knowing Setbacks: End of Section Exercises

1. Which lessons do you retain from this section? How would you apply them?

- In your relationships?
- At work?
- On a spiritual level?
- In other ways?

2. In what ways do you take charge of your life? In what ways are you complacent?

3. Describe your sense of significant personal, professional, spiritual, and emotional setbacks. How did you respond? How do you view your current setbacks?

4. What sorts of inner conflicts do you recognize? What do you accept/reject? Why?

5. How do your inner conflicts affect your sense of purpose, progress and life choices?

6. How has self-sabotage, lack of plan/initiative shaped your expectations and behavior?

7. How have you changed or how would you like to change? What are you waiting for?

8. When you invest a while and feel no progress, how can you become motivated again? Reflect on a situation where you gave up. How did you feel? Reflect on a situation where you were inspired to react differently to redirect energy and reframe progress.

ORDER AND DISORDER

> *"A miracle worker is not geared toward fighting the world that is, but toward creating the world that could be."*
>
> —*Marianne Williamson*

> *"Order is never observed; it is disorder that attracts attention because it is awkward and intrusive."*
>
> —*Eliphas Levi*

The more I learn, the more I believe the ideas of order and disorder baffle people.

The reality you perceive has points of reference. Love guides order or what works. Disorder is grounded in fear. Your reality is shaped by how you love and why.

It is hard to fathom that I dream up reasons for disorder. And yet, I experience that.

Inner conflict is a symptom of disorder. It awakens dormant ability to love. Images of crises lead human beings to imagine disorder where none exists. Order is linked to things that build faith, trust and hope. Disorder evokes discomfort.

As I listen to what you are saying, I know in my heart it is accurate, yet disorienting.

If you express love and believe others only do so in terms of what they can get, your defenses go up, and you withdraw from what comes from forging a connection. Fear creates imbalance, fragments relationships, and obscures your ability to sense choices. It all goes back to why you chose to stop loving everything about yourself.

Examining my beliefs is like a way to rescue part of me from ignorance. If I was always aware of love, no tests for my understanding of order/disorder would be unnecessary.

Human beings forget they know unwavering love. You create your order and disorder. You decide how you feel about spontaneity, people, and your conditions. As you learn to be receptive to positive energy, you create more spiritual awareness.

Human beings create their own chaos. What if I do not want that?

You get what you think. As you imagine duality, you create limits, and query if behavior is outside a comfort zone. Your sense of order can be someone else's chaos. You are redefining freedom, rediscovering sides of the greatest force you know—love.

What about self-improvement? If anything that is not love provokes internal disorder, then maybe this is the cause of destructive situations. Is the answer always love?

Improvement suggests things can be better or worse. Everything is static. Perception blinds you. If you do not recognize the power of your spiritual side to build positive energy, then you live under the tyranny of your inner judge. You postpone exploring the spectrum of abilities that are unfolding inside of you.

Stepping back to realize perception clouds my senses leads me to wonder what is true.

Separate how you think from what you feel. What other humans describe is not your experience. If you feel empty, then you are unaware of love inside. You do not require words to discern your truth or to conjure the fairytale you already live. You create order and disorder and resolve what suits you to help unveil your truth.

As I reflect, sometimes it comes to my attention I have unknowingly defended lies.

Beneath what you choose to see, you always know exactly what you are doing.

I recognize I have deceived myself and suffered unnecessarily. How do I stop?

As you rise above guilt and regret, you recognize meaning in perceived order and disorder at different periods in your life. You work though it and learn from it. This is a lesson to learn to love yourself regardless of what you do or how you feel.

Each relationship develops my inner power. Still, people think magic is superstition.

Human beings create superstition to perpetuate fear. The scope of order and disorder form the framework of your identity. Images, what you are told, and what you read, all contribute to your dream of knowing more sooner. Sift through the lies.

I sight desirable choices, but part of me hesitates to take action. I am not yet fearless. I have not yet isolated what is fully dependable about my senses and thoughts.

Choices exist that are not yet on your radar. Undesirable external opinions reflect your ego and fear to prevent you from expanding your perspective. As you think, you generate energy. You are always molding energy within and around you.

Okay, reasons exist for everything. Energy is a silent teacher. What is to be avoided?

As you learn to stop thinking and feeling what you have been taught, you will learn to rediscover the reasons behind situations that you sense cannot be avoided.

Discomfort seems unavoidable. So do pain, suffering and awkward moments.

Impermanence is another wise teacher. Fear dissipates when you get wrapped up in the moment, or the unavoidable. You give everything meaning. Love becomes romance when time shrinks. Love becomes fear as time stretches or expands.

What you say implies I can decide some situation or relationship has no significance.

You decide what matters, what does not, what loses meaning, and when.

I sense inner disorder as I further detach from what other people think and do. Yet, it feels right. Love sharpens instincts and makes sense of the unexplained. I am speechless.

Order and disorder are labels. You use them to clarify a sense of pain, love, and growing awareness. Energy communicates through sensations you like or avoid.

Order and Disorder: End of Section Exercises

1. Which lessons do you retain from this section? How would you apply them?
   - In your relationships?
   - At work?
   - On a spiritual level?
   - In other ways?
2. What examples of order and disorder exist in your home and work life now?
3. Do you see yourself as organized or disorganized? What would you like to change?
4. How do your views about order and disorder differ from those views of other people
5. who are close to you? Why might they seek to influence your behavior?
6. Based on this section, what new action might you take enhance your life's meaning?
7. How do images of order and disorder influence your feelings and behavior?
8. What environments and people make you feel more comfortable or uncomfortable?
9. Do you tell yourself the truth? What would trigger changes in your mindset?

INSECURITY

> *"Little by little, through patience and repeated effort, the mind will become stilled in the Self."*
>
> —Bhagavad Gita

> *"If we knock on the door until it opens, not taking no for an answer, our lives will be transformed as we step up into a higher awareness."*
>
> —James Redfield

I did not realize how much I learn about my own guilt through that of others. As I gain insight into how to uplift others, I detach from certain illusions. Tell me about insecurity.

Few humans really know who they are or how they got to be the way they are. They rarely self-examine. If you are aware enough to experience victory and defeat, you are beginning to distinguish sources of wisdom from what does not matter.

Experience teaches me exceptions exist, but does a general process create security?

You hold inside whatever is required. The restless ego seeks new conditions.

I sense abilities inside me now I have always had, but not used. A person notices changes in conditions before abilities or mindset. You have to notice something to desire it.

Attitude shapes your journey, but does not change your destiny. It does not allow you to avoid lessons. No matter how you learn, you have potential to expand your mind. As you get-to-know yourself, you sense who you were, is not who you are.

Sometimes I fear. As I think of spiritual development, visions of séances and spiritual circles enter my mind. This brings me face-to-face with what makes present interaction scary.

You only ever fear yourself. As you bring an issue to your attention, then this invites you to explore how you think and what you tolerate. To be happy, you must be satisfied with yourself and help others satisfy some of their needs.

I have been unaware how my own insecurity carries over in energy to others.

Everything takes form in energy. You only sense what you are consciously ready to handle. After satisfying survival, you discern higher-level needs. Teachers appear. You hurt your growth if you only satisfy other human needs or ignore yours.

Many people ask themselves if they are doing "the right thing." People judge every choice. I have learned insecurities dissipate as you have faith you know what is best for you.

A desire to feel more secure means you are willing to take responsibility for all your actions. When you no longer separate thoughts from feelings, you realize you discern how close you are to destiny by the intensity of self-love.

Well, that resonates. The more I take pleasure in life, the more I express and feel love. I am starting to feel so light on my feet that I must ask you if this an Earthly process?

As you move beyond the past and believe in a future, you will recall other things of importance. What something is or is not, helps you uncover your reason for being. Earth's real role is less important than what it means for you at this moment.

You always talk around things, huh?

Actually, I echo you as I move through you so you realize you choose destiny.

How could I forget? But wait! Energy changes during dialogue. I feel the vibrations.

When you deny your feelings, you mistakenly believe discipline enables you to accept situations. To listen inside is a soul-level exercise. Infinite wisdom is in every situation. To change what you see or feel means you get something different out of it.

Turns out I have not even asked your name yet. That was an oversight on my part.

You resist labels and behave based on your level of consciousness. Words resonate energy, yet also distract you. Not having a name, you learn about me in other ways. Your mental state vibrates at different frequencies, just like mine.

Not having certain details teaches me to release thoughts of what I need to feel secure.

Pause to reflect on what reassures you. Polarize your mind at any vibration you choose. Your energy grows as you learn which influences to shed.

I feel mental habits distract me. I make a conscious decision to become unaffected.

Self-confidence is a sign. You move beyond conditioned insecurity as you realize nothing you assumed is required. You can never be a victim of your choices.

I have been disillusioned as a lesson. I begin to lose count of emerging abilities.

Abilities are not possessions. You are a channel. They operate through you.

Since you do not reveal your name, will you offer another way to identify yourself?

You have a way to go before you believe in the impossible. As your mindset evolves about insecurity, then your energy shifts. You realize you already identify me.

Frankly, it is easier to sense who you are not. Funny, you are teaching me it is natural to use my senses to discern the truth of what you are. Society conditions me to use labels.

Natural law and the natural flow of energy do not require labels. You see them in action, experience them to know them. The power of spirit is always at your service. Moving beyond reflex or rational explanation is a divine plan. You channel energy. It tells the truth.

Insecurity: End of Section Exercises

1. Which lessons do you retain from this section? How would you apply them?
   - In your relationships?
   - At work?
   - On a spiritual level?
   - In other ways?

2. How do define security in your life? Describe your models. What reassures you?

3. What causes you to feel more insecure? (If nothing comes to mind, then think harder).

4. How do you define mistake/failure? How do you feel about them (past/ present)?

5. What is it about uncertainty that may hold you back from realizing certain goals?

6. Describe where you have felt danger. What made you so certain? Did you imagine it?

7. What causes you to feel disturbed? List calming words or ideas that compel thought.

8. What makes you believe you know yourself? What is unacceptable? Why?

9. How well do you think you know friend/family? Would you like to change that?

10. Describe external influences on your view of security? What about internal ones?

11. Beliefs about life and the way it is create views of security. How do yours change?

VULNERABILITY

> *"There's something about vulnerability that helps us connect with people."*
>
> —Jan Denise

> *"There can be no vulnerability without risk."*
>
> —M. Scott Peck

Relationships of the past and present raise vulnerability. It can be scary to sense how much intimate detail is appropriate to reveal or hide. How can I heal these insecure feelings?

You do not speak to a grandmother the same way as your spouse or friend. Subtle discretion and judgment mean you choose not to evolve. You are given opportunities. By loving, sensing, and acting, you move toward the serenity of spirit.

You continue to reveal you know things that I do not. I mean, this life being what it is, I still have not figured myself out. I grapple with my relationship to energy, that is, what I can do with it and what I am meant to do with it. Would you help me become more familiar with these processes? I sense you are a guide who is leading me to my real self.

To better sense how attitude about fear influences your progress, compare yourself to a few acorns. Imagine planting one on a rocky hillside, and the other, in a dense forest. The acorn on the hillside feels vulnerable to storms like you to emotion. Yet, its roots plunge deep into the ground, creating a means of support in adversity. This tree has power to endure elements, branch beneath the surface and grow strong.

If I am to believe in unwavering faith, then I must be the rock and roots. You keep coming back to untapped healing force within me. Why do I not see the way?

Degrees of power exist. You experience this yourself as a channel.

But, I am not a television.

No, you transmit frequencies off the scale. Some physical power is generated biologically. Faith underlies your spirit and what is naturally projected to it.

This is starting to sound a bit like science fiction or a crash course on metaphysics.

What you think you are on a conscious level hides the depth of who you are.

If I consciously knew what I really was, would I not be doing it right now?

Not necessarily. You develop skills via this dialogue. Unlike the forest acorn that becomes a weak sapling, your life prompts you to take risks and survive. You choose your entourage. You choose what you learn and how you will love. This defines you. Your physical life transforms as per your growing awareness.

Exploring the unknown comes naturally to me. Yet, I have met people who feel vulnerable to technology and bureaucracy, people controlled by electronic messages, financial and food issues, beliefs on health, exercise and work. People can be indecisive about what to eat, when to eat it. I ask how often do I do things while not under influence? Just when I believe I think and act independently, I realize I do not.

Human beings are not robots. They exist and function based on will power. Many people are born with the intent not to remember certain truths, at least initially. Attempting everything all the time is not required. You have nothing to prove. What matters is that you are always loved, accepted as you are. You can choose to see that.

To feel overwhelmed as I have is to be upset or discontent with how I am living at a given moment, but not necessarily to be unhappy with my self-view. I accept what I am.

People often deny or cover up confusion or uncomfortable feelings. Becoming consumed by views of what is "possible" or "impossible" can lead you to feel vulnerable to unrealistic goals or expectations. Return to the present moment.

That gets down to identifying questions that have been answered and which remain.

Some people believe sharing feelings makes them weak. This is a lie. It is a strength to be honest. Whenever you direct energy vibration, this is shaping you.

I recall when authorities seized equipment from my office. That investigation that did not involve me personally. It made me feel vulnerable that things could just be taken and I had no power or control over it. As I remained calm, the situation evolved to resolve itself.

To face self-limiting beliefs is necessary before you work through them. As you react with love, you expend energy. Sources of discomfort magically vanish.

Magic certainly takes many forms.

When humans experience defeat, they could choose to view this as a source of inspiration to love differently. You work toward the core of what holds you back.

The more I think about it, the more vulnerability relates to distrust. I may distrust my instincts or the behavior of others. I struggle to verify what matters or what is worth keeping.

Only when you become ruthless with yourself, replacing self-pity and self- deception, will you begin to own and strengthen your untapped power and magic.

When I withdraw from life, this brings attention to fears of treachery or rejection.

You have progressively given your power away. It takes time to get it back.

Vulnerability: End of Section Exercises

1. Which lessons do you retain from this section? How would you apply them?
   - In your relationships?
   - At work?
   - On a spiritual level?
   - In other ways?
2. Which thoughts or experiences evoke feelings of vulnerability? Why?
3. Which thoughts or behavior cause you to feel empowered? Why?
4. Describe a situation where you felt vulnerable. How did you deal with that?
5. What could you learn from admitting you feel vulnerable?
6. What have you learned about your own fear and vulnerability?
7. How does feeling overwhelmed enable you to become connected with who you are?
8. What sorts of life experiences have caused you to rethink the meaning of vulnerability? Where have you felt this was a good thing or bad thing for you?

AVOIDING FEARS AND CONSEQUENCES

"If you look into your own heart, and you find nothing wrong there, what is there to worry about? What is there to fear?"

—Confucius

"Our society must make it right and possible for old people not to fear the young or be deserted by them, for the test of a civilization is the way that it cares for its helpless members."

—Pearl S. Buck

I am beginning to realize I have been thinking and acting in many ways that no longer make sense to me. I was consciously unaware! Incredible, how the invisible becomes visible.

Fear blocks your view, prevents your growth. It holds you back from being all you are and expressing it freely. Yet, fear is only unpleasant if you see it that way

Is it really so simple? To take everything you say at face value would change my life.

How you live is a choice. Imagine you avoid fears. This is not the same as facing them. Consequences are just as easily overcome. If you had not been given strength, you would not be where you are.

Fleeting sadness is a kind of vulnerability I rarely show. I really do not believe in it.

To know energy for all it is, you experience what you do not think you need. Sensing fear invites you to love more and forgive. Eliminate judgment, expectation, quest for approval, and perception changes. You are stronger than fear. Anyone can overcome it. Realize what fear is, why it controls you, why you do it to yourself.

Many people succumb to fear. I did not believe that on some level this is on purpose.

If all human beings believed they were perfect, then life as you know it would cease. How you react is personal. People learn they delude themselves about fear. When confronted with worry, humans tend to avoid facing the source. Backing away only represses anxiety temporarily. It diminishes the creative energy that drives you.

I have heard people say it would take a miracle to overcome their sense of fear.

Miracles are illusions. All events unfold due to universal laws. Ask yourself why you use third person perspectives. Even subtle behavior reveals underlying fears.

I did not believe generalizing did any harm. For example, to meet people who say they are not alcoholics before they polish off a bottle, or say they care for themselves when they visibly self-neglect, sends messages of denial and hypocrisy. I learn what not to do.

You are the master of yourself. Rather than worry what other people do, it makes more sense to raise awareness about what you do to yourself. If you do not pay attention, then you will pay the price in weakened character and lower energy vibration.

Avoiding Fears and Consequences: End of Section Exercises

1. Which lessons do you retain from this section? How would you apply them?
   - In your relationships?
   - At work?
   - On a spiritual level?

- In other ways?

2. Describe situations where someone you know felt afraid. How did you feel/ react?

3. Specify some of your fears and reasons why you might experience them:

4. What are strategies you could use to overcome these fears?

5. Who and what do you avoid? How does each source of avoidance teach you? Describe an experience where you allowed your fear to control your decision-making.

6. In retrospect, would you make the same decision again? Why or why not?

7. How did this affect your attitude and approaches to other problem-solving?

8. Describe a situation where you did not permit your fear to control your action.

9. How did this affect your attitude and approaches to other problem-solving?

CHOOSING FAITH OR FEAR

"No one can make you feel inferior without your consent."

—Eleanor Roosevelt

"Faith must be enforced by reason. When faith becomes blind, it dies."

—Mahatma Gandhi

Many people will pay dearly just to avoid temporary discomfort and possible ridicule. In the long run, retreating does not solve problems. I sense that. Though it is hard to tell when shifting focus is not effort exerted to escape fear. Faith and fear are sometimes blurred.

Motives change based on awareness. Your perception changes how you react. No matter what you sense, you could learn to discern more intense energy forms.

This must be where magic comes in, right? I sense I must know more on this topic.

Magic is a human view of phenomena that seem beyond scope of explanation. As you evolve to realize how and why you limit your own scope, you also begin to realize that what you thought was "out of reach" for you has never been out of reach.

Huh? Each time I deliberate a decision or perceive a situation, I choose between having faith in an outcome and fearing it will not arise. What I want does not always happen.

Yes, it does. You forget your power. It has not occurred to you to give up the thoughts that do not serve you. Loving something creates a sense of miracles. Faith and doubt enable you to realize you always imagine uncertainty on purpose. You desire to learn. It goes as deep as you choose. You hesitate to enter psychic space.

What about those of us who would prefer to see through it, transcend it, overcome it?

Human beings have the freedom to change how they perceive all conditions.

That was a welcome ability when authorities abruptly removed equipment from my office based on a huge misunderstanding. That situation tested my resourcefulness.

You have choices to focus on what other people tell you is reality or, to decide on your own. Magic explains how you redirect energy to reframe where you are.

I would really like to use my innate wisdom and energy differently. I am unsure how.

No human who did anything meaningful knew exactly how he would do it.

My first thought to learn more about magic is to refer to a variety of local resources.

That is not thinking outside-the-box. Imagine living without the fear of being loved unconditionally. The more you visualize and imagine this, the more you love.

Now you imply I do not already imagine things. I do. That is why things happen.

What you seek is not going to be found by depending on what you think you already know on a superficial level. Take what you know on one level and transfer it.

According to you, I am not yet beyond the superficial. I thought I made progress?

When you hesitate, step back and review your reasons for choosing to feel hope and fear. You will grow to feel different energy. Vibrations are like a code.

Over time, I have met people who believe it is easier or more logical to be cynical.

You attract people to reinforce ego, what you feel or what you desire to learn.

I suppose I misinterpret a lot. After all up until now, I have not yet figured out if you are animal, vegetable, or mineral, or something else. I do not know how to describe you.

Categories are human inventions. You creatively transcend the physical.

Such a reply suggests to me that whatever you are, you are not a human invention.

Let us say humans exist in their reality as I do in mine, but in a different form.

Well, I do not fear your energy or words. I sense I also have no reason to fear myself.

During a period of suffering, you do not grasp why you endure it. You may be quicker to blame anything but yourself yet, until you do, fear remains. Whenever you recount disagreeable experiences out of disbelief, you miss the point. The lesson is you are learning to love people as they are, without conditions. You must learn to open your heart to permit energy to flow more freely through you. Learn to consciously expand your senses.

I used to share frustrations when things did not seem to be going well. Yet, I stopped. As I listened to others complain, I sensed complaints gain strength in echoes.

You sense energy on levels you do not comprehend and yet, you live based on your faith in your reading of this energy. You act based on vibrations and frequency.

Excuse me?

Are you ready to be truly honest with yourself? I really mean it this time.

I no longer blame myself for events past that I did not control.

That dodges the question. When will you accept all that you are?

It is my prerogative to disregard the power of intention. You said I choose to forget.

But, that is not why you exist. That is not why I am here either.

I do not know if I can give you a straight answer.

"Can't" means won't. You choose to wallow in doubt, frustration, and a sense of imprecise direction. Each focus you choose marks a pivotal moment in your life. How you interpret what you are doing has substance. Light is what you wish for.

If I add meaning to events with my thoughts, then why does the lag exist? I do not get why it takes so much time for things to happen. And why is my conscious awareness behind?

Becoming more attuned to causes and patterns of your hopes and fears enables you to make more conscious choices. It is a process. You respond to signals within that urge you to make certain choices, not only your desire to be with certain people, but also your instinct to perform certain roles. The signs are in your aura. They are evident in your energy vibration as well.

Why did I not see it coming? I did not foresee that double rainbow outside either.

Events unfold in your life when you are ready to accept what you had rejected.

So, I know what I rejected on some level and it emits energy to raise my awareness.

Yes! I am present in your face because you heighten your sensitivities with such tenacity. During stages of growth, you only perceive parts of the puzzle. Why? Feelings you generate send mixed messages through your mind to confuse you.

I am so used to comparing and describing that the invisible is leaving me at a loss.

In life, you seek to be empowered. Human beings like control. You make choices to feel inspired and increasingly whole, yet choose to feel perplexed. Each action is a means to reframe your place in the physical. You either move closer to a sense of purpose or, increase distance between where you are and your desired focus.

Enough already!

Do I detect you are losing faith?

In what?

In this process; to reflect on choices of faith and fear reminds you that you can focus on opportunities staring you in the face. Shift perception and you sense them.

Whatever my situation, it could always be worse. What I do not or have not achieved is conditioned. The hard thing in my mind is to desire to achieve what is immeasurable.

So, you raise the topic of your beliefs and they are rejected as you feared.

I believe I move to focus on transcending those things that keep me where I am.

Choices always reside in your soul, along with your sense of truth and love.

I did not think hidden fear of disapproval had so much influence over my choices.

Think back to energy that travels through your body like a bolt of lightning.

Well, it makes sense to find significance in my own energy changes. I have not been struck by lightning nor had multiple near-death experiences (NDEs) like Dannion Brinkley, but I have sensed more than a spark from wall outlets. I would like to know how it works.

Consider how you build strength rather than how you might save face.

If I have no need to prove myself, then what am I doing here?

Society orients you to appearances. As you focus more on how you feel, you identify your true self. Concerns reveal inner conflicts. As you identify what is genuine, you overcome conflicts, change how you view them. This builds faith in soul.

Who told you that?

You did. It is my job to help you remember. You know soul energy exists.

To view each moment as growth period, I am drawn to return to do more martial arts. Knowledge I gain through Aikido enhances my capacity for insight.

You shift experiences to help reveal your salvation. Deep down, you sense the nature of activities that will enable you to stop seeking to measure satisfaction.

As a matter of fact, I have been thinking more about miracles and those I can create.

Your quest to stretch your faith may arouse tension in others, but what they think is not for you to decide or change. You move to create clarity, higher thoughts.

Yes, beings known as seers, gurus, masters, or wise ones set noble examples.

You would like someone else then, to save you from the lies you tell yourself?

That is not what I mean.

The more you talk, the clearer you get about who you are and what you want. The more you dream, the more you attune to guidance and energy that help you.

I seek to stretch faith differently. The art of invisibility is something understood by masters at martial arts academies. I seek one. Their ability to move swiftly and silently, made them mysterious, giving rise to stories of amazing exploits and supernatural powers.

Now we get somewhere. How do you know that you have not found one?

Choosing Faith or Fear: End of Section Exercises

1. Which lessons do you retain from this section? How would you apply them?
   - In your relationships?
   - At work?
   - On a spiritual level?
   - In other ways?
2. Note situations that cause you to complain. How does this serve you?
3. Write three life plan outcomes you fear and, conversely, optimistic views.
4. By adopting optimistic attitudes, you profoundly influence your thinking, behavior,
5. happiness and potential for achievement. How do you wish your life to change?
6. Describe what would be involved for you to be living at your full capacity.
7. Do you characterize yourself as an optimist, pessimist or optimistic realist? Why?
8. Explain two experiences that show you blame yourself for things you can't control.
9. How does your mindset shape your relationship choices and your life direction?
10. What do your choices of friends and co-workers say about your belief (or lack of belief) in yourself? What would you change about yourself or these relationships?
11. Identify some of your expectations. What do they tell you about how you justify fear and doubt? How could these perceptions assist you to reframe your life direction?
12. Whether or not you consider yourself to be a spiritual person, how might developing faith in yourself help you to better deconstruct and understand reasons for your fears?
13. What are some of your negative beliefs? How do they affect other areas of your life?

GOING FURTHER

> *"I tried always to do better: saw always a little further. I tried to stretch myself."*
>
> —Audrey Hepburn

> *"Nothing goes further toward a man's liberation than the act of surviving his need for character."*
>
> —John Ciardi

Nothing and everything ceases to amaze me. I recognize that wherever I am, I can go further and move beyond fears. I redefine progress with every breath. It is all moving ahead.

Assuming you only move in one direction is a limited view.

You know what I mean. As Elizabeth Kübler Ross said, "[W]hen you learn your lessons, the pain goes away." You view events differently. You focus on what you gain.

More directions exist than you are consciously aware of at this moment.

If you are a master, then what would it require for me to see you, do what you do?

Whatever you discern outside can be developed inside. Direct your thoughts and energy with pure intent. Anything is possible in the necessary conditions.

In order to be like you, part of me believes I must learn to think like you.

You are worthy as you are. You have no reason to emulate anyone.

Going further then, does it not necessitate growing bigger, going higher or faster?

Growth is multi-dimensional. Your sense of space is limited to what you know.

This whole process is puzzling. For years I have been conditioning images of what I think I want and hope to experience. I have listened to people who have offered advice, courses, structure, and rules. Now progress comes down to teaching myself to forget it all.

Part of you has always wanted what you already know how to do.

I am coming face-to-face with my fear of not finding meaning in my life where I am. To move beyond self-defeated thinking requires I accept myself fully. That is a process.

Individuals underestimate how far they have come, the extent of their accomplishments. Extend your vision. People accept what you accept in yourself.

I attract what nurtures me. I draw people toward me who invite me to open my mind.

Nothing is beyond you. Teachers appear. You build faith your way.

I admit I explore something within myself that seems more than mere curiosity.

What a shame it would be to ignore your gifts and talents. If you expend time and resources and you feel exhausted and unfulfilled, this invites you to rethink how you expend energy. As you choose to deepen your connection to higher forces, you realize you have more ways to learn about existence. You have no reason to give up.

Discussions teach me who I am can change based on how I learn to sense the world.

I am fascinated that I choose which reality to experience and whether to trust my senses. I wonder how long to stay in the reality I now inhabit. Whoops, forgot there's more than one.

You are learning that "going further" has nothing to do with geography, time, or measurable distances that humans use to define their sense of experience.

That is right. Teachers and mystics have written about shifts in consciousness. For a while I have been mysteriously drawn to particular books which help me make sense of things. Wait a minute! You know about this. You helped me find them!

You silently asked for help with your search for meaning. The depth of your inner power may defy explanation, but in some form you always get what you ask for.

Incredible! I have been drawn to biographies, psychology, and varied subjects that follow a common thread. That attracted people who are on a similar track, exploring and expanding their faculties. I began to notice the nature of unique jewelry on friends and to discern energy vibrations. I would feel the urge to contact certain organizations and then meet like-minded people. It has all been connected, planned.

To evolve to understand your motivations and perception brings you back to the core of your authentic personality. Every choice, physical, mental, or other experience distorts your self-view. As you raise your awareness, you come full circle.

Situations that stifle my growth do fade away, but only after I accept their lessons.

No experience is meaningless. You choose when to stray off your chosen path.

"To go further" used to represent a linear stretch. Then, it was measurable, physical and psychological. Yet healing now seems much more than what I imagined. It goes far beyond the visible. It also requires effort to redefine growth and movement based only on feeling.

How you value yourself is reflected in how you use your time and where you channel energy. In order to sense energy, you hide from your conscious perception, heighten your sensitivities and also remove mental blocks you created.

With all I know, and sense that I have learned, I still know nothing. It boggles me!

Think again. You focus on what you desire or permit someone else to fill your schedule or define you. What you love heals you, enables you to eliminate irritability.

I believe I am always loving. You help me realize I read and experience love differently at different stages. As I reexamine my livelihood, I know it is not based on my true passion. Yet people moonlight in one job while preparing to pursue dreams.

When human beings have a health scare, how they spend time changes. Most often people revisit self-acceptance and choose to make the most of where they are. You feel you make a worthy contribution not when people tell you, but as you serve.

I am prompted to eliminate non-essentials and wish I could be sure what they were.

You are. Read your energy. People who do not value you, do not make you feel valued. Those activities that you do not feel truly passionate about or connected to are not serving your core development. Use your energies in ways that enable you to feel excited and energized. It is never too late to change or open to change.

The idea of gifts is relative. How does a person recognize meaningful choices?

As you attune to feelings and energies, you realize some of your issues are already behind you. You learn to accept the essence of each person. You may not like everything that happens, but you can still choose to grow from it.

I also believe pushing myself implies offering friendship or assistance to others.

Recognize it is neither your role nor responsibility to ensure people are happy. Each person has responsibility. To expand yourself, focus on taking your own.

Going further is starting to mean discarding the image of who I thought I was by choosing to lift my own burdens. Small issues become minor irritations I can shrug off.

Irritations are illusions. If you do not acknowledge them, they do not matter. Decide not to permit people or conditions to determine how you think or feel.

Part of the learning curve is figuring out what to keep or discard in a given moment. What seems appropriate or not changes.

All blocks arise when you are not being authentic, or true to yourself. Only you can answer what that means decisively for you.

How reassuring! You can be reluctant to accept the truth and still know what it is.

When your thoughts, feelings, and actions align with your core being, you express the qualities of soul. Always trust that your soul knows what is best for you. Believe. Encourage yourself to do what you want, so long as it does not do harm.

Every life journey has phases. I gain insight into mine as I create points of reference. At different periods of my life, different ages and states of mind, I have defined fear. My life evolves based on how I become aware of what I avoid and why, then overcome it.

You are learning wisdom grows from experience. Every human being finds his or her own way. What other people choose to see is for them. Do not presume what others need to learn.

So, expanding my understanding of learning goes beyond the typical five senses.

Power cannot possibly unveil itself when you hope to identify or describe it. Part of the process is to learn to see beyond ordinary human eyes, beyond what you thought were your limits before you began to expand your awareness.

This is not about redefining activities or relationships I already feel are fulfilling.

No. It is about learning to explore your consciousness more deeply. What you have been preparing to do underlies everything you have ever done and written. All this introspection is leading beyond the familiar realms of your imagination.

I must not be far off the mark now. It is exciting to close in on my purpose for being.

You are never far from the truth. In fact, you are closer than you think. No human is far from his or her own truth. It is not an issue of distance. It is a case of the willingness to mentally prepare and discern. Sensing abilities and using them differ.

Who I am is who I have always been, but I have yet to realize how to adapt and align?

Brace yourself. Your soul is aware of how and why you incarnated in human form. You choose different emotions to learn and build a perspective. Your sense of love energy expands. Your sense of guides expands. You encounter different people and experiences at different stages of awareness and then you move on to help others.

This is a curious way to see the other side, to view all I experience as self-directed.

All human beings have free will. If ever you encounter something or someone that encourages you to do anything that seems unreasonable or not right, then you have the choice not to listen. You send mental requests. You decide what work to do.

This applies to the physical world, and I would presume worlds explored beyond it.

It is up to you to decide of your volition what you will accept as the next step.

Going Further: End of Section Exercises

1. Which lessons do you retain from this section? How would you apply them?
   - In your relationships?
   - At work?
   - On a spiritual level?
   - In other ways?

2. Based on where you are now, describe where you sense turning points or big changes. This may relate to a particular area of your life or, a variety of different areas. What are you learning from this experience? How has it altered your perspective? Values?

3. Which steps would you imagine taking do to progress further to your goals?

4. How do you feel about milestones have you reached? What is the next step for you?

5. Brainstorm ideas that would help you define new goals once old ones are achieved.

6. In what ways would you benefit from using your time and energy differently?

7. List emotions you feel about your personal, work, health and leisure choices. Each life area may have a positive and negative emotional column. What do you learn?

8. What area of your life merits new kinds of attention? Why?

3

Reassess Your Evolution

MOVING AHEAD

"Reasonable people adapt themselves to the world. Unreasonable people attempt to adapt the world to themselves. All progress, therefore, depends on unreasonable people."

—George Bernard Shaw

"I have learnt silence from the talkative, toleration from the intolerant, and kindness from the unkind; yet strange, I am ungrateful to these teachers."

—Khalil Gibran

LESSONS

1. To dream of the person you would like to be is to waste the person you are.
2. It is always possible to reframe your conditions.
3. What you think is reality, differs greatly from the truth.

Frankly, I desire to move forward in a truly evolutionary way, but I do not know how.

Progress is relative. Thinking differently means moving in unfamiliar directions.

So setbacks bring opportunities for me to gain wisdom, and take me to the next level.

You take yourself where you desire to go. Nothing controls your movement but you.

The voice I hear does not come from me, but it comes as sure as I pinch myself right now.

You have heard my voice before, but you were not always willing to listen.

Often I know I search for something. I use up most of my power and part of my reserve energy. The mind guides me through relationships and situations. Yet old patterns, ingrained thinking, and unfinished business distract me from fully experiencing what I could.

As you become aware of patterns, learn to anticipate and resist the familiar. Inner dialogue invites you to view change as desirable. Opinion echoes ego. The unconscious mind waits to be understood. It does not seek approval.

At times I have felt I do not understand what I should be getting out of a particular experience. I consciously ask for teachers, and sense I could get more out of each lesson.

Dreams enable you to explore more of who you are. Part of you never sleeps. You observe and participate and are mostly more attuned to one role than the other. As you discover you sense with eyes closed, you realize your dormant senses awaken.

I used to expect people would treat me in ways I did not want to be treated.

And you got what you expected. You sent energy and attracted as you wished.

Part of me expected to shatter my illusion, but I did not. I learn progress is not just focusing on the good, but understanding reasons for discomfort I resisted or overlooked.

You are filled with teachings you have been given and experiences you store. These reveal colors, textures, and infinite layers that expand your growth. You are learning to convert hardship into strength. You also harness greater inner power.

I resist asking myself why I am not moving differently. When I view something as "hard," it is like I am telling myself I do not want to do it. I unconsciously resist. Doubt in any form distracts me from why I am where I am. I adopt a mindset that will resonate higher.

Consider how life's hardships drive people of all ages and walks of life to develop destructive thoughts. All of this defines a personal learning curve.

That reminds me how some people have been conditioned to view their situations as reasons to pity themselves. If people manifest what they need, then they do not always see it.

At some point all human beings hit "rock bottom." This could be experienced financially, emotionally, mentally, medically, spiritually, or in other ways. Those who define life in pain, suffering, or failure, do not only come from broken homes. Where you come from does not define you. How you choose to feel in the moment does.

Many people create some baseline or point of reference. They like to orient spatially. You have a better sense where you go, whether you move, if you can describe where you are.

Imbalance prompts action. Recovery emerges from conscious choices to initiate self-healing. When you forgive yourself, others, you rise above negativity.

Faith inspires healing. It is said this concept reaches infinity. I have never been there.

Not seeing serves you. If you believe physical illness grows from energy imbalance, then you can shift energy frequency and heal issues before they manifest.

I have come to the point where I believe what I have done in life makes sense for what it is. I value jobs, relationships, and upsets and redefine progress based on how I feel. For a long time I believed my dreams grew from my imagination. I still believe it and they do.

Whenever part of you denies your feelings about anything, another part of you is wrestling to get your soul back. When you give your energy away to any thought or action that does not nourish you, realize you have power to shift what you do. This is part of your process of remembering. You have not yet learned what full expression is.

I have many things to remember. Selective forgetting is as useful as is selective recall.

You are always brave. To sense what you are not, you realize what you are. The more you deny how you feel, the harder forces within and around you work to enlighten and redirect you. Guides are always present. Each one serves a purpose.

I sense many changes go on inside me, but I do not track or grasp them all. I used to worry more about that. I used to think I do not know how events will affect life as I know it.

Disrupted routines are useful. They remind you that you possess knowledge.

As I realize I need not know how to use what I know, I learn to adapt and cope as events unfold. I realize I am never empty-handed. My capacities unfold to build character.

When you are aware of the law of attraction at work, it is not such a mystery.

Words do not adequately describe what I am experiencing. The frequency of my energy teaches me to redefine possible. I have never encountered anything I did not manage.

Fear disturbs vibration. Recognize your misunderstandings. Be conscious of your abilities. The universe equips you to deal with everything. You emit and receive energy. Ask where you are going. Answers are always given.

I realize how I evolve is a matter of magnitude that I am not meant to measure.

Your process is your evolving story. Power runs through your energy field. It strengthens as you notice the current and choose to clear perceived blockages.

Threads are coming together. I begin to feel adjacent energy fields. I make phone calls to people far away when I sense they are available. I discover they just arrive in the door.

What seems insignificant to others has deeper meaning for you.

On separate occasions while living abroad, I phoned my grandfather just when he needed someone. As he was slowly going blind and lived alone, he did not always see the phone. Yet, he found it when he heard it. In one instance, he had fallen and cut his forehead. Why my impulses to call?

You tap into energy flow. You do not yet grasp impulse or where it's leading.

In 2007, just before I heard news my maternal grandma died, I dreamed she regained mobility and walked away from her wheelchair. During that dream, she communicated with me telepathically. After she passed, I visited my grandfather. He desired to follow his wife. I told him angels would come when ready. I dreamed how they felt before they were reunited.

What you dream is always real. As you learn to read energy, this is teaching you how to rejuvenate inner energy you disregarded. Experience is not taken away from you or given back. You dream the presence of everything to bring new clarity.

As I wear my grandmother's scarf covered in her favorite flower, I notice more of that flower around even though it is not in season. The flower also appears in unexpected places.

Love is a memory and a bridge that transcends different worlds.

You know, I do not watch much television, but I recently flipped through channels to a documentary program. The subject was a medical ship that sunk in the Baltic Sea during World War II. I knew instinctively this was the ship that my grandparents were supposed to take to escape the bombings. They missed that boat as my mother got lost in the commotion. They found her a day later. She had been taken in by older folks in a retirement home. The Red Cross ship had been bombed overnight. When my maternal grandfather was still alive, he told me that story with emotion. I never forgot how providence got them on the right path.

You are slowly moving to the center of your truth. You are learning to trust in what is unfolding. You no longer only view yourself from a physical standpoint.

To believe in the circle of life is to recognize the soul is never ending. I sense new kinds of continuity in energy that defy how I was conditioned. The sensations grow stronger.

They are not new. Opening yourself up to listen enables you to reconnect.

During my second trip to Estonia, I was drawn back to an immense cemetery I had passed briefly a few years before. This time, I felt drawn straight to a separated area of plots. I walked directly to my great grandfather's grave. I did not even know he was buried there.

Some human beings seek to become what they decide they will not be. You accept incoming visions and feelings. You are breaking down boundaries you created in the mind. As you build on your prior consciousness, I am not your only guide.

I begin to accept what is going on in me, but is this something that naturally happens to human begins if they choose to evolve in awareness? How would other people take it?

Vulnerability becomes your greatest shield. The only thing that prompts people to hide is fear. To work through it is a choice. The inner power you discern has healing properties. This power has degrees of healing functions you can explore.

Complete strangers assist me to clarify things without even knowing what they do. During seven days of my honeymoon, I encountered signs from my maternal grandmother. She had an unusual name. One day it was on a clerk's nametag at a train station. In another city her name was on a huge store sign. On an island in a church, I came to a display of dolls in ethnic costumes. The central doll's dress was like my grandmother's. Poppy images were also encountered repeatedly where I stayed and on billboards. The signs reflected love.

On a deep level, every being knows. What you choose to discern and what you intuit only seem different. One thought leads to another. Patience, courage and confidence grow to drive your evolution. Expressing yourself comes naturally. You get absorbed in energy. It reminds you that you are worthy, gifted, and loved as you are.

I am learning to reframe all conditions.

Many people choose to sustain themselves with perceptions of trial and struggles. You may also choose to restore your energy. You are discovering options. If I tell you exactly where you are going with this, then that will disturb the continuity.

Please!

Supposing the spirit of someone you knew was around, how would you know?

That depends on memories I have of the person, associations or common experiences. If I am attuned, sometimes I will smell a particular aroma no one around me does. That aroma will come with a thought of the person. I mentioned some other examples previously.

In other words, you detect connections in energy vibration. Senses connect.

You could say that. I receive the message mentally, and I just know, like synchrony.

If you appreciate energy as it flows, then you do not doubt, correct?

That is about the size of it.

You are growing to recognize things about yourself that have largely been blocked by other destructive emotions and habits. Whenever a human being discovers he can do something, this is not because he could not do this thing before. It is because he was unaware of his capacities and therefore, did not use them.

You forgot to mention mental-preparedness.

I did not have to. You already knew what I was thinking.

Reassess Your Evolution: End of Section Exercises

1. Which lessons do you retain from this section? How would you apply them?
   - In your relationships?
   - At work?
   - On a spiritual level?
   - In other ways?
2. What do you view as achievable goals? How do you plan to realize them?
3. How would you measure progress in different areas of your life?
4. Recognize your own self-defeating judgment that limits your view of "possible."

- (i.e.: where do you say: I can't because...) (change it to: I can because...)
- (i.e., I won't achieve this because...) (change it to: I will achieve ...)

5. What it is that you long wished to do, but have never done? Why?
   - How would someone who knows you well answer that?
   - How about someone who barely knows you?

6. What in your current reality do you see as a positive step toward defining new goals?

7. Note examples where your decisions have been influenced by what people would think. What does this say about your self-confidence and the impetus for your goals?

8. What is your reference or plan for moving ahead at this stage of your life?

9. Do you share your feelings or shut people out? Are you direct or diplomatic?

10. Reflect on some experiences where you anticipated what someone would say or do before they acted. How did it feel to get confirmation?

SENSING CLEARER DIRECTION

> *"Don't compromise yourself. You're all you've got."*
>
> —Janis Joplin

> *"Common sense is the measure of the possible; it is composed of experience and prevision; it is calculation applied to life."*
>
> —Henri Frederic Amiel

Growing then, is something that I do actively and passively, and you witness it all.

Your sense of direction changes with your revelations. As you look back to see where you have been, you decide what is to be next. You benefit from re-evaluating your beliefs and determining if their current form still nourishes you. If not, then this is a sign to let go so new beliefs emerge to strengthen you. Your beliefs deter-

mine your self- value. What you believe you can do with energy differs from what you can.

Many people long for something they are unable to put their finger on. Some people seek to revisit or review the past. Others move on. As for me, I am frequently reorienting, wondering if this process ever slows down to stop.

Do not disregard the significance of high-frequency experience. If you fail a test, then you retake it. If you are not accepted into a club, then you can reapply or find a new club. If you do not earn recognition, then it is not a sort you want or need.

It is so eye-opening to reflect differently without the impulse to justify or explain. Certificates reflect external views of what is meaningful. In this world and worlds beyond, what I see and do is based on how I accept or reject myself at deeper, soul levels.

Note positive and negative vibes orient your chosen direction. Your initiatives stem from creative choices or judgments you take on. To identify what is meaningful, listen to what feels right. If you lose faith, then higher forces will catch up with you.

Whether or not I realize it, I unconsciously assess what is the "right thing to do" now. Then, I skip conscious steps because of having faith. I do stop on indecision. My impulsive side grows stronger each time I act and feel I benefit from past decisions.

Everything that helps guide you back to your soul. Feelings are energy forms that bounce off people around you. You resonate all the vibes. As you take the time to sift through them, you assist people with their own journeys, and help also comes to you.

My maternal grandmother always encouraged me to share what I learn, to encourage others to stop and think. It is not surprising she still finds ways to do this.

Names are not the real individual. This is only one way a being is known.

I know what you are saying. You think of taste preferences, hobbies, behaviors, and other ways to sense personality. This prompts me to love all, even when I feel dispirited.

Your spiritual side will prompt you to pray for others. This happens as you ask higher forces to help you listen to yourself. Human beings are not meant to understand exactly how energy triggers inner change. Conditions empower you to recognize what matters. Whatever people do will help you as long as you choose to help yourself. Even choosing not to model the behavior of others can build strength.

You can say that again!

Another thing: Everything you experience has occurred before in different energy forms. The same lessons are available to everyone. Trusting yourself includes being happy with who you are every moment. Nurture an uplifting attitude even when you do not sense good happening. What you do not see is vital to expand you.

I get it! Only impatient people sense they are experiencing lessons in patience. Funny, I get the feeling I have not yet mastered patience because those lessons keep coming.

Human beings cannot know or grasp each thing that higher forces are planning or doing. This is not to say that you affect nothing. Your choices pave the way. Your principles ground you and give you stability wherever you happen to be. You would benefit from learning to trust them more fully.

I used to think direction had to be definitive, predictable, measurable and logical. Then, I discovered that as I need strength, I just have it. Directions are not always visible or traceable. I do not always know how my strength grows. At times, it seems inexhaustible.

Higher guides urge you to open your heart and mind. You choose to face difficulty. It is not your job to seek, but to find. You willingly confront challenges. Even when you may not feel very strong, you have the power of higher forces within you from which to draw upon. Tap into that strength. Develop it as you will.

It is like you know what I do and you want me to do it, but I do not know how. I sense shifting and aligning energy. I sense inner peace that enables me to reframe dimensions unseen. I have lost my previous sense of self, detaching from those activities I felt were me.

No matter what happens or what you influence to happen, look ahead. Keep believing. Be grateful for whom you are and the talents you have been given. Cultivate them. Each day you are faithful to yourself, you nurture seeds toward a brighter future. Opportunities always exist for growth. Lessons never stop. You are beginning to sense implications. This goes beyond a physical or emotional condition.

Sensing Clearer Direction: End of Section Exercises

1. Which lessons do you retain from this section? How would you apply them?
   - In your relationships?
   - At work?
   - On a spiritual level?
   - In other ways?

2. What criteria or conditions led you to choose your partner, job, and fields of interest?

3. How could you act to develop new strength and more courage inside yourself?

4. Offer three ways you could use your current conditions more to your advantage.

5. What does your view of advantages say about your evolving sense of purpose?

6. Choose five traits and five skills you will strengthen to help you move ahead.

7. Write three things in your life which cause you to feel joy as you work toward them.

8. How would you describe what you think is worth having? Or doing? Is it clearer?

MONK IN YOUR MIND

> *"If you always do what interests you, at least one person is pleased."*
>
> —Katherine Hepburn

> *"There are no accidents...there is only some purpose we have not yet understood."*
>
> —Deepak Chopra

I like analogies. To me, what matters is to experience situations and recognize they are worthwhile. I often find myself asking what a serene monk would do in my situations. This periodic reflection reminds me the power of peace, good will and courage in giving.

When you sense unfavorable circumstances and suffering, you can also imagine absorbing the suffering of everyone. This would lighten their loads and enable you to sense more with soul. A monk in your mind seeks seclusion to give soul voice. A close relationship leads you to rediscover your deepest, truest, highest self. Experiences distance you from inner peace only if you permit this.

As I put pieces of this puzzle together, I am at a loss about what you want from me.

I want nothing your soul does not desire for itself. Doubt means you resist true intimacy. Part of you desires reassurance. You need to believe you are strong enough to set boundaries, create structures for safety.

Maybe I hope to mold a future in an activity that is beckoning and ever-insightful.

Whenever you reach out to touch someone or something, something invisible touches you back. This is not a figment of your imagination, but spiritual reassurance.

Part of me believes my choices have not always been ideal. No matter what my efforts to become more aware, I have encountered negativity, criticism, anger, and aloofness.

Every situation offers reasons to believe in yourself and gain new confidence in all that you are. Those people who seem to be your greatest burdens and frustrations are wise teachers. Consider how they lead you to realize you do not know everything about yourself or the world. Just when you begin to assume you grasp patience, understanding, love or anything, experiences humble you.

During all experiences, I develop awareness that strengthens parts of me. I am ready to take a leap toward a voice and a mindset that guides me to evolve as I express how I feel.

As you move to understand yourself, the way to discern is to risk everything.

How can standing and sensing my inner power come if I opt to give it up?

No matter what you do, you cannot lose who you are, even if you are a seeker.

For whatever reason, I convince myself I am unworthy and mixed up with nothing.

When you feel malnourished, it can be difficult to value and trust yourself. If you believe you find the point of all this, then you may fear or feel it is too good to be true. Before now, it may have seemed easier to shut yourself away with books or to change focus. Habits dissolve as you turn to invest in experiences that generate inner light.

I have been looking to sources that I now realize are unlikely to provide what I need. This is a great irony. It is a lesson to challenge myself on levels of my being I had not seen.

Humans often seek love and affection in people who do not know how to give. Until you become aware of what you need, you look for love where you are least likely to find it. Monks look inside. People bring you to face fears and insecurities.

Monks teach me value in simplicity. I send out love and light and exert effort to stop focusing on separating dependence and independence. I attended a few monastery retreats.

To intensify your light energy, you must identify deeper soul questions.

I admit I get lost in a kind of abyss. I stare into a timeless wall hanging with a man on a pilgrimage. He walks barefoot up a mountain toward the isolated cave of a spiritual master.

Your continued questioning is changing your energy vibration. You learn lessons as you climb your mountains. Regardless of where you think you travel, the furthest distance you ever go is within yourself. You explore the infinity of the mind.

Amidst everything that unfolds around me, to read poetry permits me to refocus:

> Let me not pray to be sheltered from dangers
>   but to be fearless in facing them.
> Let me not beg for the stilling of my pain,
>   but for the heart to conquer it.
> Let me not look for allies in life's battlefield
>   but to my own strength.
> Let me not crave in anxious fear to be saved
>   but hope for the patience to win my freedom.
> Grant me that I may not be a coward,
>   feeling your mercy in my success alone;
> but let me find the grasp of your hand in my failure.
>   —Rabindrinath Tagore

During such moments, you begin to confront yourself. That is an intrinsic step in your quest for a higher level of consciousness. Wait till you see where that leads.

So the key is to ask different questions and grow more confident with my answers.

You begin to grasp how and why you exist. It is a journey, full of turning points.

Monk in Your Mind: End of Section Exercises

1. Which lessons do you retain from this section? How would you apply them?
   - In your relationships?
   - At work?
   - On a spiritual level?
   - In other ways?

2. What are some of the most difficult questions that preoccupy you about yourself?

3. What are some issues or questions about the world that interest and challenge you?

4. How could this information act as a clue for the next step in your life path?

5. Which talents do you discern emerging within yourself? How could you use them?

6. Describe a life situation where you have reason to compare your imagined and real needs. In what ways does making this distinction assist you on your life journey?

7. Reflect on a situation which hurt your sense of pride. How do you feel about it now?

WHAT'S MISSING?

> *"The real voyage of discovery consists not in seeking new landscapes, but in having new eyes."*
>
> —Marcel Proust

> *"Something very important is missing from my life: consistency."*
>
> —Nastassja Kinski

As I arrive at points where I discover and admit something fundamental is missing in my life, or in my attitude, I become willing to figure out why.

This implies the willingness to reconnect to higher forces beyond you.

I do sense I am edging closer to something.

To fill the void you discern within, refine your needs. Explore ways to serve. Helping others helps you, whether it is enabling someone to reconnect with a passion or a source of comfort, or encouraging them to explore options to find what they need.

Many people believe a fulfilling relationship or pursuit is missing from their lives. That was a fundamental feeling I had. And yet, I had to sense completeness inside me before I found opportunities to add to a sense of completeness in other forms.

Your mind wanders when you feel uncomfortable with yourself.

It is so confusing. Social structures feed our illusions. Messages constantly tell people to plan for tomorrow, yet the people do not know how to notice or value the "now."

Social structures teach you how well you know or do not know yourself. People hesitate to change. Why? You choose what you will and will not accept. If you feel misguided at soul level, then you will not recognize other wavelengths. Your energy determines how and what you perceive.

I am able to recognize you and ideas you are sharing but I sense I am not exactly on your wavelength. To interact with you, albeit briefly, sort of contradicts what you just said.

You do not always acknowledge me, but you have always sensed me on some level. To realize voids exist, you have to become aware things are unbalanced inside. As you sense these voids and gradually accept more of yourself, you start to hear frequencies you did not detect or hear as clearly before. Many more energy levels exist that transmit messages. Open yourself to be more receptive and listen.

When you put it that way, I do discern resources I have not been using regularly. I realize I have untapped skills and potential. Many people hesitate to act or fill their voids.

To be flexible and willing to transform means you gain a stronger sense of who you are. As you move beyond excuses, you enhance invisible spiritual ties and enrich your life force. This is drained each time you give into destructive emotion. Work though that. Arrive somewhere else. Your state of mind and soul expand.

People often say, "How can I find someone or something that really satisfies my needs?" Or, "I once loved that person, or that activity, but I stopped when key needs in me were just not being met." In different situations I have sought completeness outside myself.

Inner dialogue enables you to reevaluate your changing needs, if you choose to listen. You are not meant to fulfill yourself by establishing lasting ties with every person you meet. If over time, you grow to feel starved and empty, if you sense a lack of sharing and nourishment, then a relationship or situation does not work for you. Recognize you do not have to be compatible with everyone or everything all the time.

In retrospect I suppose failure does not exist, only negative judgments inside me. I do not wish to neglect myself in favor of altruism or sacrifice myself for people who do not care. It can be hard to set boundaries for my devotion and commitment. I want to give it all.

Recognize no person or situation will meet all your needs. As you discover new aspects of yourself, some of them may scare you or other people. Do not expect other people or even you to know exactly all the things missing in your life. Each step is a new discovery. Everyone will not accept all of you, but you can.

Some people believe that companionship can make life more enjoyable than solitude. Where love evolves in two people, they can talk and share perceptions of needs. I have found interaction with others helps me discern needs I had not seen. In this way, love helps detect and fill holes. Awareness of holes leads me to seek new sources of fulfillment.

Talking about thoughts, dreams and initiatives can connect beings. Love is the cement of experience. It adds a sense of completeness and satisfies unmet needs.

Each new experience helps me recognize inner voids I did not know I had. Things that seem missing invite me to sense and experience differently. Darkness becomes light energy.

If you sacrifice too much light to support another need, this is unhealthy.

You continue to mention light and energy in ways that had not jelled for me before. It is as if something about you offers guidance to my soul. You help me to view truth inside myself. A kaleidoscope of color brings me a fresh perspective.

To evolve as a seer is an experience that defies words. It is a path that requires deep insight, unwavering faith and support.

I am not an oracle or a prophet. I have no crystal ball. At the same time, I sense that I am changing and moving away from a physical frame. Since birth I have been dreaming about traditional and nontraditional healing practices. In waking life, I also recall disguising myself as a medicine man for a Halloween party for hospital volunteers, staff and patients.

To recognize you are endowed with spiritual insight is a personal revelation. You do not have to read palms or take on a title to sense energy. Everyone does it, but not everyone is aware or accepts the implications. Understanding comes when you are ready is. It requires discipline to unlearn knowledge that is misinterpreted. Intuitive skills grow to shake you up.

For as long as I can remember, I have been described as unconventional, but...

Teachers are where you are not looking or expecting. They tend to the energy field around you and empower you to reevaluate and redefine dialogue as you are.

A common view is that I must accept myself as I am. Yet, my sense of this is changing more rapidly than ever and is increasingly hard to follow.

Remember what I told you about following anything. It is like a carrot on the end of a stick. When you find yourself pursuing anything, stop and listen.

To accept myself as I am implies taking all voices I hear in stride. It is not up to me to discern what is missing in others. Only they can decide to change, if it is their will.

You can ask another person to change, but more to the point, you can change how and what you see. You grow constantly and are unaware. You adapt for what you think has value, but you actually adapt for something else.

As I stand back and gather my thoughts, I sense how this conversation began with me talking, going through the motions. Here you are now telling me it was all leading to this.

I say nothing you do not already figure out for yourself.

The ups and downs of day-to-day living seem irrelevant. Much of it drains my energy.

You had a vision that predicted what it would take for this book to arise.

So I adapt my life to growing insight. We cooperate on a task.

You empower others to figure out what is missing while you remind yourself.

What's Missing? : End of Section Exercises

1. Which lessons do you retain from this section? How would you apply them?
   - In your relationships?
   - At work?
   - On a spiritual level?
   - In other ways?

2. What makes you feel comfortable and/or uncomfortable about change?

3. Detail what circumstances you believe you need to feel satisfied. This could include personal, professional, emotional, spiritual and/or other elements. Next, describe your current situation. Reflect and compare that to what you wrote about satisfaction.

4. Recount any daydreams or night dreams that may have offered you clues about where, when, and under what other circumstances you are unsatisfied. What do the dream images tell you about your feelings in relation to your actions?

5. What are your most urgent desires? How might you begin to satisfy them?
6. Describe an experience when you thought a person or activity would fulfill you and it did not. What did you learn about you? How did you react to the person or activity?
7. Describe your top three noticeable inner voids. What might you do to help fill them?

GIVING LIFE NEW MEANING

> *"If we knew the meaning to everything that is happening to us, then there would be no meaning."*
>
> —Idi Amin Dada

> *"Since it is the other within us who is old, it is natural that the revelation of our age should come to us from outside—from others. We do not accept it willingly."*
>
> —Simone de Beauvoir

Giving my life new meaning is all about timing.

You foresaw this book through the eyes of spirit. Relatives came to you amidst seagulls above a beach. They said it would happen. In their own way they foretold a process you had to experience to manifest the truth. They did not tell you how, but they told you why. You had to figure out the rest yourself.

I evolve to think events have no meaning. That dream gave no impression of time. Significance and purpose are created by my own interpretation and understanding of things.

Your perception of events defines the directions you wish them to take. What you learn is a choice based on awareness of how you feel. The knowledge you detect may initially seem unreasonable. And yet, you decide what is reasonable and why. Selective ignorance or indifference keeps you where you are.

People are unaware how they define their goals. When I feel good vibes about things, I tend to head in that direction. When I feel apprehensive, I tend to pull back, retreat, give up or rationalize its good training to overcome fear.

Much of what you do is grounded in morality. Pride is a serious obstacle to spiritual progress. Your life choices and experiences tell you it must be completely removed. You gradually face all those traits that have prevented you from seeing.

It would be helpful to have a checklist. Would you be willing to assist me with that?

The set of values you adopt brings you face-to-face with traits to form your list. Perceptions are diverse. Take steps to better sense and accept who you are now.

This is similar to a vein that tells people to glimpse the workings of their hidden self.

Even rigid thinking guides growth. Unchanging principles mean a person will constantly struggle to control emotions. For instance, you were taught to always obey your parents, in-laws, or boss, but you may grow to disagree with their views.

You cannot expect a child to always agree with everything he or she hears from adults. I do not, yet this can be seen as disobedience, disrespect of elders, or even rebellion.

Overly flexible morality imposes restraints out of convenience. Yet morality that expands based on maturity leads to selective changes. Evolutionary morality based on experience adds new dimensions grounded in awareness and intention.

My own experience has taught me people will view intent and intention differently.

Intentions manifest through your thoughts and words. Intent is a concept that allows you to explore infinity. How you see differs from what others see. Sometimes it is difficult to go out of your body, but you have done it, you do it now, and will again.

In my life I've met people that create their own sense of meaning at a given moment.

You plant seeds of ideas in your mind like magic beans. You make a wish.

So we are each under different spells. I believe I can do certain things and I refuse to do others for reasons that bring me back to fear. I define what feels right at a given time too.

Whatever goes against yourself takes your attention away from what gives your life depth. A broad spectrum of codes, customs, and traditions guides how you live. Instincts prompt you to control or free impulses. Public opinions move with new scientific facts or court verdicts, but such views do not alter your inner sense of who you are. They simply postpone your recognition. The more you speak to yourself and develop fascination with magic, the more you are creating and receiving visions.

I sense certain laws or principles are unchangeable, but those are not in the press.

Be aware of your recurring thoughts that communicate the frequency of your instincts. This has nothing to do with what goes on around you. Self-mastery means you can control your moods, energy levels, and polarities. In order to get to that point, you must learn to disconnect from what people think or do in the physical world.

It is hard to stop pursuing. Conditioning runs deep. To stop and realize I feel good halts the feeling or leaves me in a state of suspended animation. I naturally resist many situations that evoke discomfort, but only to a point, because I learn those teach me a lot.

It has always been that way. Some of your deeper soul work is just beginning.

My instinct used to always prompt me to avoid certain people. I used to assume they were the problem. In one case, I learned a very negative person who initially alienated me had never really known love or compassion, only abuse, violence and hate. In choosing to confide in me, she learned of love while I learned patience and understanding, among other lessons.

To shatter your myths and theories compliments you own increasing inner harmony.

You know about that too, huh? Many avenues exist to explore life mysteries. Even books about stones sort of fell into my lap and really feel right. They are tools.

You follow instincts without knowing why you do it. Another book appeared on a familiar library shelf and you were prompted to drive 900km to a conference that just felt right as well. Impulses reflect unspoken wisdom. All you must do is listen.

I reflect on people I have met who suffer health setbacks. Some permit themselves to be debilitated. Others use physical hardship as occasion to deepen spiritual awareness and to address self-destructive behavior. Morris Goodman, the Miracle Man, is a fantastic example. All experiences are meaningful, but I do not always have a clear idea what I gain from them.

Core learning is immeasurable. What you sense during an experience differs from how you feel later. As you raise awareness, you become conscious during every experience and have no reason to reflect back. Do not expect the same experiences to unfold as those which have happened to others. That is not how soul magic works.

My values give me points of reference. I do resist certain choices or behavior when I feel it's not the best thing to do. I am still learning about control. I still desire to minimize what I view as unacceptable conditions for people around me. The judgment must dissolve.

You need discipline when you dream. You just assume you are awake.

If I am dreaming as my life is unfolding, throughout all the trials and tribulations, and the pleasurable experiences, then I have a far more vivid imagination than I thought possible.

You have no idea! You have a limited conscious sense of dreaming, but an unlimited understanding on other levels. You are elsewhere in symbolic ways.

When I imagine more acceptable conditions, my mind wanders to sponsoring foster children, supporting disaster relief, literacy, and things like vaccination, education and peace.

Such ideas are grounded in opinions focused in the physical plane. They are also based on your values of desirable conditions or standards that are not universal.

It is hard to believe intentions can be misplaced. I sense that awareness has different levels. Maybe this helps explain lack of consensus? Natural disasters only inspire some proactive thinking. Human minds develop methods to protect society and biodiversity, yet people disagree about the most meaningful initiatives, what they cost or who should pay.

To see the bigger picture gives meaning to how you think and how you behave, as well as increases your understanding about your belief systems. Move beyond them.

So we are getting into multiple words and dimensions. Preparation to go is exciting!

You are already there. Implicit in your personal acceptance of a code of right and wrong is the notion that you are of lesser importance than higher forces and the bigger picture beyond you. If you internalize that your personal well-being is less important, then your self-worth suffers and you neglect your soul.

Where I am is meaningful, but I struggle to detach from that to get where I am going.

You struggle to detach from expectations. Taking care of yourself adds meaning to your life now. This part of a journey invites you to learn to care for yourself differently. It is not reinforcing physical realities you have come to know. You move geographically and you also distance yourself spiritually and emotionally from people and circumstances that are no longer on your wavelength.

I still do not know how I exist in more than one place at once. Will you explain that?

It is all encoded in the energy you are learning to decipher. You do not always have to understand what you do. You do what makes sense at soul level.

When everyone figures this out, imagine world economies may crumble. Jobs related to manufacturing, sustaining and replacing transport will be obsolete. Taxes generated from energy consumption will no longer be available. Energy as humans consume it and all the related industries and lifestyles would transform. Mindsets and beliefs would have to change

Rather than get into possibilities for the world you think you know, it makes sense to revert back to your own sense of self. Teachings that stimulate your awareness may affect other people, but you dream the answers you need now.

Different belief systems alienate me from myself. Perceptions of injustice differ.

What goes on around you does not affect you unless you take it personally. As you transcend that, you cease to be obsessed with control and only sense magic and power in yourself through other people. That pulse is no longer imperceptible.

Whenever something becomes perceptible, I assume other things are still unseen.

To choose to attune to energy fluctuations does not appeal to everyone. The Akashic record is a public space. It stores energy of everything you think and do.

Now the sound of that place intrigues me!

This is an exercise in developing patience. We will get to that.

Giving Life New Meaning: End of Section Exercises

1. Which lessons do you retain from this section? How would you apply them?
   - In your relationships?
   - At work?
   - On a spiritual level?
   - In other ways?
2. What aspects of leisure and work-related pursuits add meaning to your life? Why?
3. How can you make them your principle focus and reorient your life directions?

4. Describe how the goals that add meaning to your life conflict with the goals of

5. people who know and care for you. How does this make you feel? What will you do?

6. When would you feel it would be an advantage to adjust your views about acceptable behavior? How would flexibility enhance your self-confidence and esteem?

7. Describe a situation where you took (or will take) action to expand your knowledge.

8. Share a life experience which caused you to change your views about morality.

9. How do your existence and efforts add meaning to the lives of people around you?

10. In what ways do they offer clues about and connections to your life purpose?

APPROACHING SELF-ACCEPTANCE

"God, grant me the serenity to accept the things I cannot change, the courage to change the things I can, and the wisdom to know the difference."

—Dr. Reinhold Niebuhr

"The best effect of any book, is that it excites readers to self-activity."

—Thomas Carlyle

Arbitrary human determinations distract me from approaching self-acceptance.

Nothing is arbitrary. You give away inner power and postpone soul love each time you believe your state of mind is not directly related to your choices. Why create hierarchies? What you experience shapes your perception every moment. How much you are paid in a job reflects social value. Another way to look at it is to see it as a reflection of ego and perceived self-importance. Acceptance is beyond that.

Factors beyond my control, like supply, demand, and market trends affect some salaries and stretch gaps between highest and lowest so that they seem out of proportion.

You imagine everything, including what you measure, judge and compare. When you assume inferiority or superiority, or not getting enough money or anything, this conveys messages on conditional self-acceptance. Working to achieve unconditional self-accep-tance is key to higher self-mastery.

Hold on! A well-known movie actor might make a million dollars per picture. A professional athlete may receive enormous sponsor-ships. Musicians and artists are often paid according to their popular-ity. A CEO may earn twenty even thirty times what his employees earn. Scales of salaries in public and private sector jobs change based on gender, politics and seniority. Educators are low paid. People who risk their lives to protect are rarely high paid.

What people earn does not define who they are. It does not reflect their inner joy. Intrinsic value is not measurable. You grow to qualify your value based on varied factors, including how you feel, how others would like you to feel, and how you permit people and situations to affect you. The mind lives in more than one dimen-sion. You have the right to believe or disbelieve what I am telling you.

It is like a game. My mind has areas of conflict that are at odds.

When humans meet, often one inquires what the other does for a living. Why not resist and instead ask what gives life meaning? This kind of reflection helps you separate what you value from how society defines value. Once you separate your views from those outside, you get to the crux of the matter, that is, you clarify your deepest desires and devote yourself to listening to your soul. Other people can say one thing and do another, but not you.

Somehow, somewhere during the evolution to becoming the best I can be, the idea of an occupation defining personal self-worth became a problem. I no longer feel defined by what I do. A shift has occurred as to how I perceive myself and engage with the world.

Human beings spend more time taking steps to clarify identity than they do peeling away the layers of delusion. Survival of soul is a given. Your sense of earthly survival does not hinge on a job unless you let society base your self-worth on limited skills, traits or contributions. There is more to you than how you make a living. You must learn to see beyond how society defines you. Transcend self-created limitations.

From early childhood life gains meaning through family and other relationships. You relate to and define yourself in part alongside sib-lings. Meaning evolves in the form of where you feel you belong or to which person, organization, community, or group that you are associ-ated. I lose track of all the activities that filled my childhood schedule.

Your choices of human interactions cause you to think about what influences your behavior, promises, expectations, history, motivation, and connectedness. You are reminded you are not an individual functioning alone, but a viable part of a larger picture. It began long before you and will continue long after you transform.

I do not presume to be the beginning or the end of anything for anybody but myself.

The big picture includes your imprint and adds to your intrinsic value. Your contribution is meaningful. Relationships gain or lose value evolve based on your emotions and mindset. Your energy imprint evolves in the physical and ethereal. The desire to be appreciated means you forget you are loved and cherished always.

To stop seeking reasons for hope and meaning in life is a kind of reverse conditioning.

Any search is grounded in hidden dissatisfaction. You sense value in people and things that inspire or nurture you. Distance yourself from chaotic or fragmented existence of simply "doing." Balance relates to a new understanding of "belonging."

I already feel I belong. Many people live a process to find communities. I reframe my personal identity which used to be more closely associated with aspirations and labels.

Certain roles only seem to choose you. Interpretation clouds the truth.

Yet what is not interpretation? The police interpret your speed. Everyone interprets.

You sense differently when you decide to dream and live differently. Being faithful to your intrinsic value creates profound, inner peace. Each time you feel inspired by some person or situation, this enhances your self-worth. At any given moment, your value is what you decide to ask for. This message resonates in energy.

This suggests that many people read energy around them and do not even realize what they do. Each place resonates. Each person resonates energy based on mood and thoughts.

Your feelings are a gauge. That sixth sense and additional senses show you a different side to yourself as well as energies that resound from different beings.

For a long time I have noticed nuances in body movements and facial expressions. I sense anger, discomfort, pain, or tension other people do not choose to see in themselves.

Your level of self-awareness determines what you think, see and feel. You do not realize if you lean on a chair until your muscles tell you so. You permit your conditions to escalate before you choose to realize you are responsible. You go to the library and forget a library card, and sense energy shifts when you feel accountable.

Based on what you say, if I was more highly-aware of myself from birth, then I would not be who I am now. The "humanness" is clear in my emotions, my perceived errors, and my evolving abilities. I contribute to collective consciousness when I do not see because I learn.

Disciplined awareness is a state you arrive at. It is not a chosen menu option. Forces beyond you are working every moment, resonating in response to thought and feelings. Energy materializes in form based on where you are and how you got there.

The going and coming part of energy movement is so fast, I feel things, but miss loads. I do not know exactly where energy goes when it resonates from my thoughts and feelings. Yet, things that happen around indicate I am on the right path. I sense light on the horizon.

Musings can be helpful. Every thought is adding substance to your awareness.

I recall one workshop I was doing helped me to develop a distance. Then, I started to feel like it was time to move on. This feeling was reinforced by a passing class participant. He was present long enough to interpret a drawing I did and to say he knew I was a healer.

Part of you waited for a sign. He was amazed you did not notice the obvious.

A person can sense something inside and not know exactly what to do with it. I had the sense of untapped energy, potential and felt I had the ability to create value. I just had no plan, no recipe. People around me offered clues, but my mindset was not quite "there."

Three-dimensional thinking limits how you sense infinite dimensions beyond.

Approaching Self-Acceptance: End of Section Exercises

1. Which lessons do you retain from this section? How would you apply them?
   - In your relationships?
   - In your work?
   - In your spiritual pursuits?
   - In other ways?
2. What kinds of connections do you recognize among events and choices in your life?
3. Describe a situation where your attitude assisted you to recognize self-acceptance.

4. Who are your two great inspirational role models? How do their lives encourage you?

5. If you have low self-acceptance, what kinds of things can you do to change this?

6. What is the most useful thing you have learned about yourself through this section?

7. How do you associate your job with self-acceptance? How do you measure value of your job? Why do you think salaries may become a factor in self-acceptance?

8. What gives your life meaning in ways that differ from social or monetary value?

9. How have your family and other relationships influenced your self-acceptance?

10. Follow the thread of three events and three people who have inspired you to great re-orient your life choices or direction. How did they influence your mindset and action?

BOOSTING SELF-ESTEEM

> *"Don't be afraid to go out on a limb. It's where all the fruit is."*
>
> —Shirley MacLaine

> *"Every act of conscious learning requires the willingness to suffer an injury to one's self-esteem."*
>
> —Thomas Szasz

Many people I meet are at odds with fear, anxiety and negativity. It is a challenge to figure out if you are compensating, in denial, aloof, indifferent or a master of your true self.

Rather than self-reprimand about lack of morale, tap into feelings that are not reactions. Move away from everything else. Be grateful for moments of realization.

I already sense I would be better off discarding certain habits and not looking back.

As you linger in low energy vibrations, you prevent yourself from connecting to higher ones more consistently. Higher healing energies include kindness and love.

To strengthen confidence in any area of my life affects my energy vibration in others. As I assist people, their boosted energy uplifts me. People help each other evolve. How?

The "how" never matters. The fact is, you ask. When you reach out for healing energy in form, it comes to you from unseen places and unseen sources.

Although we converse on many subjects, we keep coming back to energy.

I do not speak for you, but I never move. Energy is what I am, all you are.

Knowing that is supposed to boost my esteem in areas of uncertainty?

Light is a source of illumination that empowers you to reframe all uncertainty.

Of course! We reviewed the topic of fear and I am still not over it. When people are hurtful and destructive, part of my own mind seems to conjure up undesirable visions. I could take it all lightly, learn, and forget. After all, I have done it through this life.

It is a common human reaction is to absorb these vibrations and lower energy. Individuals are often unaware of how they are conditioned to drain energy or to allow themselves to feel drained. You have choices to set new boundaries.

I am attuning to something. I desire to develop and connect differently to energy.

Be careful what you wish for. You summon it and create it and the universe brings it. Fear only evokes fear and traps negative energy. Choose to sense and discard it.

Boosting Self-Esteem: End of Section Exercises

1. Which lessons do you retain from this section? How would you apply them?
   - In your relationships?
   - In your work?
   - In your spiritual pursuits?
   - In other ways?
2. List ten things you can do to uplift your spirits and boost your self-esteem.
3. List ten of your skills or talents and how you use them to feel good about yourself:

4. List three things you wish the courage to do. What would cause you to take a shot?

5. List your thoughts/ actions at each area that increase and decrease your self-esteem:
   - In personal relationships, I boost/lower my self-esteem by:
   - In job situations, I boost/lower my self-esteem by:
   - In spiritual (and/or religious) pursuits, I boost/lower my esteem by:
   - In school (or learning situations), I boost/lower my esteem by:

6. Describe a situation where someone injured your self-esteem. How did you react?

7. How do you believe you now sense the cause and effect of your feelings differently?

BELIEVING AND ACTING

> *"This thing that we call "failure" is not the falling down, but the staying down."*
>
> —Mary Pickford

> *"Action is a great restorer and builder of confidence. Inaction is not only the result, but the cause, of fear."*
>
> —Normal Vincent Peale

If I evolve based on what I believe, then why am I not a magical being? After all, I asked for that as a child, and that has yet to happen. I do not see a magical being in a mirror.

What you view in the mirror is not what you are, but what you choose to perceive now. How you draw on your senses shapes your self-image and actions you take. When a human being really desires to do something, a way is created.

That reminds me of the lesson about "why." When I identify that in a given situation, "how" works itself out. People may even lose everything and redefine pleasure, as related to things different than what they had before.

Options are unlimited. What you choose to see reveals what you believe.

On the topic of "seeing is believing," I believe astral travel changes me for the better. To practice exploring dream realms teaches me to see differently while awake. As I awaken, what I believe has expanded. It is as if I sense a ripple effect. I connect differently to energy.

One view is humans are actually asleep while awake and awake while asleep. Everything you do is preparing you for things unforeseen. Choices enable you to develop beliefs and act in different ways. All events deserve your complete attention.

Wait a second! This teaches me more about freedom. I have freedom of choices for what to think or not. I choose to attend functions, work or play hooky. I care for the mind, body, and spirit or I choose to neglect myself. I determine all I do, but not how aware I am.

You determine beliefs about what is good or preferable action in this moment. Each option leads to an outcome. Everyone is not on the same plane of awareness. You resonate energy available to everyone. Thought and feelings translate as energy.

I like how what I view as "meaningful" changes. I find new ways to learn and grow, to realize my worth. Spiritual questioning reminds me to dream of the person I would like to be is a waste of the person I am. When I move from believing everything matters to discard what no longer resonates with me, I value all that happens differently.

Inside every human being is a place of knowing, a place where your wisdom lies. You can deny it as long as you want, but the world around you brings you back.

That sounds predictable. I believe life experiences are unpredictable.

As I peer through you, I sense you shift gears to transform your inner power.

It is a learning process to grow to understand that moving away from conditioned goals is not the same as evolving away from my true desires. The experiences I work toward are not conditioned goals, but those parts of me I had forgotten about or not acknowledged.

Negativity blocks you from seeing your true beliefs and accessing your power. The more you diffuse bad energy, the greater the lightness that suddenly picks you up.

It would have been nice if you had prepared me for the fright of my life.

Everything you do prepares you to live.

Yet, I imagine you always foresee the consequences of your choices before you act. As I learn more about myself, I attune to how I permit beliefs and adversity to shape me.

This is how you evolve to reach higher-level goals. Humans are conditioned to expect quick results. So long as goals are based on views about fear, legitimacy, and approval, conditions will shift energy to encourage you to recall why you really exist.

If I get your message, then a person will experience struggle until such time as their choices align with their soul?

Every human being is energy and feels energy. Destiny is encoded in you. As you reconnect with it, and believe in it, then your perception of everything changes.

If that is true, then would you say that is fair? I mean, no baby I have ever seen was born with a guidebook containing lessons required to graduate from the school of life.

No two paths are ever the same. The order and nature of lessons differs. Your life takes shape based on how you choose to experience what you create.

I was unaware life is teaching me to dwell on where I am. I am a conditioned planner. Each test I take is with thought of a result or diploma. Every internship was attached to a vision of a permanent position. I had to stop thinking of future in order to rediscover now.

It is not the action you take or do not that matters, but motivations behind it. At any given moment, every action is an effort to magnetize and magnify energy. A level of love or fear determines how you harness energy and how it ricochets.

To begin to sense the degree of energy fluctuation is to realize how little I know. What began as an exploration of my own bottled up frustration about a recent situation has brought me to a completely different place of peace in my own mind. I have raised the bar.

As you discover the goals and opinions of others may not be right for you, it does not mean their paths are wrong for them. You must disconnect in order to move beyond the limits of physical existence. This is a step toward a different sense of you.

I am learning observing differs from judging. I find I can turn the judge off. It is like my mind moves elsewhere, beyond limits of undesirable energy vibration.

Whenever you believe problems could arise, energy unfolds accordingly. Each action you take or do not, reinforces what you believe, justifies why you act. You are moving beyond it. The answer to whatever you have been deliberating is you.

At different moments I recognize I experience different levels of consciousness. I am selectively aware and make sense of what I can the best way I know how. From my vantage point, I harness energy in consciousness without knowing how many layers of knowing exist. The energy is immeasurable, but I believe it brings me to greater understanding.

When you believe you nurture peace energy, you block negative energy from your conscious radar. You do not choose to acknowledge fear-based beliefs in anyone. You sense no value in negativity. You do not permit it to exist or drain you.

I have to figure out why part of me believes consistency is such a challenge. Why is everything outside me only transitory? People around me can get negative and upset at my calm reaction. That does not mean I always get upset, but I notice external reaction.

You are only responsible for your own awareness and reactions.

That is exactly what I say, but people act in ways to provoke. I aim to hold my ground, but at times I admit I can get rattled. I want to believe what I do is right for me.

If you truly want to believe, you do not doubt. Inner peace, health and well-being are always accessible in forms you can access in your mind. As you discipline your mind and apply yourself, you move to accept yourself more fully, whatever your conditions. You act based on what you believe, and believe based on what you feel.

Believing and Acting : End of Section Exercises

1. Which lessons do you retain from this section? How would you apply them?
   - In your relationships?
   - In your work?
   - In your spiritual pursuits?
   - In other ways?
2. What aspects of your belief systems or perspective make you feel happy/unhappy?
3. Explain some of possible reasons why you think this way.
4. What obstacles do you see in front of you? Which ones do you create? Why?
5. What kinds of people or circumstances may lead you to become misdirected?
6. Recall a time when your beliefs were incompatible with your actions. How does this cause you to think about the usefulness or desire for change?
7. Describe some of the things you did today to learn more about yourself. If you have yet to do anything of this nature, what could you do to learn more about yourself?

MAKING TIME MATTER

> *"I have a problem when people say something's real or not real, or normal or abnormal. The meaning of those words for me is very personal and subjective."*

—Tim Burton

> *"It has done all that is possible from the angle of the present opportunity."*

—Alice Bailey

Amidst all these changes, I cannot help but realize time is not what I thought it was.

Human beings use time to measure position and action that are immeasurable. You identify experiences. You see color, hear sound, and feel texture to differentiate. You forget senses are versatile. Some human beings visualize color of music in the air, taste light and feel rainbows. You create boundaries to ground yourself and to verify existence. You choose to perceive your world with limited use of senses. Why?

What I choose to sense led me to acknowledge you as more than a figment of my imagination. I now reframe how I view and use time. I could do other things, but I do not.

You acknowledge lots of things now that you did not choose to notice before. Even with no clock, you sense when "timing" for action is right. To explain infinity, you may use words like love, eternity, inestimable, but part of you does not grasp it.

I make an analogy with foods, languages, and places. People are unsure how to describe foods they have never tasted, unfamiliar landscapes, and unpronounceable words. Instinct is to compare what they know. I feel its right to explore a few less-developed talents.

Perceiving time is multi-sensual and multi-dimensional. How and what you emphasize relates to how you translate your feelings.

I used to feel odd to say I see, hear or can feel time pass. People say they try to catch it or slow it down as if they could hold it in their hands. You can come to believe anything.

When your senses stagnate, you detect notice movement by changing thoughts.

I used to wonder how people would get by without a watch. It seemed as though that was unreasonable. After all how would they know if they were late for an appointment?

The world around you sends signals in the form of energy. You interpret them as you choose. If you desire to work with energy, you require a deeper insight as to where it is located and how it affects the human perception of time and space.

To put perception of time aside, people sense payday, intuit hunger, or tire before bed. I become more aware of intuition. As I discard what I was taught, I sense time differently.

Exactly! You do not need numbers read from outside yourself. You read vibes.

I had not thought about it that way, although I meet people who do not wear watches and notice I have not been wearing a watch as often as I used to do. It is like I choose to be aware of "time" in terms of what my body tells me, or what energy around me resonates.

This signals you move beyond ego. It exists in the past and cannot understand the present. Since time differs from events, as you grow, you do not perceive time, but rather, changes in events. You notice how you react. You do not perceive events only, but also their temporal relations with respect to other objects or events you see.

Somehow I suspected there would be more to it than my fleeting impressions.

It seems natural to talk of perceiving one event following another. How often do you say, "time has run away," "time got the best of you," or even "time flies"? Such impressions may be excuses for not rethinking your use and views of time.

Some people view procrastination as everything that is not their big purpose. Since I believe everything I do contributes to my destiny, then dawdling is a foreign concept.

Consistent, positive feelings are reality when you stop ignoring your true self. What you choose not to believe does not exist. If you say one thing and do another, energy vibrates differently. To align your beliefs, parts of you must still awaken.

I have heard time used as an excuse and also as an historic explanation for behavior. Civilizations evolve to be affected by cycles of the sun and moon. A monk sleeps little, prays at sunrise and sunset, and easily changes certain plans. His mind energy flows and he does what comes naturally. Fishermen and farmers live based on light and darkness. Solar and lunar cycles guide travel, suggest when to fish or harvest. Light and darkness guide animals to eat, sleep, give milk, and lay eggs with an inner rhythm. People also attune to themselves.

You are evolving to sense the essence of soul. It not only guides your path, but also your connection to me, to density, speed, light and energy. Yet get a sense of where you are not and what you are not doing. Signposts enable you to realize time is just a tool, not what you think. Feelings differ from beliefs until you reconcile this. As St. Exupéry said, "What is essential is invisible to the naked eye."

Personally, as I attune to my soul, I sense an indescribable connection draws us together right now. Students meet teachers all the time, but they do not always value what is.

What If I invited you into this space to learn from you? Could you handle it?

I am not going anywhere where you cannot find me. I find I lose track of something when it becomes unimportant. What time is matters less than what I do with time and energy. As an employee, I functioned based on someone else's clock. Self-employment enables me to work at my own rhythm. You also empower me to sense "time" differently.

You constantly challenge yourself to derive deeper meanings of words. As you put them in context in your life, you learn to step further outside yourself. This is teaching you that you are invisible when and where you desire. Your sense of time and space is expanding so that you travel further and without knowing it.

And yet, to hear people speak of rigid schedules, based on twenty-four-hour days, seven day weeks, and a twelve month calendar year, increasingly baffles me. It is not natural.

As you permit yourself to be distracted from what you are not, you tense up.

The military, disaster responders, and emergency medical technicians (EMTs) require people move at short notice. Some people move geographically based on timed contracts. Missionaries travel based on the schedules of a destination, custom and country. Women have children based on biological clocks. If you are unemployed or imprisoned, bill deadlines and forces outside yourself dictate time. Are we not all sort of on borrowed time?

Experience is timeless. People are actually faceless. What they teach matters. More than one version of time exists. More than one sense of emptiness exists. You deceive yourself if you believe you grasp all subtle nuances at once.

You remove the personal to connect me with the universal. At times, I perform tasks for myself and others and feel I accomplish little. Others are content to do what they do.

You create expectations. You imagine anyone else's. To rush means you aim to compensate for things you wish to do or avoid.

You create limits and rationalize self-defeating thoughts about the concept of time. You are under your own spell.

It seems I am working magic already and very unaware of my own power.

How you perceive your daily life has distracted you from the magic you are. You are going through change to raise awareness of your own inner light. As you grow, you sense a relief because any reason you thought to worry is groundless.

I find it a humorous exercise to reflect on associations I have adopted about time.

Perception of time in the present separates you from a clear sense of eternity. You separate your life into particular periods or frames to find ways to put pieces together. Time is ultimately your reference for personal experience, nothing more.

Time Matter: End of Section Exercises

1. Which lessons do you retain from this section? How would you apply them?
   - In your relationships?
   - In your work?
   - In your spiritual pursuits?
   - In other ways?
2. How does your perception of time influence your life choices?
3. If you had no time constraints, what would you do? Who influences your use of time?
4. How do/ would your views of time and priorities change according to:
   - Childhood and Adolescence
   - Adulthood
   - Single-hood
   - Partnership/Marriage
   - Parenthood
   - Employment
   - Unemployment
   - Retirement
   - Health
   - Other
5. If you did not wear a wristwatch, or focus on time, how would your behavior change?

6. List some of the different ways you use to measure passage of time in your life.

7. How do your uses of time reveal what you value and what motivates you?

8. How do you think about time? In what ways does perception shape your life choices?

9. How does a sense of routine influence your evolving purpose and desire for change?

LIFE IS A TEST

> *"I believe the first test of a truly great man is in his humility."*
>
> —*John Ruskin*

> *"All of us have moments in our lives that test our courage."*
>
> —*Erma Bombeck*

Each time I tell myself that all experience is worthwhile, that does not mean I overlook hardship or ignore the suffering. I would like to detach completely from the past.

To know "where you're at" is to begin to tap into your hidden power.

Maybe those Akashic records you mentioned offer the answer. Please expand on that.

Akashic records are energy imprints left in the anti-matter realm by your progress of awareness. You record every thought, action, emotion, and experience that has ever occurred. The universe compiles behaviors from this life and past lives. You cannot erase energy from the ethereal. You can learn to read energy from this realm, to sense things that are not discernible when fully in the physical realm.

I do not want to erase detail per se. I sense to pass tests requires I learn and heal.

Whether you believe in God, Allah, a Tao, Hindu Spirit or some other universal force, never a moment passes when your perceived higher forces do not know how you think and behave in this world. You can be an atheist and recognize you do not control all that happens, or erase the past. You choose how to see it now.

To what degree is something beyond me in charge? How much control do I have?

Mystery is like the form of a higher power. It constantly tests your faith, trust, and sensitivities. This force prompts you to determine your own limits. You grow to discern what causes you to question faith and courage in order to know they exist.

Obstacles I face do not discourage because of what they are. I sense they are keeping me from where I would prefer to be. Yet I believe the more I believe, the more I am tested.

That is impatience. At a given moment, you are exploring growth, aging, change, and a variety of processes. Where you may get to distracts you from where you are. You aim to evolve in other realms. The present instant is training ground.

It is reassuring to know a greater force cares for my well-being and growth. Whatever I used to believe, I sense my faculties evolve beyond that. I am meant to recognize benefits in challenges. I grow stronger, resilient and directed by understanding the usefulness. The Akashic encourages me to learn to read myself, to discern progress through my mistakes.

Circumstances change. Akashic is not a tool to help you predict coming responsibilities. Every human being is tested. Every choice is a means to better understand the self and others. You store all of your choices in consciousness.

The more I raise my awareness, the more I sense I tell myself not to believe anything, but to question, explore, doubt, and discover for myself what is the "truth" in a given moment.

You are not meant to impose your choices. You may choose to believe higher forces test your patience, maturity, composure, and ability to support or love unconditionally. Feelings exist beyond words. You may see obstacles and think only you can resolve the situation. You can choose to be alone. You chose to seek help.

Part of me obviously knows why I summoned you. Other parts of me are in the dark.

You hover between realms without believing you are your own compass. You ask for bearings. I assist you to raise awareness about spirit. Avatars like Edgar Cayce, Buddha, Krishna, Jesus, Mohammed, and others wrote on consciousness.

I trust you will expand on that.

You are drawn to what is termed the "anti-matter realm." As you evolve to enter consciously, you are entering the realm often linked with the death experience.

Is this a test concerning life and death? I do not fear these subjects.

Higher forces did not plan for everyone to be the same or to evolve the same way. All lessons are available to everyone. You notice lessons you are ready to learn. While alive, some beings choose to explore and relive their past lives and previous experiences in backward motion. It is all about growing, loving, and forgiving.

It would be great to know how higher forces think, how they sharpen perception. They are not hindered by emotion. I develop my own rituals for connecting and disconnecting to what matters. I channel and receive energy in ways to give my life meaning.

What comes naturally to you at this moment is not necessarily "natural."

I spend a lot of energy working that one out. Erasing all conditioning is a chore. Higher forces may consider me to be like a mineral or gemstone to be worked on, shaped.

You shape yourself. Believing in my presence tests your faith. To realize external approval is irrelevant, passes a test. To express your gifts, passes more tests. See yourself for what you have been, who you are and the soul expands. You already planned your life. You just need to remind yourself to fulfill what you planned.

For me certain kinds of expression are a challenge. I do not recognize the answers.

That is a test of integrity. Seeking recognition is a quest for self-validation. Human beings spend their lives seeking what they think they need. They are convinced they will find things or they do not "see" properly.

It can be scary to admit what I desire and to go after it, against many odds and against my own judgment. I have so much to work through to get to where I want to be.

You never go against your true self. You are working your way back to it. As you act on impulse, it may be because you trust yourself and do not let anyone talk you out of it. What is created and exhibited in the universe is given to you. You are tested, retested, renewed, and prepared for roles you do not see.

I refine and extract useful things from my life journey. The challenges I face can be viewed as priceless after the fact because I sense value in lessons learned and what I gain.

Repeated tests arise wherever you are, to remind you of your abilities and integrity. You grow to clarify what makes you, you. You gain wisdom and faith in your potential. Tests are a way you visualize your learning curve.

Even now, I realize I am being tested in all that I have, think, feel, and do.

You are your only judge and jury. Higher beings have universal knowledge of all possibilities. You work through your own misun-

derstandings so that you are no longer inhibited to express your true self. Higher beings have universal knowledge of all possibilities. They see what you do not. If you were them, then you would not be you.

All of that is fine. Yet I have this desire to clarify where any kind of learning is leading. That is, what motivates it. This enables me to better evaluate benefits of a test.

Your body, thoughts, and feelings are all the opportunities you have been granted to use to define priorities and act to prove whether or not you have integrity. There is no hierarchy or comparison with anyone else.

Let me get this straight. I am not graded. It is like a self-designated, pass-fail system.

Your conscience and deep awareness decides how you are tested. The goal is to become more aware you are constantly testing yourself. Examine your feelings.

Honesty and respect may develop a conscience, yet not every human being has one.

To have faith in yourself requires evolving in your life and outside it. As you learn to recognize everything that happens is a test, you ask yourself if your decisions make sense considering who you are, how you feel, and what you wish to become.

As I reflect I feel very fortunate. Each phase of my life has given me a sense I earn things. Some are tangible. Others involve intangible appreciation that makes me feel good.

Pain, suffering, and hardship will be constant companions to growth.

In many areas I have persevered and expanded how I view success. Although I have been discouraged, I am always learning. Life experience shows me I overlook talents I was not ready to acknowledge. Higher forces have been testing me. The more I think about it, the more I realize each experience opens my spirit. Some people forget their life is up to them.

How you designate positive and negative does not determine the pace of your life, or affect what is beyond you. Every moment, you move closer to accept destiny.

At certain times I sense something wants to challenge me, as if to tell me I must work harder or in another way to reach my goals. In such instances I feel bombarded with tests.

You always move in some direction. If you allow doubt to kick in, you may feel you move backward just because you sense backward is negative. You may dream in reverse, as if you were rewind-

ing your life. You have not yet accepted more directions exist than those which you use to frame your thoughts. Conditioning limits you.

Yet much of humanity is motivated by going places or getting to a destination.

Hardship may cause you to think something beyond you aims to teach you. In your impatience, you may assume they take things away that made you feel stable. You may feel like you did things wrong or were confused. No reason exists to feel bitter or angry. If you wish to feel you have nothing, or that what you seek is out of reach, you will have these experiences. You know what it means to have something. You take the space you require to review and digest what makes sense, then grow.

Before this conversation I had less strength against self-doubt. I often feel life is a big test. Something beyond me is showing what it is like to feel alone and in need.

As this begins to solidify, your sense of a spiritual role trans- forms. It does not just appear. You find strength and perspective within. You register everything has a point. As your knowledge of spiritual energy grows, your capacity to be intimate in other ways also grows. You sense space contracts and time speeds up in good feeling.

It is hard to fathom I regularly convince myself I need new kinds of understanding. I read about people and their experiences. They man- age to work through almost unimaginable obstacles and pressures. This builds self-confidence. Many admit to a spiritual connection.

No human being ever does anything alone. That is pure love. To be aware you conjure, create and devise every instant is a step to recognizing what you are capable of and gathering courage to see that through. You chose what to become and do it.

Developing intimacy with higher forces is not described as some- thing that comes quickly. Not everyone is interested in reading scrip- tures or meditation.

Spiritual intimacy is built on an attitude inside yourself. There is no one way to go.

You mean, people may consider themselves spiritual if they engage in behavior they believe would open them to a comforting presence?

That's right. You have chosen to develop something you already have within yourself. You have power to make it far more useful. Then, you will move to teach as you learn, to be tested on different levels. You are a student and teacher in this life.

I also note that leaders and other people will associate personal failure or other crisis with a weak spiritual relationship. It is like a test of their will or who to blame. I learn from that. I wonder how seeing spirituality as a test empowers people to find what they have lost in themselves. It is a challenge to stop imagining what other people do and to focus on myself.

Human beings seek to develop closeness with higher forces for varied reasons. They may seek answers, guidance, escape from problems. People desire to help themselves. You act knowingly and unknowingly. You pull situations and mindsets to yourself to learn what they feel like and how they affect you. It is all transforming you.

Just what I need: to feel like tests are frequent distractions. From your words, it is like I am unconsciously distracting myself from what I really want. If everyone does this, it is no wonder people evoke negative emotions? Even our discussion goes on, as if like a distraction.

You create situations that draw your attention to different levels of ignorance. This is reality. The emotions you choose to evoke are your response. If you do not feel ready for the next stage of your growth, you will hold yourself back. You may decide you wish to learn more lessons or deepen your understanding where you are.

Can you give me a timeline, an estimate of when I will realize the mystery of my life?

It is not for me to tell you what will happen. You create what unfolds. Many possibilities exist for any person's future. How you think influences everything. As you learn to discern and focus your energy, you become aware of how you exert control.

If you are a seer, what good are you if you are unwilling to foretell my future?

I tell it like it is. You choose whether to accept it. I do not offer lotto numbers. You interpret based on the level of control you exert over your emotions. If you desire to create a different life, then shed the old and discipline your mind. This is a test. As you appreciate yourself in thoughts and gestures, words become unnecessary.

Life is a Test: End of Section Exercises

1. Which lessons do you retain from this section? How would you apply them?
   - In your relationships?
   - In your work?
   - In your spiritual pursuits?
   - In other ways?

2. Describe two situations in your life where you thought you were being tested.

3. Explain why you felt you passed the test or, why you felt you did not.

4. What did you learn about yourself and the "bigger picture" from these test situations?

5. Which kinds of new skills did you learn that you apply to refine your life goals?

6. How are you strengthening new kinds of connections as the result of tests?

7. Explain how spiritual pursuits may be connected to your sharpening purpose.

8. What is the key thing you learned about yourself and your purpose from this section?

9. How would you explain things that happen to you which are out of your control?

10. What kinds of life tests do you think would help you to better understand yourself?

11. What sorts of qualities and goals have you developed as the result of life tests?

12. Which results dishearten you? Why?

13. Notice how you react when you believe in things you cannot see or do not understand.

14. If you drift from believing something lies beyond physical existence, or if you never believed in that, how could belief in something beyond you be developed? Why do it?

15. When you distance yourself from or disbelieve higher connections, does your life gain or lose meaning? How does this affect your sense of life direction?

COMPELLING WORDS

"The tongue like a sharp knife...Kills without drawing blood."

—Buddha

"Words mean more than what is set down on paper. It takes the human voice to infuse them with shades of deeper meaning."

—Maya Angelou

To sense a track you are on has significance. Each soul meets silence alone.

You use few words, but they always strike a chord.

As you rediscover your true self, you learn to omit the extraneous.

I suppose that your presence and this dialogue remind me anything is possible.

Imagine that from this moment, you only speak of feeling happy and complete. To further dissolve negative thoughts, focus on words you choose. By changing what you do and do not say, you reinforce thoughts and beliefs about yourself.

I hear words I use but I do not always listen. When you ask people how they are and they respond, "not bad," this rings stress and frustration. Words contain powerful energy.

Each person is invited to think before speaking. Words chip away at esteem. You create suffering and hold yourself back from developing. As you notice words in your vocabulary that evoke negative feelings, reinforce what you do not desire, or have a harsh spin, train yourself to stop. Decondition that impulse.

Come to think of it, is it wrong to use the term, "want?"

Right and wrong do not exist. Ask instead if using certain words serves you. Take a closer look to what you really say. Notice how some words drain you and others energize you. Discern the mood of "want": inadequacy, lack, and discontent.

You know, to feel unsatisfied has an energy vibration. To feel satisfied also has one. I have not always chosen to notice how words trigger and strengthen emotions in my mind.

You already believe in the invisible and know what it takes to make it real.

There is a hint of magic again. I do not know my own strength, but do I need to?

The term need is a self-delusion. If you listen to yourself and others closely, then you describe a need based on longing, not on survival or knowing yourself. Your views are biased by external influences. Nobody knows you better than you. As you sense your abilities, you are obliged to awaken them.

In retrospect I believe I use "need" in order to motivate myself to take action. I have not been mindful of other, far-reaching reasons behind my choice of using this word.

Recognize that your basic needs for survival are actually food, water, shelter, clothing, and love. These things are self-created. Everything else is a luxury. As you hear yourself explain or justify your needs, discern what each statement hides about beliefs.

Unnecessary desires are nurtured by assuming you do not have enough.

I had no idea of all these hidden motives. Another term I aim to avoid is, "can't."

That term is self-defeating. You use it to prevent from doing what is most meaningful to your soul. "Can't" is a substitute for won't, but few people admit it. The meaning of "won't" is grounded in fear. Consider why you think you cannot do things. Someone told you to believe certain goals were inaccessible or inappropriate. When you challenge a theory that you cannot do something, you discover you can do what you led yourself about before. Revise your word choices. Boost new confidence.

Society defines what is "legitimate" or "desirable." I did not realize how that affected me. Awareness is required to consciously change.

Yes, but you are doing this. My presence is partly explained by a call from your deeper consciousness. It prompts you to develop new kinds of faith in skills you had put aside. You buried these abilities with your word choices, entourages and activities that distracted you rather than acknowledge the creative soul you are.

I am drawn to the word "should." I keep asking myself what I should be doing.

This is a word you use to exert power over yourself and impose things on others through guilt. You tell yourself what you should do even more than you say it to others. Do you listen to your advice? If you catch yourself before you say this, then you will sense should echoes self-importance. When ready, just choose to change this.

I am finding it increasingly obvious that attitude is not always my friend. I am controlled by beliefs. They surface, regardless whether they are unfounded or off the mark.

Worry imprisons human beings. They nag about issues; such as how appearance does not measure up to an imagined ideal, how someone has not yet got something right, or how undesirables are reasons to complain. You can also choose to focus only on thoughts, feelings, and actions which promote well-being.

It is useful for people to realize they control the direction of their energy vibration. When I identify sentiments that reflect worry, part of me knows I create illusions. I still ask myself what exactly is enough reflection and when is it preferable to avoid self-reflection?

Define it precisely for yourself without comparing with others .

Clearly I use certain words that do more harm to my mental processes than I realize. I sense the world raises my awareness about my word choices as I encounter people who utter words I do not wish to say. This is part of my learning curve.

Indeed. In order to master yourself, you increase your consciousness. As you become more aware of what you say and the meaning behind each word, then you will discover more freedom of movement in other ways. Everything is related. You are not conscious of everything happening now even if it is all within reach of your mind.

Okay. I make a mental note to pay more attention to destructive words in my vocabulary. I catch myself more before I write or speak. I did not think it mattered so much.

If you utter them, then correct yourself with a powerful positive statement. You will feel empowered as your vibration changes. Choose language to reflect the responsible, powerful, masterful spirit you are. Solutions are always available to you.

I have heard many idiomatic expressions about words that suggest they actually take on a life of their own.

Words offer a subtle exercise in listening to yourself. Consider the sounds you utter by expressing each word. You use your tongue, vocal chords, mouth and other parts of you to convey a message. The meaning you understand as the definition of a word is only part of that. Harsh sounds send a different vibration than soft ones.

There are so many subtle things I had not noticed and do not notice, but would like to.

You notice things when you decide they are important. What you do not see can harm you. Your life evolves based on impact of lower consciousness, ego and parts of you that prevent you from seeing a true self. You miss more than you think.

If this is supposed to humble me even more, then it is working.

You are choosing to readopt what you had discarded because you have had a change of heart. You feel no shame. You do not justify or rationalize. You just are.

You mean forgetting about my word choices and deciding to remind myself of them?

A change of heart is triggered by different kinds of experiences. You have decided to expand on your insular world. You realize there is more to awareness.

I did not grasp changes are so interconnected. They reverberate like a stone on water.

I am not here to tell you what to believe. I echo your thoughts to help you face them.

This tells me you not only know what you are doing but also why, even if I do not.

Compelling Words: End of Section Exercises

1. Which lessons do you retain from this section? How would you apply them?
   - In your relationships?
   - In your work?
   - In your spiritual pursuits?
   - In other ways?
2. Write each letter of the alphabet. List adjectives that begin with each one that you would use to describe yourself. What do they reveal about your attitude and tendency toward destructive or self-defeating thoughts?
3. What action verbs that describe you and enhance thoughts of possibility and potential.
4. How have your word choices helped or hindered your life choices?
5. How do you foresee your changing word choices will influence your life?
6. What kinds of words do you or others use which criticize or make you feel bad?
7. In which ways do negative words alter your sense of life direction?
8. When do you use the terms "want" and "need"? What do they mean to you?
9. Reflect on situations where you use the words "can't" and "should." Recognize who or what experience has led you to be self-limiting. What does it say about control?
10. Write five negative personal qualities and then write the antonyms (opposites).
11. List words or phrases you hear yourself saying often. Where did you learn them?

TRIGGERS FOR CHANGE

> *"Next in importance to having a good aim is to recognize when to pull the trigger."*
>
> —David Letterman

"If we don't change, we don't grow. If we don't grow, we are not really living."

—Gail Sheehy

The journey from solitude to facing a jungle of fears causes me to think about situations or traits I have overlooked. You got me thinking more about words, now what?

Physical, mental, emotional, financial, or other crises are triggers for forced change on different levels of awareness. As you let a stressful situation get to you, this motivates you to act differently, make new choices. Your search for fulfillment implies you would benefit from devoting yourself to those unspoken things.

Extreme experiences serve as triggers for change in my life. It reminds me of certain nightmares that draw attention to what demands urgent attention, compromise, or sacrifice.

As you realize you are in the right place, you stop believing in sacrifice. This resonates negative energy, captures your attention, and tells you something does not feel good where you are. It is a call to listen to your intuition you ignore.

Disruptions in my work routine or health compel me to reexamine my life, but I do not often zero in on the links to a bigger picture. I hesitate to slow down or alter choices.

Human beings rarely listen to themselves as well as they could. All reactions have consequences like all causes have effects. It's a huge energy-level domino-effect.

It appears I do not always know how attitude affects my identity and how I sense life.

Unconsciously, you think about all that. You do not have to know how triggers for change work on an energetic level. It is the awareness that concerns you.

To be aware of some things does not mean I am aware of others in ways I would like to be. It is the "others" that concern me, the others that I sense and heighten my senses to see.

Your awareness is growing. Events trigger your automatic thoughts. You evolve to discern when the conditioned thoughts no longer serve you. Your feelings and beliefs offer a perspective. You can choose to keep them or explore alternatives.

That is easy for you to say from your "higher" vantage point.

Your soul has been expanding and continues to expand.

I know you are an observer. I am becoming a different kind and I am unsure yet what.

Triggers for Change: End of Section Exercises

1. Which lessons do you retain from this section? How would you apply them?
   - In your relationships?
   - In your work?
   - In your spiritual pursuits?
   - In other ways?

2. Describe a life experience that was reason for you to change things about yourself. How did the situation cause you to reconsider your feelings and perspective?

3. Describe a crisis in someone else's life that changed you and your perspective of what you consider to be important. How did your priorities and goals change?

4. Based on your beliefs, how do feel about change? How have you reacted to perceived crises in different areas of your life?

5. How would believing in something beyond you could help you cope differently? If you already believe in spiritual things, in what ways have they assisted you?

EMBRACING CHANGE

> *"No change of circumstances can repair a defect in character."*
>
> —Ralph Waldow Emerson

> *"Perhaps we're too embarrassed to change or too frightened of the consequences of showing that we actually care. But why not risk it anyway?"*
>
> —Princess Diana of Wales

Change is inevitable, from your body language and gestures, to your mindset, and your emotions. As you evolve, you realize change is good for you. If you choose to dwell on fear, then you forget staying as you are is not enriching you.

I would imagine you know I am not a pessimist. I nurture faith. Admittedly, I do not always know the kind of faith I nurture. My faith is not yet unwavering, but I work toward it.

To have faith means you believe in something other than what you know. As you observe the world, you will recognize aspects of reality you dislike. As you view your localized reality, you will find areas where change would be a good thing.

Cleaning can be good for the soul. I have learned that to declutter a living space is a step to declutter the mind and life. Life is about discarding what you no longer need.

Whether you look at world events or your own life path, change always has potential to bring good. Even when it seems your work or personal world seems crumbling, stepping back enables you to see advantages to wherever you are.

Moving among different places, I have met various people, made friends, known people who come and go. I sense constant transition. That is partly why my identity is confusing.

Having no reference is itself a clue to your evolving being.

Change can certainly be liberating, enlightening, and empowers me to define who I am. Each experience teaches. I do not aspire to predict the future, but I would benefit from discarding lower thoughts so I could surrender to what is growing deep inside me.

That "something" is you. Each time you create something, you also hide it.

If I change much and often, I obviously do not realize how much my mind influences my evolution. I would like to blossom into this hidden self but do not do it fast enough.

You are doing it. I see what you are. You do not choose to sense it yourself.

That is a bit scary. You are telling me I do not see myself for what I am?

Consider your entourage, the evolution of your writing, activities and workshops that appeal. This energy sends you messages about your mystic side. You not only find your soul there, but the renewing energy resonates back at you.

I guess I grapple with how I can feel separate from who I am, my truth as you put it.

You believe in rotating planets, the coming and going of tides and the evolution of creatures, belief systems and society. You sense change brings good things. This process is about being convinced of positive things in your own changes.

I have been told I am a person who makes complicated what is really simple.

Each experience you have shapes your view of change. When results enable you to feel good, you are receptive. If results are undesirable, then you hold back.

In retrospect, how people have treated me influences how I perceive the prospect of change. It is about conditioning my expectations, my sense of anticipation. I have options to trigger changes I do not know about yet. This is incredibly exciting.

As you admit your fears, one-by-one, and face them, then you acknowledge them, master them, and are equipped with knowledge to replace them. To know what you feel enables you to heal and transform your beliefs. Note what triggers attitude.

All this is telling me that when I think I love and forgive, sometimes I am blind to my own misunderstanding. To become aware of change is always useful.

Whatever is happening in your life is meaningful. You personalize each event. You decide what you await. Beings have been guiding you about energy.

Excuse me?

To acknowledge the unseen is the beginning to sensing differently. You may not get all the outcomes you desire on the physical plane, but the results you do get draw you to situations that require attention. Change is all leading you to bridge the gap between your conscious and unconscious mind. This is key to be able to traverse unseen boundaries at will, to sense places beyond realms of the familiar.

Where are you going with this?

Exactly where you have been hoping and praying to go.

I have long been fascinated with places. I even visit enchanted sculpture gardens.

No place you visit will fascinate you so much as realizing where you are.

You already dream and experience the answer. Every human being attunes to symbols, signs and events. When you learn pure intent, you catch errors in your thinking. You take steps to progressively raise your energy vibration and connect.

Embracing Change: End of Section Exercises

1. Which lessons do you retain from this section? How would you apply them?
   - In your relationships?
   - In your work?
   - In your spiritual pursuits?
   - In other ways?

2. How do you feel about change? Who or what has influenced your beliefs?

3. List ten errors in your thinking about change. Why have you assumed it was bad?

4. Make a list of affirmations to express where change is good for you because…

5. What strategies would help you be less likely to get caught up in fear or self- doubt?

6. To address your wavering attitudes about change, answer the following:

   • The reason I resist (or fear) change is…

   • The reason I feel comfortable about change is…

   • The reasons I do not feel ready to embrace change are…

7. What is it about present or past experience that can reinforce your feeling of security?

8. Reflect on valuable changes you see or foresee in different areas of your life.

9. How does consistent thought or behavior make you feel? Secure or insecure? Why?

LIVING A MORE FOCUSED LIFE

> *"Face a challenge and find joy in the capacity to meet it."*
>
> —Ayn Rand

> *"Be occupied, then, with what you really value."*
>
> —Melvana Rumi

I figured we would connect to this subject eventually.

If you wish to reach your potential for this lifetime, a plan to live a more focused life would enable you to recognize and overcome your fears.

We already covered that.

You grow to reframe discipline, to become more intuitive. Opportunities always exist to get involved in things, to take risks, to get hurt, broaden your overall scope of experiences. At each stage you evolve to take it with you and share it.

We have still not actually clarified my mysterious destiny.

Infinite targets exist in your mind. How you choose to get there is what counts. Through a process of eliminating what does not serve you, you slowly uncover how you desire to live a more focused life. You naturally grow more selective when feeling how to channel energy. The universe is evolving such that you will no longer engage in things unrelated to your goals. You already strengthen your mind-soul connection.

Part of me seeks to define and realize these unspoken goals. I make adjustments to move closer to the people and activities that inspire me. I invest myself differently to develop relationships along current interests. It is not as if I explore anything that pops into my mind.

All activities develop you. Your mind functions to enrich your energy and discernment. What you choose to see and what you choose to do with it is up to you.

It is wise to be selective about the people I include in my life.

Incompatible companionship does not nourish your inner self or compel you to reach out and develop who you are. Each choice you make has the power to bring you further away or closer to what you have been hiding from yourself.

How do I know what I am hiding from and when I stop hiding?

Humans learn what distraction means to stop being distracted.

To think I hide from my authentic self out of fear seems like an easy thing to change.

As you listen and love yourself, you eliminate activities that no longer serve to enrich you. To accept everything happens now, you do not have to grasp it all.

Focus never escapes me. What escapes me is a sense I have the best focus for now.

You always have the right focus at a given moment. Doubts dissolve. You define priorities or adopt someone else's priorities. When you do not choose a focus and trust it, someone reorients you on their terms. Decide on meaningful directions.

I have no qualms about reframing priorities. I move in directions of positive energy.

You focus more on intensity rather than other aspects of energy that serve you.

I focus on how it resonates from within me and wonder where it goes after that. I sense energy build-up in certain places. This tells me I am moving away from the crowd.

You are effective at what you do. Yet you are unaware of the implications. To recognize your gifts is part of the process of using them differently. Do not expect people to tell you the truth about yourself. People unknowingly lie to themselves.

For me, living a more focused life seems to be about listening to guides I already have within and around me. It is about reevaluating everything, not jumping to conclusions. I learn to tune out from some energy vibrations and attune more closely to others.

You realize you are not ready to do everything all at once.

If I am tired, then I am less apt to exercise, but I still think about it. Multi-tasking makes sense to me. My body and mind do this without my conscious knowledge or consent.

You attune to yourself as a way to constantly work on your psychic power. You send energy signals throughout your body even as your mind focuses beyond that.

I rarely stop to interpret energy. I do not query its origins or inner connections.

Inner knowing is second nature when you listen to your authentic self.

I sense it is never too late to change how I view the world and my place in it.

Shifting focus is a process. Your thoughts and feelings draw your attention to energy flowing at certain frequencies. Then you shift to focus on different energy movement. You are redefining a sense of space and time, how you feel and resonate.

Another way to understand this is I am gaining more trust in myself. I am learning to perceive from a distance, with detached emotion so I that will not cloud whatever I see.

Every human perceives based on their level of awareness. You do things already without thinking. You acknowledge them or not based on your intuition. You are learning not to question. You gradually allow energy to filter though you freely. This redefines health, stability, inner peace.

This certainly takes the cake! Everything and nothing I have done relates to this.

You are getting the picture. In fact, you are beginning to understand the sense of many pictures passing through space simultaneously. You only glimpse a fraction.

Maybe that helps explain why I went through a stage in my life where I made videos.

Every choice you have made got you to your current state of awareness. You have the discipline you need to go further. Enjoy each moment. Gratitude begins within you. Faith in yourself and in events you do not explain reinforce new insights.

So no definitive path exists for me, for anyone? That changes everything, yet again.

From a spiritual point of view, recognize whatever you think is a living, breathing thing. Obstacles are only a passing phase to endure. See beyond that.

I already see beyond it. I am not always aware I do.

A focused life perspective enables you to deal with whatever situation that evolves. Convince yourself consciously that you can deal with anything. You do.

This is a valid point. I have been unaware I did not really know myself. I am full of untapped energy. It is very empowering to redefine my sense of "normal," yet again.

Do not merely endure a challenge or an experience. Consciously make the effort to get something useful out of it. You are meant to share wisdom as you grow.

I thought that is the point of this exercise: to share what I already know with myself.

Actually "the point" is always changing. The side of inner power that is unfolding now is merely a segment of what is reminding you who you are.

The prospect is certainly a mouthful.

You are unable to say with integrity that you did not foresee that coming.

I…

You are learning how to find places between illusions. Go back there. Curiosity has your mind peaked. Energy awareness leads you to personal freedom. Peace enters your soul when you trust your life force.

I have rediscovered a space of transition between sleep and awakened states. It is a place where mental barriers do not exist.

As you can rebuild aspects of your life, it is only natural you will deconstruct or dissolve elements of your previous perspective. This is part of redefining what is.

Living a More Focused Life: End of Section Exercises

1. Which lessons do you retain from this section? How would you apply them?
   - In your relationships?
   - In your work?
   - In your spiritual pursuits?
   - In other ways?
2. What have you learned about your life focus?

3. Explain how you see your personal evolution. Which stumbling blocks do you notice?

4. Who or what might you turn to for assistance to overcome your fears you? How?

5. How do your beliefs about what is real and possible evolve after reading this?

6. Where do you spend time with people or interact in environments that bring you down? Which steps will enable you to develop a different focus?

7. Which life relationships no longer serve to enrich you? What will you do about it?

8. Consider what your current focus. Outline three priorities for this point in your life.

4

Raise Awareness of Perception

MOTIVATION

"Hope is the thing with feathers that perches in the soul, and sings the tune without words, and never stops at all."

—Emily Dickinson

"Be miserable. Or motivate yourself...It's your choice."

—Wayne Dyer

LESSONS

1. Your senses empower you to master your visible and hidden self.
2. The soul seeks evolution and experience beyond the physical.
3. The process of raising awareness teaches you learn forever.

My sense of motivation is changing. It is in my blood to explore new unknowns. Not surprisingly, when I was a child, my father thought I was developing "the travel disease."

As awareness expands, your hopes are no longer limited to prior expectations.

I feel energy differently than before. Where do all these sensations come from?

The origins of energy vibration spark great curiosity. To decode messages raises awareness, then what? That which is desirable is often hardest to achieve.

Discovering hidden sources of motivation is a revelation. I especially mean feelings that boost energy. I ask myself, who will relate to this? I used to envision mainly results while I was oblivious to the power I have to influence the journey of vibrations.

Faith empowers you to shift focus from the purely physical. How you react to a situation determines the unfolding reality. Your inner perspective adds depth.

That helps. I recall when people I know have been diagnosed with serious illnesses. My choice to think only healing and positive thoughts has an uplifting effect. You can send healing to anyone. If people are receptive, it works. Heal if you choose.

You instill hope as a service. This encourages people to face their resistances.

I am aware different parts of me have ideas or functions of their own. Do they align?

Every part of you has a personality. Even individual cells make choices and sense your level of awareness. As you align energy you realize a concentrated period of evolution. No experience raises awareness within you that does not relate to something you already knew, but forgot. As you hold the palms of your hands close without touching, you sense energy that connects you to everything, everywhere.

I sense things turn out for the best. As my sense of "best" evolves, I feel different.

When you sense deeper confidence inside, your self-respect grows. To awaken untapped energy reminds you that you think and act without complete awareness.

Okay, so sleepwalking was a short-lived phase of my childhood. Why does it recur in different ways now? I outgrow phases and then later, I revisit them. Many people say the same thing.

Many human beings sleepwalk through life unaware. As you awaken the mind differently, you respect other beings for who they are. The urge to react dissipates.

The more I think about it, the easier it seems to raise my awareness about others. I certainly notice what bothers me in people before I realize what it tells me about myself.

What you are unable to explain or control alienates you less, and instead begins to fascinate you. You are viewing energy from completely new angles.

What I used to perceive as bothersome challenges and endless struggles, no longer provoke my inner judge like before. I sense emotional reaction blocks my sense of a process.

Great strides are made each time you decide nothing has to be resolved.

I think to the irony of conditioning. It seems to exist to confuse the way things are.

Being motivated means recognizing your reasons to focus on learning. As you clarify your desires, you learn which sources of motivation boost your esteem and energy. You learn to differentiate between the "I" and "me" views or motives within you. Motives that serve your highest good do not serve ego and lower consciousness.

This brings us back to what I hope and trust will be **good** or **bad** for me at a given moment. I am not alone in doing this. To reflect on my choices, what I used to view as desirable behavior now seem like lower consciousness. I resist categories, yet, here they are.

You have to recreate your own sense of decency and honesty, to acknowledge the reasons for your values. As you dissolve your inner critic, negative energy goes.

Listening to my inner voice reframes meaningful motivation. I learn to read vibes. Yet to view changing positions on morals, principles, or ethics can seem random around me.

Nothing is random.

I guess people resist coming to terms with their own self-betrayal. Only by facing it does it become possible to live an authentic life, to be true to soul and carry out the soul plan.

While in physical form, your ego struggles to clarify a single reflection about your origin or, let's say, where the entity you came from. You grapple with how soul abandoned all it knew to embrace the unfamiliar. That is how your journey began.

How did we get from Earthly motivation to my soul origins? Words are sly. My conscious and unconscious do not agree on the role magic plays in my life or on the extent of illusion. I struggle to grasp how my body, mind, and soul have motivations that disconnect.

You sense separateness because conscious parts of you fear other parts. You are willing to deal with fear in steps, as you do in work or romance. You do not grasp ego fears the infinite perspec-

tive of the soul. Magic is what you feel as fear dissolves. Magic is not a figment of your imagination or a reason to evoke sheer disbelief.

I have searched for signals about a clearer soul identity. My mindfulness deepens.

You know and have always known who you are. All beings know. You take risks to remind yourself of key sources of motivation. This deepens emotional contact. It is a ploy. You move out of comfort zones and unconsciously move into your element.

I get a sense that where I am, is never the only option. A person can always find or create another job or relationship if you sense where you are is not working. Yet society urges people to stay where they are, improve, narrow a focus, and be motivated like others.

Nothing outside of you knows you as well as you know yourself.

To be motivated in a given moment only ever seems significant to me in that moment. I'm losing the short- and long- term perspectives I used to base motivation on in goal-setting.

The illusions of separation merge as you embrace light and energy. You can feel when you have abandoned the truth of things for self-interest. You are motivated by where you are to rediscover what you are. Beliefs resurface on how you got here.

I encourage my self-sufficiency, yet, that does not enable me to answer my questions.

Your mind has no limitations. You have not really begun to explore it.

What is it about my own self-esteem? I imagine new awareness is available. I hope it exists and I experience it. As I discern mental blocks it becomes a never-ending exercise.

High-vibrating souls realize you learn at the rate you need to know. Each human being works toward existing at a higher vibration. This is where emotions do not interfere with thought.

Part of me hopes that nothing and everything is planned. I mean, my name was given to me. Parts of my life seem laid out, meant to work out or not. The questions keep coming.

Before you were born, your soul chose a name. Its spelling and vibrating rate invites action and reaction. You foresee you will reject parts of you until you evolve to accept the beautiful whole being you are. Each incarnation enables you to discern.

Hey! What makes you think that I believe in reincarnation? I tend to, but…

Imagine you accept the truth. Be loyal to what you know. Your level of personal power, your experience, is based on beliefs and the integrity of your choices.

The more I live, the more I realize taking everything in stride strengthens and heals me. Earlier in my life I assumed children grew up to have adult logic, to see the same way. Then I grew up and realized adults say they are motivated by one thing and hide the truth.

Children are innocent and direct. They verbalize as they perceive. Adults have conditioned themselves to self-question, to anticipate disproval, reprimand. They fear judgment, grow to withhold their instincts and core perception of the truth, unless...

To think I would choose to hide from my own self-awareness. What good is that?

You raise awareness as you recognize you have erred and why. You choose to relish a journey, attune to energy, and explore endless possibilities of the unknown.

All this comes rushing back to me. If I was asked what I am right now, I would not relate this sense of identity to particular training. In fact, I would discard what I used to think.

Motivation can be understood by realizing you have nothing to worry about.

To a degree the definition of motivation confuses what matters, yet, it gives me hope.

Enthusiasm drives you to do what it takes to get more of the good feelings. No matter what you do, you realize you never left your sense of legitimacy. Everything you do enables you to grow more aware. You do not have to exert effort as you think.

That view allows unmotivated people to sense no reason to exert effort or evolve. Are you saying that to be lazy, or doing nothing, will yield the same result as being motivated?

You have the freedom to choose to go around in a circle or, to stay where you are. What you learn is different in degree. You raise or lower your vibration at will.

It is desirable then to make choices even if I am unhappy with results. Some people think it is better not to make choices and not to gain any life experience.

Not choosing is itself a choice. Selective ignorance is a choice linked to fear.

You know, what if I am supposed to hope and become more clairvoyant? This would help explain why people describe me as being "out-of-my-mind."

You must be outside the mind to apply your psychic abilities.

Yet, the mind offers a perspective that seems confined to the physical body.

To see over, above, or beyond the physical means you sense with your psyche, your soul. The nature of your energy determines the kinds of energy you receive. You use your will to pull yourself along. At pivotal moments, your choices transform you.

I could swear I glimpsed an image, like a golden ball out of the corner of my eye!

Orbs are the product of the mind. They awaken the soul. This is another sign.

The more I think about it, the more I sense I would benefit from taking notes.

If it helps you then go ahead. When you give into your passions, you discover forces within you become more pronounced. Experiences that unfold defy what you originally thought possible. That is because your mind was not in this space before. Dreams result from giving into what resonates on levels not explained by logic.

You have something there. When I feel increasingly motivated, I could be driving along and I encounter a series of green lights. Someone ahead of me at a toll booth will spontaneously pay for my parking. I will miss flight connections, but others fall into place.

This happens to all human beings who are true to themselves. The universe cooperates. When you exert effort to rediscover the gifts you have been given and also to use them to the best of your ability, obstacles will seem to fall away. You forget they were never there. You only imagined them to distract you from a source of light.

What you point out confuses me. I thought obstacles appear for everyone as a means to stretch and learn. This is what reassures people who otherwise feel overwhelmed.

Events unfold for reasons you choose in a given moment. You are not meant to plan ahead in ways to avoid decisions and tests that will arise at each crossroads.

When people are unmotivated, what can I do about that? It is a challenge to stop motivating myself. It is my hope I will always be motivated to do something meaningful.

You are slowly beginning to grasp everything you do is meaningful. It will always be so long as you do it with pure intentions.

The pure intention part is tricky. How does anyone really know what this means?

Regularly step outside yourself. Think before you speak and act. As you move to greater awareness, you evolve to no longer reflect the same way. You naturally do what you love if you permit that. Simply attune to energy as it flows. You feel it.

To be conscious of how I am changing the way I see things, is rather remarkable. Human beings are often conditioned to motivate themselves based on incremental goals that encourage them every step of the way. Milestones are perceived rewards. They motivate me.

Human beings evolve to where they attract and regenerate love energy.

As I join the pieces of my life together, the dynamic, positive developments are all connected to love. Learning to love myself has enabled me to open my senses and learn to love other people and my conditions differently. It is natural to be brave, daring and loving.

You are motivated by movements and non-movements. You are motivated by opening up and closing yourself off. You are motivated by dialogue you overlooked.

Since I realize I am going through such a far-reaching metamorphosis, part of me looks in the mirror differently. I more pay attention to gestures, facial expressions, and subtle nuances of my physical form. A while back, you did imply shape-shifting.

If that motivates you, do that. When challenging situations unfold, your mind, body, emotions and spirit all react separately until you realize this is unnecessary.

So, it is like connecting invisible dots. If I get what I am meant to get from a given situation, then, a similar situation will not unfold to reteach me the lesson. And yet at different ages and life stages, I have revisited situations to reinforce lessons. This reveals what might have happened if I had made different choices in my past.

You are loosening up. I detect a budding philosopher.

It's funny I make a big deal of trivial things. I am on a journey I cannot see, motivated by inner power. This tells me I will not fail, even when I do not know what lies ahead.

You send questions into the universe, and energy stimulates the subconscious.

Motivation: End of Section Exercises

1. Which lessons do you retain from this section? How would you apply them?
   - In your relationships?
   - In your work?
   - In your spiritual pursuits?
   - In other ways?
2. Write down five things that motivate you right now.

3. Describe how you motivate yourself. What else could you do?

4. How could you connect to something beyond you to motivate you differently?

5. What can you do to feel better about your present life condition? If you have very little motivation, or if you aren't motivated at all, why do you feel this way?

6. How do people act to boost your self-esteem? How could you reciprocate?

7. Describe five initiatives you take (and will take) to lift your own spirits.

BE HAPPY NOW

"The moon is the first milestone on the road to the stars."

—Arthur C. Clarke

"Do not seek to follow in the footsteps of the wise. Seek what they sought."

—Basho

Rediscovering deep happiness is like a revelation. Joy is everywhere I feel it.

As human beings stop using obstacles as excuses to be negative or judgmental, they remove shades from more than a third eye. Perception widens toward infinity.

Many books exist about the concept of happiness. People describe how they lost it, found it, buried it, hid from it, and even forgot they had it. They talk how revelations trigger rediscovery.

Hardships show me joy is like angel wings that embrace everyone who asks.

You encounter perceived difficulties as a means to find yourself. The senses you open, enrich, or close, all depend on you. Self-growth stems from your will.

Or, I would say efforts to boost self-growth stem from ignorance about alternatives.

If you do not feel happy where you are, then you find peace and contentment unattainable. Life challenges enable you to develop your potential, to open your mind and absorb what you can. You are always right where you are meant to be. It may shock you to realize you never leave one place.

People who hide their true selves wonder why they are not content. Complaints are like a heavy repository of energy stored in the soul bursting to get out. Happiness is rediscovered. Do people somehow lose what seems to mean the most to them along the way?

Negativity urges you to stretch. It is part of a larger plan. Things you do not yet see are shaping you as you are busy learning to discern energy differently. Energy always resonates off your current radar. As you decode energy, you uncover more.

As I tell myself that I am happy and fulfilled, I attract conditions that bring the experience or evoke what I imagine. In some sense I reach out to help energy express itself.

It may come as news to you, but you are always in the process of motivating and creating yourself and others. You are what you have been until you decide to become something else. All of what has shaped you brings you to your current understanding. Energy is a tool. You act to unfold your character and inspire.

Never before have I felt so awake and conscious as I have evolved to feel at this moment.

Be Happy Now: End of Section Exercises

1. Which lessons do you retain from this section? How would you apply them?
   - In your relationships?
   - In your work?
   - In your spiritual pursuits?
   - In other ways?

2. What sorts of thoughts and activities enable you to feel happy? Which memories trigger happy thoughts? Where are you when you feel this way? What are you doing in these places?

3. Explain things you know make you feel sad or unhappy.

4. Which things don't you do now, but you imagine you would be happy doing them?

5. How does this section assist you to clarify sources of meaning in your life?

6. List five things you did today that evoked positive energy in yourself or in others.

7. Which words, sensations and vibes would you use to describe happiness?

8. Name people who behave in ways to make you feel happy. What do they do?

SEEK AND YE SHALL FIND

> *"What we seek we shall find; what we flee from flees from us."*

—Ralph Waldo Emerson

> *"All that counts in life is intention."*

—Andrea Bocelli

Come to think of it, I do not always have faith in my senses or what I discern.

Consider where you are, how you feel and what you have in your life are partly based on fear that you have allowed to grow within and control you. As you reflect more on goals, ask yourself honestly what is happening, where you wish to be.

One possibility is I do not desire situations that surround or absorb me. Lots of people are wrapped up in a job, lifestyle, relationships, self-image, or state of health. What I desire evolves to focus on intangible experiences. I connect with the idea of not having, and of not living, in order to realize what it really means to be alive. My findings change me.

As you sense your innate abilities, the key is to use and develop them to grow.

I relate to that with languages. When you do not use them, you forget words, details. When it comes to inner power, certain "what ifs" will arise in my brain. I desire to empower people to discover who they are while I am in a continual process of this myself.

As you evolve to fearlessly attune to your intuition, your skills strengthen. Even now, you find it easier to know which thoughts hinder you and create more effective choices. Do not seek outside yourself. As you write, you discover the truth within yourself and in all situations. Everyone can choose to do this, but they do not.

Okay, if I already know the answers I seek, then why not stop seeking?

You stop seeking anytime you choose. At this juncture, you clarify meaningful directions by identifying certain lies you tell yourself. You dissolve those and grow.

To realize the goal is to break down my own defenses is humbling.

You take up the tasks that await you. As you accept your desire, you find it, create it, manifest it. As you love where you are, you transform. It is up to you how.

I sense I create and shape an evolving reality. When I had an operation and desired to heal, I learned thought energy is always in motion. People have been known to heal pain naturally with the mind. They write uplifting books on healing and trigger chain reactions.

Humans selectively ignore how gratitude influences healing. You are evolving to realize regeneration is a lesson. Individuals relearn to align, heart, soul and mind.

It takes effort to move beyond conditioning. For instance, what causes people to assume a psychic is a fortune teller? To write feelings you associate with a word is revealing.

If you believe fear is stronger than hope, then you nurture self-defeating beliefs and act in self-defeating ways. People who seek out oracles secretly seek reassurance or guidance about their own knowledge, esteem, and life choices.

I will channel more uplifting energy. Negative thoughts about anything foster doubt.

Watch your word choices. Rather than dwell in the future, stick with the now.

We spoke about that in some depth. I did not realize the gratitude that fills me now.

Listen to what you tell yourself. You whisper what you are not when deep down, you know. You talk about what you would like to have when you already have all you need. Everything you think triggers actions some part of you will experience. How this brings you to reconnect body, mind, spirit, and emotion is yet to be seen.

A person has to desire to live differently to be motivated from inside to make meaningful changes. A good example is someone I love dearly. When she discovered she had cancer, it was a blow, and a message from her body to shift how she lived, her choices.

How you view your reality at a given moment emerges from how you view the past. You have power to develop inner strength, courage, and to escape the pull of negative patterns. Your body and emotions send messages and you interpret them.

If I do not interpret and I resist comparing and judging, then that leaves a what?

It leaves free-energy flowing and experiences that will transform awareness.

No restraint as all?

The only restraints are those you imagine and attach.

I would like to learn to attune to more subtle vibrations.

Many factors determine on which levels you detect energy. Your body takes readings. You have done it since birth, but sense more as you reach new awareness.

I have heard gifted people read other people using different techniques.

Senses heighten in different ways. Some beings form images in their minds with particles of energy. Other beings nurture thought forms to trigger other senses.

Part of me wonders whether this evolving ability is not becoming intrusive.

Energy reading on the Earth plane is not what you think. All thoughts are not read; no thoughts without permission. To block feelings is to resist all that you are.

What about beyond this physical plane? Do you see through to my intimate details?

My perception permits me to view all possibilities simultaneously. Whatever you have felt, presently feel or could feel, already exists. Thoughts created await for you to align your energy vibration to make each experience more real.

Oh, is that all? I thought fleeting rewards are not reason for living.

You have no reason to apologize for the part of you that is a seeker. You learn what it means to go deeper further, beyond any cave or mountain you have visited.

I suppose it should not surprise me you are aware of my experiences at Jenolan near Sydney, Australia, Postojnska Jama in Slovenia, and Werfen ice caves in Salzburg, Austria.

I was there. You progressively reach new heights of conscious choices.

Am I to believe you were in these places when I was?

You are beginning to sense a whole new reality connected with your existence. When a person resists innate gifts, that person hesitates to take responsibility for what the soul represents. You went to great lengths to avoid your truth. You have traveled extensively to explore different realities. What you have not yet learned is you cannot assess the value of spiritual endeavors based on physical duration. You are unable to measure the immeasurable. You seek answers that do not yet make sense to you.

Whenever I am asked why my life turns out the way it does, the only answer that comes to me is based on my idea of "normal," my idea of creating a meaningful life.

You are the only person who defines your own benchmarks in eternity.

You act as though it is insignificant to find myself.

You interpret how I feel as a way to externalize what you fear about yourself. Each person lives in the world he or she creates. You discover your destiny in a linear, logical, or some other way that makes sense. All your vibrations begin and end with you. Energy moves in ways you discern until you begin to realize universal laws function within other laws. Your behavior affects some of these laws but not all.

I am beginning to think it does not matter what I will find. The seeking itself matters.

The process of seeking is all about letting go of how you used to view yourself and the world. Your reason for hope is to believe that each lesson you learn in life is valuable enough to become unforgettable. When you love everything is worthwhile.

Seek and Ye Shall Find: End of Section Exercises

1. Which lessons do you retain from this section? How would you apply them?
   - In your relationships?
   - In your work?
   - In your spiritual pursuits?
   - In other ways?
2. List ten strengths and weaknesses in yourself.

   - What would a person who knows you well say? Why?
   - What would someone who does not know "the real you" say?
   - What do you conclude from a comparison of these three lists? What does your quest for healing tell you about the evolution of state of your life?
3. What is the most useful thing you have learned about yourself from this section?
4. How could your current situation be at least partly due to your fear and unwillingness to get uncomfortable or move closer to a goal? How could you seek new inner peace?
5. Describe a time when you lied to yourself. How might you be lying to yourself now?
6. Which signs does your body give you that something is not right? How do you react?

BE LIKE A SPRING FLOWER

> *"If you never heard opportunity knock, maybe you're never at home."*

—Marilyn Vos Savant

> *"The quality of a person's life is in direct proportion to their commitment to excellence, regardless of their chosen field of endeavor."*

—Vince Lombardi

I sense benefits in highlighting the positive and eliminating the negative, but my life experience does not always permit me to experience the onset of rebirth and renewal.

The priority of the moment is your focus. It motivates you to get out of bed and to act to get something in return. You awaken at sunrise to embrace new days filled with possibility. You work as programmed until you evolve to transform your dream into the natural one. This connects you with the sun, the air, and the water. You become aware of the fog you create and clear away like the wind.

Why is it then that just as a new business is up and running past financial issues arise? This moment is when rebirth is desired.

Reprogram the mind. Adopt new beliefs. If you listen to honest voices inside, clouds passion. Rebirth comes from complete surrender to another way of seeing.

And yet more recently, situations arise where I have no way to defend myself. It is a lesson. I must stop misdirecting energy.

Like a spring flower, you are a creature that still has much growing to do. Flowers do not focus on the changing weather. They function in the moment.

It just does not make sense based on my current thinking about success and progress.

Recurrent discomfort urges you to shift focus. You are being oriented to why you exist. You have moved to a stage where your heart and soul vibrate on a frequency to stimulate your dormant memory.

One way to trigger feelings of rebirth is to visualize myself as a flower budding in spring. I would open up in response to changes in weather. I affirm the presence of forces and events beyond me. It would be refreshing to wake up and embrace forgotten memories.

Recognize nature has stages as you experience yours. You are not alive by chance.

At times I have the best intentions, but optimism is challenged by physical obstacles, by my concern for others, and situations that do not provide the encouragement I desire.

Like the flower, you are your greatest source of energy and encouragement.

Very often, it is easier to ignore perceived problems than to believe I create situations that draw attention to my unhealthy habits and thought patterns.

Each event is like the aroma of a flower. Aromas exist to trigger memories. Notice how the focus of your thinking shifts to where you experienced a flower before. As you float above a vision of problems, you have more energy for uplifting activities. Flowers are tools, helpful reminders. You are naturally able to reframe all situations.

This is easier said than done.

To focus on your strengths is not meant to deny the existence of weaknesses. Move away from a source of stress.

I tend to forget I work at different levels simultaneously in practice.

Move in directions that evoke positive energy and feelings. Any thought or feeling that dies is reborn where you do not see. Rebirth is like spring. It touches all.

Curiously, I sense how the nutrients of the earth connect with the flower.

A wilted garden reveals many things. You can decide you have tools to become a gifted gardener in the garden patches of your life. Human beings unknowingly mistreat people and themselves. As you recognize what is not working, you can change aspects of your secret, inner garden.

Discussing pain does not make it go away. If I drove down the road facing backward, it would be hard to see my path. Flowers do not grow upside-down. They grow toward light.

Understanding why you feel alienated, mistreat people, or feel mistreated, means you will be less likely to behave in ways that made you unhappy before. Each event helps you better sense or move toward what energizes you, not what drains you. When a child burns himself, he is apt to learn a valuable lesson and not do it again.

The plant analogy is helpful. To focus on the sun does not mean I forget the value of clouds and rain. As I relate my emotions to nature, I gain wisdom to transform my life.

To tap into hidden sources of energy helps you turn your thoughts toward the rejuvenating light. Your attitude determines your direction. The light is generated from inside yourself based on how honest you are about your pure and boundless spirit. You are your own creation with love and peace in your heart.

Honest dialogue with myself leads to engaging in meaningful exchanges with others. This leads to healthier attitudes and behavior. I sense this is vital to my soul's well-being.

Remark how spring flowers are versatile and impressionable. When aspects of your life evolve to discourage you, transplant your attitude in more nourishing soil.

It is possible to sense hardship teaches how to stand tall, sense the warmth of the sun.

Note sunflowers shift their physical position toward the sun. How you grow is limited or expanded by your perceived source of energy. As you choose to believe in yourself, no matter what, you shift thoughts and action to what brings you energy.

Come to think of it, flowers have been grown in natural and artificial environments. When requirements are provided, the love, water, and light provide reassurance and energy.

The truth about you is similar to the truth about flowers. You have ability to grow wherever you are. How you feel matters. As you gather insight into what enables you to feel good, you rise up higher. You channel energy more productively.

If I was truly honest, then I would admit all memories inside me have teaching value. It is enlightening to realize I unconsciously remember what it was like to be a bud and a flower. To recognize connections to nature is like the healing balm of spirit that connects all.

Before you uncover deeper sources of meaning in your life, you create analogies to clarify what you are not now.

People can learn a lot about themselves from flowers they choose or, are drawn to. You can look at the color, shape, origin, aroma and many other details. Flowers speak to us. They resonate energy. They all reflect what you can learn or be more attuned to about you.

When you think about a person, you may not be able to describe the sort of person that is. Yet that person, like you or a chosen flower, resonates energy vibrations. When all boundaries and emotions fall away, all that is left is self, like the open personality of a flower, whose characteristics are physically in front of you.

I note comparisons are ill-advised, yet they enable me to step back, be more objective.

A sense of purpose is vague without knowing about the authentic you. Soul emits energy to empower you throughout this process.

If judgment is discouraged or transcended in higher realms, then why do messages echo that some analogies are better than others? Why does true contentedness seem silent?

The more you know about duality, life and death, and cycles or rejuvenation, the more effectively you will clarify roads you forge or follow. What people say is true or not is irrelevant. Listen to yourself. You learn as you go. Phases of flora exist that you have not yet seen. Stages of natural life exist beyond your knowledge.

Amidst all of this, cycles of living and learning, life and death seem inter-connected.

Be Like a Spring Flower: End of Section Exercises

1. Which lessons do you retain from this section? How would you apply them?
   - In your relationships?
   - In your work?
   - In your spiritual pursuits?
   - In other ways?

2. Name some positive, uplifting thinkers. How do (or could) they influence you? What measures can you take to enhance your sense of hope?

3. If you're already an optimist, how might you act to share some of this positive thinking in order to motivate and inspire people (and, reinforce your optimism)?

4. How would positive thinking assist you to better clarify your current life purpose?

5. What are reasons you feel discouraged? What action can you take to change this?

6. Describe a difficult situation you had. How can you see a bright side or grow from it?

7. What have you learned about your own emotional baggage or that of other people?

EXPECT THE UNEXPECTED

> *"Freedom means the opportunity to be what we never thought we would be."*
>
> —Daniel J. Boorstin

"Well-behaved women rarely make history."

—Laurel Thatcher Ulrich

Perception alters everything. It brings you to face your highest and lowest self.

What prevents me from imagining the unimaginable?

You do. You define what is possible, impossible, and everything in between.

Inventors devise new ideas and put them into practice. I sense I am like an inventor.

You too can live as nobody else, and do it with enthusiasm. Joy is found when you live your life in ways that enable you to touch souls.

People find or experience happiness through me and my experiences. It gives me joy to share stories of where I have been and what it has taught me. Many people complain about being alone, and fear taking action to change. My life illustrates my choices and results. Each person can live vicariously through others or, be inspired differently.

Human beings reprogram themselves constantly. Anyone can. Reflection brings revelation. You imagine conditions of choice, exactly how you could explore new purpose, how faith in friends and forces beyond you can help. As you listen to your impulses, you realize the universe will not always agree with your conception.

You already sensed I would return, did you not?

I never doubted it.

Reality is that external conditions often exert pressure, bring burdens, and enforce deadlines on themselves. People expect to give into stress. It prevents them from believing in, or focusing on, possibilities.

Other people do not define you. Your only ever exert pressure on yourself.

Physical references are useful guides. In the rush of my hectic life, I have resisted allowing the world around me to dictate my agenda, yet it has. My life used to have different structure. I now expect magical experiences, spiritual realities. This is what life has become.

Magic has always been part of your innermost soul. As you disregard negative interpretations of this term imposed by history, skeptics and those with undesirable intentions, then what you have left is what you are evolving into.

Yet as I permit this, I am aware of the subtle erosion of standards and values. Media and society influence what I have come to expect. I would go so far as to say I desire to expect the unexpected because I have never truly felt comfortable with predictability.

You create notions of what you view as normal, acceptable, or essential ways of living. When you accept complacency or things you dislike (and there is always a choice) then you expect whatever is undesirable for you.

Anyone who becomes unhappy or unfulfilled then, only has themselves to blame.

Guilt and blame do not exist. If people focus more on understanding what they hear about and acting to evolve the inner selves, nourish their souls, and inspire their imaginations, these people will evolve to break out of molds that confine them.

Some people feel comfortable in their self-created worlds. Why would they leave?

Human beings may or may not choose to evolve. Any change of perception arises from within. It is initiated at any point. Some people remain longer in certain stages. Each person is endowed with their own reasoning.

At times if a person feels hurt or uncomfortable, that person feels as though the best choice is to avoid sources of uneasiness. Identifying them makes it easier to avoid them. I have known people to pretend situations do not exist. This can prolong emotional turmoil. What can I do to empower people to shed tears?

Come into the light.

Excuse me?

You heard me. Reach out to the sources of magic within yourself.

Anxiety or depression can be frustrating symptom of uneasiness. Perceived weakness leads people to know feelings of helplessness. How can this be desirable and beneficial?

Everything is expected and desired. Do not revert to fooling yourself.

Negative views of the unexpected can also be based on impatience and self-deception.

You have reason to believe you are capable of adapting to the unexpected. All you experience is expected by parts of you and unexpected or feared by other parts.

Expect the Unexpected: End of Section Exercises

1. Which lessons do you retain from this section? How would you apply them?

- In your relationships?
- In your work?
- In your spiritual or religious pursuits?
- In other ways?

2. If you could go anywhere and do anything right now, what would you do? If you couldn't do this (at least right away), how could you live through or be inspired by someone else?

3. In what ways can you teach yourself to look at the bright side of uncertainty?

4. How do you deal with uncertainty? Do you get anxious? Take it in stride? Why?

5. Describe three situations where you dealt well with uncertainty.

6. Describe three situations where you didn't deal well with uncertainty.

7. What can you learn from these experiences?

8. How does this influence your sense of purpose and current life directions?

FAILURE IS A STATE OF MIND

"Failure is the key to success; each mistake teaches us something."

—Morihei Ueshiba

"If you ever need a helping hand, it's at the end of your arm."

—Audrey Hepburn

I choose to recognize failure is a state of mind. Fear of failure controls people and keeps them where they are. I had to evolve to redefine meaning in life to see through this.

Resolve is a mental state. Success is often measured by humans in outcomes. It shapes wisdom that evolves within you during changing circumstances. When you exert effort, all phases of learning have meaning. How you view success at a given moment reflects your level of unconditional self-acceptance, fear, self-love.

Since I learn from all experience, I always achieve a result regardless of whether this is what I initially envision. I desire insight into the deeper and more far-reaching meaning of success. People often get wrapped up in what standards or norms are imposed from outside.

Perception is like your magic compass. You hold the mental map to soul.

To think that I am a soul-level magician! Success is partly defined by sensing what gives me purpose. As I surmount obstacles, I inspire my own growth. This is divine magic.

Every human is a soul magician. What you do with your tools is up to you.

I have sensed disappointment, but I am never possessed by failure. I have no reason to worry what I do not choose to say, do not choose to develop. I choose to be myself.

You always have the inner power to choose to celebrate your life.

I learned that a sense of failure is an illusion. The physical world is structured to nurture this illusion, to encourage human beings to stay ignorant to what is happening.

Voluntary accountability is the key to freedom.

People around me impose their ideas of success. I have learned I choose whether to accept and agree with people. What is your assessment of my inner evolution at this stage?

A mentor does not sense failure. A mentor does not judge. A mentor observes.

In my view your role in my life is far more than that. You guide me to find myself.

At every moment you redefine your sense of intelligence.

To sense success on any level, it is useful to realize my vision is mixed with conditioning. I have the ability to sort this out. You empower me to figure it out for myself.

Success is shaped by your conscience, mind, or soul. Sensing failure means you feel unlucky. You may feel you do not work hard enough, or disbelieve a higher power or guide exists to reassure you. Failure is not an experience someone wishes you to have. Rather, you bring on this feeling to understand what you are not.

Life does not always turn out the way I initially thought I would like. Then, I evolve.

Not achieving what you plan, like pain, is the route to strengthen yourself. Success is a feeling you sense, you earn. If you sense failure, you may simply forget the bigger plan which is to enable you to grow and use your skills to awaken yourself.

So I am not meant to distinguish between failure and success?

You reframe all experience as progress that changes your state of being, your appreciation of life, and your perspectives. If you qualify experience as defeat, then it is your personal sense of defeat. As you qualify experience as useful or character-building, you become increasingly spiritual, wiser about yourself and the physical world. You learn to defeat the ignorance that aims to consume and defeat you. A sense of success means you overcome ignorance in its changing forms.

I like to think of myself as a magician of thoughts and feelings. I change when I like.

When you attain a goal, you believe you have reason for feeling successful. When you do not achieve exactly what you set out to do, success is experienced within you in the forms of hope, positive inner thoughts, and anticipation of clearer identity.

Young people may not get accepted in teacher's college or the school or discipline of first choice. Yet a meaningful livelihood can be anything. It does not have to be what your ancestors have done, or even familiar to people. All skills have meaningful applications.

How you react to not achieving one goal actually helps you to develop skills useful to a very different destiny. You get instruction from outside yourself, yet you must do the preparation and learning to rise to the next stage of transformation.

Whenever I experience suffering, it is teaching me how to feel no sense of loss.

Facing your sense of fear and failure is key to knowing success and happiness. To be grateful for the ups and downs in your life is to realize difficulties enable you to gain insight. You would not be where you are if you had not grown already.

I gradually gain deeper understanding into this world and my own illusions.

What about needs? Failure seems to gain momentum based on my own mental reference of what is desirable, purposeful, and achievable for me. Let us discuss that.

From the moment you accept you want nothing, need nothing, and have everything, your point of view changes. Failure is not possible and you move on.

Everyone will not believe they have all they need. All they must do is look in their own mailbox for a reason to think differently. Then the media and marketing tell you stuff.

What if I told you that you create a mailbox as an object in the physical world to send yourself messages from other realms, from dimensions of the mind you have yet to explore? What if everything in the physical world reinforces what you are not?

It feels real enough. I have not yet figured out a way to push my hand through walls or other physical objects with consistency and without injury. This would offer perspective.

Before you transcend what you use to define the physical world, you must first rediscover personality traits you have come to dis-associate with yourself. To grasp the invisible inside is key to expanding your understanding of what you do not yet see.

To live a routine life, to feel confident and secure in the same, unchanging job and predictable existence, leads some people to wonder what else exists. As I have seldom done any one thing for too long, stability, security, and change all have different meaning for me.

Be the architect of your universe. Accept the path you have defined and live it.

People know people who encounter obstacle after obstacle. Some people feel cursed.

Life is all about stepping back from others and allowing energy to flow freely.

When a person faces difficulty, I find myself able to detach from their problems. I have learned that at any given moment, you choose to wallow or do your best. To procrastinate, make excuses, and expect the worst or blame others, pulls you back to expected failure.

Some people are still at a level where they are unaware of self-betrayal.

To decide on moving at all, even in small steps, gives me a sense of exerting power over conditions. People forget that a sense of moving and success change. To give into fears closes you off from what you want most, even if you are unable or unwilling to clarify that.

From outside your life may look wonderful. Only you know if this is the truth.

I choose to learn from tough times and emerge even stronger than before the let down. This mindset serves me. I learn benefits from looking positively at obstacles I encounter.

You believe what will happen in your life. Do not be surprised as it does.

I think of political crisis and environmental disasters. People lose everything and leave all they know behind. They can choose to focus on the loss or choose to believe they will know a better situation. Health problems arise and people choose to be victims or victors.

Problems are created by the soul to draw attention to neglect and ignorance.

I have placed myself in situations where I learned to get by; in foreign environments, new workplaces, changing conditions. I adapt.

Life just unfolds, like magic. Not everyone is as courageous. In fact, I am unsure of the origin of the deep courage that got me started.

Your connection to the source of all that is resonates. Magic is everywhere.

Magic is a term I associate with transformation and inner power to create and evolve. As I continue to challenge myself to experience a fulfilling life, I choose to be a pioneer. Learning comes from taking risks, from listening to my impulses or going out on a limb.

Frail trees are like people who are afraid and prefer not to take chances.

I do not believe that sounds like me.

At birth your memory of truth fades. Human beings perceive themselves as frail trees. With no grasp of what sustains them, nothing to challenge their breaking-point, delicate trees do not survive long. They may grow tall, but stay skinny.

Life teaches me the value of stress, but I need not prolong it to get the lesson. Tough times stimulate the mind and empower me to grow stronger.

The changing tides of life, and all encounters with people, project parts of you. As you learn about elements of your psyche, you are removing layers of illusion.

Failure then is a skill needed to learn forgiveness and to live a more meaningful life.

Failure is what you choose to see when you do not live your life with integrity.

As I recognize reasons why I hold myself back, I realize that I have lingered on experiences with negative energy. It is all about cleansing the pores, dissolving hard feelings.

Each time you reflect on the direction of winds you face in life, you realize the winds are not the reason you face in a particular direction. It is the source of winds. You are drawn to pure energy. This brings you closer to re-experience pure love.

Amidst all of this I am beginning to realize I am pure energy. I have been seeking energy and feeling energy in different forms all around me, but that is not what matters, is it?

As you vibrate, you are reconnecting with the universe and everything that you would sense is part of you. Every feeling you express is an effort to revert to balance.

I receive many messages about the meaning of balance. Societies that function based on economies and a tax base encourage me to generate income any legal way they can benefit. Religion imparts belief systems. Politics offer a view that balance requires conflict.

Whenever the skeptic inside you surfaces, you dwell on any perspective that carries you further away from the truth. Part of you does not wish to see or believe it. That part takes the view that ignorance is bliss or the physical world is all there is.

That is why you are here—to remind me of worlds beyond that?

Each person chooses the type of life journey that is most suitable in a given lifetime. Some people decide a short visit to this particular physical world is enough. Other people choose long journeys. Each person takes steps they feel are necessary.

I fail to see the relevance of this to where I am at now. I mean, I am learning stages of detachment. I feel encouraged to stop comparing and judging myself based on what other people think and do. I dream and seek middle ground between creating and letting things unfold in inexplicable ways. I am less apt than ever to measure the length of my journeys.

This is the way.

The way to my destiny?

The way to approach greater enlightenment and deeper self-understanding.

This dialogue is reminding me that I do what I feel I must to recreate a zest for life. In order to heighten the intensity of my energy, I seek constant challenges, but these do not have to be those which are imposed from outside myself. They lead me to define failure.

Greek philosopher Aristotle put it well when he said, "All men by nature desire to know." He also said, "Dignity consists not in possessing honors, but in the consciousness that we deserve them." How you develop knowledge can bring dignity.

Failure is a State of Mind: End of Section Exercises

1. Which lessons do you retain from this section? How would you apply them?
   - In your relationships?
   - In your work?
   - In your spiritual pursuits?
   - In other ways?
2. Reflect on some kind of personal triumph you consider to be a success.
3. Consider a time when your vision of success was different than what other people wished for you. How did this make you feel and behave?

4. Relate a character-building experience you have had where you were not defeated.

5. How might you get by with less money and develop skills you didn't know you had?

6. What kind of events in your life make you feel like a frail tree? How can you grow?

7. Describe three situations in your life which have made you a stronger person and why you believe they were character-building.

8. How you define success and failure in your past, present, and envisaged future.

   - my past, success/failure meant...
   - In my present, I feel I succeed/fail when...
   - In my future, success will mean...

9. How has your sense of direction and self-confidence evolved based on what you have learned about yourself in this section?

10. Write a story about a character you once felt like. Enable this character to have choices about a life direction. Who or what would influence this person's choices?

11. Describe a situation in your life that made you feel discouraged and weakened. How would you react to a similar situation now?

LAUGHTER FOR LIFE

> *"At the height of laughter, the universe is flung into a kaleidoscope of new possibilities."*
>
> —Jean Houston

> *"Laughter is the shortest distance between two people."*
>
> —Victor Borge

The modern world brings on pressure. Deadlines and demands orient behavior. I sense people around me have a distant memory of laughter, laugh less or, forget value in humor.

To forget humor, means you forget the value of learning to laugh at yourself. Laughter is an effective means to heal. Laughter is an invisible friend that reminds you of an incredible lightness of being. As you laugh, you vibrate and see differently.

So I have more than a handful of invisible friends? I suspected that when my passport was stolen in Estonia. I laughed out of disbelief at how a stranger who only communicated with me in Estonian appeared to assist me to obtain new documents in record time.

Everybody has invisible friends but few talk openly with them. Invisible hands lead you to recognize incongruencies within yourself so you sense reasons for humor.

What would it require for more people recognize the value of laughter?

Humor is conditioned or learned. How you use it is always up to you.

I slowly become less tense about the here-and-now.

What kind of humor do you sense in the, "now"?

For me humor reframes everything. In a sculpture art gallery I recently visited, I was amazed at how the sculptor even crafted a mouse beside a mousetrap on the floor of his gallery. It is clever to stir humor at different levels, to encourage people to open their eyes.

Humor is never out of your scope. It is based on how you adjust bearings.

Humor is also a teacher. It prompts me to smile despite apparent foibles. I laugh when I get confused and mix up directions. Laughter enables people to break down barriers of language, culture, and emotional baggage. Laughter is like a key that unlocks hidden doors.

Laughter is a source of that twinkle in your eye. It reminds you how to get the joy. Laughter brings lightness. It helps soul find light. You reconnect with yourself.

I have done that in places like Kyoto shrines and Thai Wats (temples). I am drawn to spiritual places. Everyone smiles. I smile back as if to say we all have healing potential. People relax when they choose to find humor. After the fact, I laughed at my impulse to ask a monk to take a photo using my camera. I forgot interaction with women is not their way.

Laughter reframes feelings. It empowers you to release tension.

I believe I balance life on my terms. I move beyond racing to find answers.

You do not need to dwell on what is not reality or what is out of your hands. Focus instead on what you can rely on.

What would that be?

Yourself.

I tell myself laughter is free. It is fresh air that reminds me what happiness feels like.

Laughter is within reach for all. It enriches soul in ways you do not see.

So, why is it that people do not laugh more?

Ignorance and fear. They do not know what they are missing or they forget.

Yet the incentive to learn! Longevity evolves in peaceful, joyful people. Good things relate to and evolve from laughter. Why is it that some people do not sense that?

Each human being progresses alone through stages of self-awareness.

Self-imposed constraints prevent people from enjoying sources of priceless joy. I evolve to realize any role in life brings me my destiny. I begin to realize that you are not me.

I am not you in the same form you are. We laugh at ourselves, not each other.

I am learning to deliberately think and feel what it is like to feel constantly uplifted.

Laughter is not rigid or something learned from a textbook. It is meant to be a jovial reflex, instinctive and refreshing. Think of laughter as a window to your soul. It is a thoughtful and inward-looking sense of place, somewhere to feel comfortable and in control of optimism. Laughter is energy expressed freely. Part of you yearns to break out and take form. Laughter is but one form of joy. You have infinite choices.

Laughter echoes thoughts and ideas. The more I laugh at lost luggage and travel foibles, the more growth and wisdom I receive from some mysterious source. I am grateful.

Where you create the means you choose to express energy is less important than the thought process behind it. Tools to convey and experience joy are endless.

I sense humor is a form of magic. It permits me to let go of old ways of seeing.

Magic is where you choose to experience it. Spirit energy is widening too.

A physician can find humor in the intricacy of his stitches. An engineer can convey joy by building machines. A farmer can do a little dance as he bails hay or milks cows. In terms of how humor relates to who we are now, people are only limited by their imagination.

Magic and spirit power are in everyone, yet not everyone chooses to sense it.

If each person laughs, this makes a contribution, and leaves the world a bit lighter than before we existed. My impression is we evolve individually and collectively.

You can feel sad yet recognize reasons for joy. You can laugh and awaken.

Laughter reminds me not to take life too seriously. What happens is what I choose.

Depth is found in a being who laughs for no apparent reason.

As I sense it, laughter is a key to open a portal to other realities.

It is indeed another tool that assists you to expand your faculties.

As I stop being who I thought I was, I start laughing at who I am. How hilarious!

Everything is part of becoming; how you feel, how you sense, how you dream.

Laughter brings me full circle. It is a teacher, a feather that tickles my chin and brings me back from dreaming of experiences which do not serve me. I sense it is a wake-up call.

You are learning you must bestow or inspire happiness to feel it yourself.

I truly believe you.

In order to do that, you are actually taking in energy and experiencing it on levels you do not acknowledge. To believe is action with mind-blowing implications.

I take it you will now help me see how I "blow my mind."

Do not take my word for anything. Reinvest the energy. Disclose to yourself those things you have mused about for lifetimes. Laughter takes you back there.

Positive energy has no limits. Funny, spirit power is only limited by natural law.

Laughter for Life: End of Section Exercises

1. Which lessons do you retain from this section? How would you apply them?
   - In your relationships?
   - In your work?
   - In your spiritual pursuits?
   - The other ways?

2. Who do you know who laughs often? How can these people enable you to lighten up?

3. List twenty-five funny things. How many have you done/experienced lately?

4. What activities would enable you or cause you to laugh more often?

5. How could reasons for laughter contribute to your sense of purpose?

6. What prevents you from laughing more? Do these reasons seem reasonable to you? Why or why not?

7. Which similarities do you sense between spiritual energy and laughter?

THE POWER TO DECIDE

> *"First you have figure out what you want. Second, you have to decide that you deserve it. Third, you have to believe you can get it. And, fourth, you have to have the guts to ask for it."*
>
> —Barbara De Angelis

> *"I think that all things are spirit and are derived from spirit. When you look at life from that perspective, it takes on a whole new meaning."*
>
> —James Van Praagh

The power to decide is a confusing human trait. You can decide you are too old, too young, too tall, too short, too fat, too skinny, too smart, too stupid or too something. In each case, people succumb to self-imposed limitations. Is that not the truth?

When the spirit, heart, and mind are willing, age and capacity are limitless.

I believe health begins as a state of mind. If you permit people to convince you that you are incapable of following a path, too complacent to change or realize your dreams, someone other than you exerts control. You are wise not to give away that personal power.

As you revert to "you" rather than use the pronoun "I," this reveals changes.

I imagine these are desirable changes.

Another view is you are avoiding or transcending thoughts and feelings.

And yet, if a person thinks he or she does not move as quickly as before, or he or she is tired, too weak or impatient to learn, then a change of pace, focus or direction is evolving.

You redefine progress every moment. Use what you have and develop it.

I have heard that if you do not keep your mind and body in shape, they fall apart or disintegrate. A person is never too old or too young to get fit, to address nutrition and diet, to consider preventative medicine or refresh the mind, body, and spirit.

This is not about comparing what other beings are doing and conforming.

To what degree you honestly believe that you have the power to decide about things in your life depends on whether you trust yourself and if you take opinions seriously.

You choose to be inspired or discouraged. As long as you grapple with the implications of your choices, then you are not grasping the freedom you have.

I met a senior citizen who actively sails around the world. I know a man who climbed the Himalayas. I encountered a "handicapped" person who chose to become a famous artist. A friend who smoked for many years gave up cigarettes cold turkey. I have known people to defeat harmful cravings for alcohol or drugs after years of addiction. I discover people who strive for full self-expression however they can. All of it teaches me self-love conquers all.

Every person is an instrument of the inner spirit that guides.

Views of age-related or stereotypical barriers segregate genders and generations. This suggests that your past, your gender or age has to limit what you can do with your life and when. I do not necessarily believe this, yet many people stay as they are because of the mind.

You are never too old or too young to love yourself as you are. People of all ages and backgrounds realize significant personal goals, return to school and acquire university degrees, write best sellers, beat the odds, go on thrill-seeking expeditions, and more. Doing what you love can mean ignoring what you are told. As you awaken your spirit, you become unaffected by anything unrelated to your authentic self.

I make decisions often. With all the layers of awareness out there, it is hard to keep track of decisions. Part of me has no desire to do so.

You are not expected to keep track. That is not your job.

I sense I would benefit from making a list of those things that are part of my "job."

Anything you need will emerge out of your own consciousness.

I do not believe I have enough paper or ink for all that.

Learn to "just be." Sense the magic of the moment, right now.

That is way too straightforward. I am prepared to list initiatives, thought processes and experiences that organize my thinking. When I mean what I say, that is integrity.

Energy flows in paths of least resistance. Being true to yourself requires flow.

I am not struggling, so my decision must be right for me.

The power in any decision is in the silence that ensues. It satisfies you when your feeling is beyond any question of doubt. Attuning to will is innovative. You may have heard the phrase, 'many are called, but few are chosen.' In actuality, all are chosen, yet not everyone is ready or willing to listen at the same time or energy level.

The Power to Decide: End of Section Exercises

1. Which lessons do you retain from this section? How would you apply them?
   - In your relationships?
   - In your work?
   - In your spiritual pursuits?
   - In other ways?
2. Describe issues or situations in your life that require serious decisions. How have you become aware of interconnectedness between how you think, act and feel?
3. What issues would you like to decide now?
4. Which key decisions have you made lately? How has the process changed you?
5. What can you decide to do to get your mind, body into better shape? When to begin?

SELF-PERSUASION

> *"At the end of reasons comes persuasion."*
>
> —Ludwig Wittgenstein

> *"One life is all we have and we live it as we believe in living it."*
>
> —Joan of Arc

I suddenly sense a wave of brainwashing coming on. There must be good reason.

Conscious affirmations are a means of self-persuasion.

Wherever I am I generate powerful and far-reaching changes in my life. No amount of insight, suggestion, encouragement or guidance from anyone shapes my behavior that way.

As you realized already, motivation begins within you. Somehow, you convince yourself of what you think is best for you at a given time, and then you do it or you do not. Your life is as simple or as complicated as you make it.

Each day I get up, eat, drink, work, and interact with people. I condition myself to prepare for what unfolds. I consciously plan for what I sense comes next. Few people look very far ahead. This does not seem like magic, only natural.

Sensing magic is natural demonstrates foresight. You crave answers.

I regularly adopt a great idea of my own and let it influence thoughts and imagination. I define the possible. Part of me simply wishes to help people to discover who they truly are.

Such thinking stretches you to unpredictable heights and depths. As you persuade yourself to change your patterns, you are encouraging changes in people. You can always turn over a new leaf. In effect, the nature of change is up to you.

Some people become motivated to change when they experience inner tension and recognize it is a sign or a turning point for their evolution. Inner tension is created when you say or do something that opposes your beliefs and when it threatens your idea of fulfillment. Your sense of happiness evolves with your life experiences.

If you always do what you have always done, then you will get what you have always gotten. Without choosing differently, you do not grow.

It is also hard to anticipate how energy will feel as I explore new dimensions.

You are evolving to give something back in forms of courage and love.

Perceived hypocrisy is another reason for stress; you can overcome this in your own mind. Who wishes to see oneself as a hypocrite? If you say or do something that makes you feel like a hypocrite, the ideal would be to stop saying or doing what makes you feel that way. Yet that is not always easy or even appropriate.

You decide what is easy or appropriate and when. Take the notion that you once believed and told everyone who asked that you are not. If life experience compelled you to change your behavior because this made you feel better about yourself, you may prefer to adapt your original principles and standards.

I did not believe I ever designate myself as a hypocrite. When I view behavior in people, I realize this is meant to teach me things, but I am not always sure I get what I need.

You always get out of a situation what is useful at a given moment.

When a change in attitude makes one feel hypocritical, how do you deal with that?

Transmutation is a process. Trace your emotional pathway and refer to Barbara Brennan's work. She describes how a creative wave forms inside as you center, contract, and merge within yourself before you can expand differently.

My! This is getting deep. You encourage me to gather power in apparent idleness.

So far I discern you are more than a little awake.

Is that all? I honestly sense a great deal of headway is being made.

Your actions are inconsistent with your beliefs. Your words tell a story that you have yet to accept fully. You convince yourself you do the best you can, but refuse to adapt your principles, standards, or actions to be more consistent. Feelings inside you can evolve. They urge you to adapt and change in new ways.

I am changing all the time, yet clarifying no sense of lasting direction. That this is okay, even desirable, goes against everything I have been taught.

You do not discern or acknowledge all your teachers.

How am I supposed to acknowledge what I do not see?

You nurture faith in things you do not see all the time. It is based on your sense of trust and self-confidence. You do not have to see love energy to feel it.

Sensing is believing? I threw the idea of "seeing is believing," right out the window.

There is no role for you to fill unless you imagine it.

Self-Persuasion: End of Section Exercises

1. Which lessons do you retain from this section? How would you apply them?
   - In your relationships?
   - In your work?
   - In your spiritual pursuits?

- In other ways?
2. List some of your self-destructive habits.
3. What are some ways you could change habits that hurt yourself and/or others?
4. When has your behavior made you feel like a hypocrite? How do you feel now?
5. Write out ways that you have procrastinated in your life. How do you feel about it? Explain some of the reasons you have for seeking to change aspects of your life.
6. How does this assist you to refine your goals?
7. What kind of role do you imagine for yourself? Are you there yet? If not, how close?

HOW CAN YOU TURN DOWN A HEDGEHOG?

> *"If somebody thinks they're a hedgehog, presumably you just give 'em a mirror and a few pictures of hedgehogs and tell them to sort it out for themselves."*
>
> —Douglas A. Adams

> *"No problem can be solved from the same level of consciousness that created it."*
>
> —Albert Einstein

If someone asked you how you could turn down a hedgehog with that longing look in its eye, you might initially reply it depends how hard you would get pricked.

Human beings will convince themselves it is hard to say no. If you repeatedly find yourself agreeing to requests that evoke distress, reasons exist why you say yes when your gut says no. You create guilt or aim to avoid hurting people's feelings. You are actually avoiding what your reaction says about you.

Part of me used to feel more responsible for other people's feelings. Their happiness does not depend on me, and yet, I feel connected to them so it is hard to detach from requests.

You can be aware that inner work is required but not know how to proceed.

Perhaps I forget or have internalized the virtues of sacrifice? Is altruism a vice?

To neglect yourself in favor of others does not serve you.

I know people who are afraid to say no. They assume they will not be asked again. It raises the possibility of bruised ego.

Mistaken assumptions complicate your life. Identify and curtail them.

If a friend asks to borrow money, do you know how many people are afraid they will be disowned if they refuse? What about those people who fear refusing a request from an employer. They fear being fired. Ever sense if you refuse a child, he will no longer love you?

None of this is true. You hide from your true feelings, something else again.

Oh, to identify expectations and understand why they are misguided.

To do anything less would be to ignore your dreams and the magic within you.

It is easy enough to desire to think differently. You may think, if I say no, my friend will be disappointed, but our friendship will stand. I will be respected for being open, explain why I have no money to lend. My boss may be unhappy if I refuse overtime, but you feel bad.

Nothing is ever unreasonable to refuse unless you decide that it is.

I realize I must decide on what reason to refuse. Underneath this, it is unwavering faith I desire so I will not feel compelled to review, self-question, or over-think.

To decide can be short and sweet. You can switch off over-thinking anytime.

People do not realize they lead other people to assume they will always be compliant. Inside, I have felt overwhelmed or powerless. I worked through it, but I sense it around me.

You always have choices. Life gets easier when you learn to appear confident even when you may feel uncertain. It can be easier to say no to some people than to others because of how you intimidate yourself. This means you fill yourself with fear.

I am learning to anticipate situations and practice behaving differently. When I have said no, I listen to myself. I listen to my intuition about things and do not dwell on what was.

Helping others is admirable, yet, you also have a right to put yourself first and feel good about it. You are meant to integrate your true feelings into your decisions and learn to stop fearing the worst reactions in yourself or from others.

Now, cases exist when it would be handy to pull out a magic wand.

You always have magic inside and around you. The voice of magic guides you more often than you realize. You tap into it each time you sense life is meaningful.

I keep imagining a magic book will appear with all the answers right in front of me.

You forget you are your own magic book. You appear and disappear in and out of the lives of people you know or do not. People notice you when you have things in common and disregard or erase you from memory as you no longer relate to them.

I have heard of black cats as companions of sorcerers, but I am not sure about a hedgehog. What about a wombat or an echidna? I already ponder additional choices.

Human beings feel compelled to choose when this is not what nature intended.

What do you mean?

All creatures are your companions. You need not choose one and exclude others. Part of you rises to a new stage. The rest of you resists your authentic self.

I am getting closer though. I do feel more comfortable with certain topics that I hesitated to mention before. When I focus on what I do not want, I get more out of what I do.

How Can You Turn Down a Hedgehog?: End of Section Exercises

1. Which lessons do you retain from this section? How would you apply them?
   - In your relationships?
   - In your work?
   - In your spiritual pursuits?
   - In other ways?
2. Identify some of your own mistaken beliefs. How can you turn them around?
3. Recall a time when you accepted to do things you really didn't wish to. Why did you?
4. Did your behavior seem to be a setback to your desired life direction?
5. Reflect on how you interact with people. Are you more agreeable than before?
6. When have you decided not to cave in to the demands of others? Why?

7. How demanding have you been of others in asking them to do things they might not have wished to do? Describe two situations where you might have acted differently.

8. Where in your life would it be advisable for you to change your attitude? How?

UNMISTAKABLE

> *"The wounded spirit is not seen, but walks under a disguise."*
>
> —Bishop Robert South

> *"When our eyes see our hands doing the work of our hearts, a circle of creation is completed inside us. The doors of our soul open and love steps forth to heal everything in sight."*
>
> —Anne Jones

At times, you sense looking out at the snow is more than looking at the snow. You feel like you see through the season of hardship to observe something deeper and inexplicable. This inner feeling, this energy vibration, is absolutely unmistakable.

I perceive a stronger connection to the earth, to my soul, to what exists around and inside me. Some voice reassures me as I proceed to explore unfamiliar directions. If I miss a bus, I reorient and take a train instead. What I learn in the process adapts and shapes me.

Just because you do not consciously predict something does not mean it is not right for you at this moment. As you grow to have faith in your vibes, you will move to no longer question your instincts. They are the most dependable gauge you have.

From this very instant, I have reason to feel reassured and connected to sources of hope that are hard to describe.

Reassurance is a voice in your mind that tells you everything will be okay. A feeling of connectedness to things enriches and transforms you. You feel the warmth of a bond, a source of unwavering encouragement and inspiration in directions that feel right. It is a belief in yourself that teaches you to live a renewed life.

As I sense an increase in intimacy with myself, I detect new intimacy with other people in my life. It is an unspoken understanding of interconnectedness.

You become more honest with yourself, about what is really bothering you or making you happy. Human beings are frequently unaware of reasons why they act. As you share feelings more openly with people, you grow closer to them. You use fewer words. They read your vibes. This openness enables you to sort through your own dilemmas. Your new confidence is unmistakable. The thinking process helps you to organize your thoughts and see things briefly from the outside looking in.

What used to seem like burdens bothers me less. The power of choice reminds me to stop noticing. I feel less vulnerable talking openly because I discover this strengthens me.

To realize what matters you feel unafraid about what people think of your views or decisions. It is grounded in confidence and unconditional, invisible support.

I sense it is useful to minimize tentative words like "think." Confidence is reinforced when I say, "I believe." A new level of self-respect, patience and calmness means I no longer react to outbursts, destructive comments, whining, sweet talk, or truly negative comments.

Humans seldom understand the meaning and implications of their behavior.

To feel valued, it only makes sense you must know what this means and how it feels in your own mind. I establish ground rules and boundaries for how I wish to be treated.

People who worry less than others usually have a kind of faith in higher forces and unspoken hope. These people are also willing to let go of the desire for total control of problems in their lives and the lives of others.

Rather than focus only on the difficulties associated with listening to the extensive needs and worries of certain people, I learn to express needs too, to not neglect how I feel or permit the other person to control how and when everything will be done. Rather than permit anyone to exploit my generosity or presence, I gradually learn to recognize how people's behavior is like a mirror that brings fears to the surface so I act to heal and change myself.

Revelations are unmistakable.

I also think about other people and their sense of obligation to themselves and others. Rather than keep key issues to themselves, these people could be encouraged to find ways to seek advice from sources they trust. This would help refresh their minds and bodies.

Yet, truly life-transforming experiences come as you move to a new level of awareness. Everyone you encounter is a vehicle that exists to bring clarity to why you exist. Everything around you is part of energy flow that goes through you.

No person I encounter is out to get me? No person then, is out to get anyone at all?

Human beings exert enormous efforts to shift their attention from the truth to illusions. The best way to learn is through your own first-hand experience. How you react or do not reveals a lot about deeper self, unhealed wounds, and sources of joy.

What you say suggests it would be useful to have a audio-video recording of how we act and what we say. This would reveal the truth we do not see.

Unmistakable: End of Section Exercises

1. Which lessons do you retain from this section? How would you apply them?
   - In your relationships?
   - In your work?
   - In your spiritual pursuits?
   - In other ways?
2. Describe three reasons you have to feel hope in your life.
3. Recall an experience where someone made efforts to control your decision-making. How did this make you feel? How did you react? Would you react differently now?
4. List some ways you are becoming aware. What have you done lately to help yourself?
5. What would you like to ask yourself or tell yourself to do right now?
6. Reflect on your blessings. What is unmistakable or predictable in your life? For what or whom are you grateful? Why?
7. What connections do you see between your life intentions and reading this book?
8. Do you have a new sense of progress in a particular direction?
9. What do you draw from this section about you and your stage of personal growth?

ORDINARY PEOPLE, EXTRAORDINARY LIVES

> *"The greatest gift you could give to another is your own happiness, for when you are in a state of joy, happiness or appreciation, you are fully connected to the Stream of pure positive Source Energy that si truly who you are."*

—Esther Hicks, Abraham

"We must overcome the notion that we must be regular... it robs you of the chance to be extraordinary and leads you to the mediocre."

—Uta Hagen

Somewhere along the line, I learned I have power to perceive life as ordinary or extraordinary. I add context, color and explore the feelings that are part of everything.

You create your reality. You have to figure out which feelings are accurate and which ones are distractions. In terms of the super-natural, you evolve to detect spirits and energy in ways that reorient your life. Your disbelief evolves to where you acknowledge what you sense yet, still hesitate to accept it.

The thought of spiritual communication itself is extraordinary to me.

Regardless of what happens, you sense connections to people and events. What you perceive as unusual is a new norm. What seems extraordinary simply lies outside your previous notion of "normal." You have always discerned vibes and different levels of energy. How you perceive and interpret it is awakening you.

As I write things down and share impressions, I realize physical objects, people and places express particular qualities to draw my attention to things. It is all so extraordinary.

It is becoming clearer as you are gradually lifting burdens from your psyche.

This is all happening so quickly. Although physical objects are tangible, and can be grasped with the physical senses, my sense of evolution here is not as straightforward.

Realizing spiritual ideals will requires practice to transform.

Creative communication has always been part of me. I think back to how long I have been intuiting things and why I have been reluctant to share my impressions. Positive feelings come from gaining insight into visions as far back as when I was seven.

The more you discover about yourself, the more you feel peace and joy. As you recognize your identity is based on boundless energy, on what you discern about your talents or abilities, you realize fulfillment is experienced as you learn to recognize goodness in everyone and find ways you can help them. You have regained a spark. This signals that your deepest awakening is well underway. Life is about to change.

Ordinary People, Extraordinary Live: End of Section Exercises

1. Which lessons do you retain from this section? How would you apply them?
   - In your relationships?
   - In your work?
   - In your spiritual pursuits?
   - In other ways?
2. How have you opened your mind to learn more about your inner thoughts?
3. What could you do to learn more about this process?
4. Describe three situations in your life that you think lowered your confidence. Why?
5. Describe three situations you think have increased your personal confidence. Why?
6. Describe five things you could do to improve your confidence in your life right now.
7. How does this enrich your sense of direction and life purpose?

PERPETUAL SUNSHINE

> *"Change alone is eternal, perpetual, and immortal."*
>
> —Arthur Schopenhauer

> *"And life is what we make it, always has been, always will be."*
>
> —Grandma Moses

Many human beings feel unfulfilled or at least have their own unanswered questions.

A sense of a lack of anything is an illusion. People create emptiness for a purpose. Everyone has the power to find constant sources of sunshine and energy.

I discover immeasurable value is found in taking more time to savor nature, to interact and connect differently with people, to reflect on the simple things, to even do nothing and feel that is meaningful. The process of de-conditioning is ongoing inside. I sense it now.

Reality is simple. Any perceived comfort zone is the opposite of who you are.

Some people change routes they take to work or ways they see the world. I change how I view everything regularly without recognizing the implications.

What you choose to learn is always useful. What you see changes with intent.

I find deeper satisfaction in interactions and relationships. I have learned that at the right moment, I define what makes sense. I realize this does not require I pursue anything.

Joy is always within you. Maybe people you know are not what you wish them to be or are not appreciative or respectful. To choose to feel content is to recognize you hold the key to your sense of balance and contributing something meaningful.

I encounter many people who feel tired or discontent. They share impressions that something is not quite right in their lives. To think this way, that life is not supposed to be the way you perceive it at a given moment, well, this signals the person is becoming aware of not being true to the self. People will say they see I am in my element and wish to share joy.

Reassure yourself. You can change this whenever you decide to turn your life around. The first step is to make this decision. You underestimate that everyone who observes you in some sense learns from you. They choose to evolve into joy or not.

I know my beliefs are grounded in what makes sense at a given moment. I find it intriguing to follow threads of my life back and review situations from my vantage point.

How you perceive lessons from choices influences your inner light energy.

There was a time when I believed I always had more to achieve, to earn, to own, to finish. Discontent may leave a person perpetually motivated and perpetually discouraged.

As you revisit places and conditions that scare you, you master your fear.

At different phases I have imagined myself frustrated, disillusioned, confused, afraid of the future, lonely, and riddled with guilt over past decisions. Restless people around me led me to wonder. To overcome ingrained beliefs reminds a person that soul can be healed.

Whatever you do or, route you take, your goal is the same: your sense of joy and meaning in life comes in varied forms.

There has got to be more to life than that. People seek more depth, clarity, and details.

Your life evolves through your relationships and chosen endeavors. A sense of connection to higher forces, intimate partners, close friends, family, and children all add depth and clarity. You have to be open to it. Aside from fulfilling relationships, your most innate need is to make a contribution to people and society.

In the human heart burns a desire to lead a life with meaning. This is connected to feeling good. People wish to feel they count and make a difference.

What you do in your own life is less important than how you perceive your behavior and what wisdom you choose to get out of a given experience. Each person is where he is at a given moment because he is happy to be there, even if he forgets.

If this is the case, why do people get so wrapped up in reasons for discontent?

From the moment people realize they are responsible for their own sense of perpetual sunshine, they become afraid. They block it, postpone it, ignore it, or deny it. A meaningful life is not only joyful. How you feel does not make you who you are.

People may find it hard to believe that they exert so much control over their destiny. How to take responsibility is not taught but learned. Intentions, like burdens, weigh heavy.

Nothing carries weight. This invites you to detach from your current beliefs about what is measurable, visible, and tangible. You sense beyond that.

Sunshine is more than light that beams down from the sky. It is symbolic of who I am.

It is not symbolic of you, rather it is you.

How can I be light? I illuminate a bulb with electricity and understand that as light.

Everything is energy. You look in the mirror and your eyes only detect certain vibrations in the form of visible color and texture. You are already expanding to see beyond that. What you choose to see is not all there is, not all you are. You are connected to everything that is happening, and all that has ever happened anywhere.

How am I supposed to feel good about being too connected to things I do not control?

This is part of the exercise of learning to let go. You have higher awareness than you realize. You are aware choices exist before you make them. You are aware of feeling temperature, velocity, acceleration, and many other levels of energy. How much faith you have in perception changes along with what you choose to perceive.

I know what you are saying. People will walk into a room and sense a heaviness or lightness depending on the mood of other people. Why each of us chooses to discern positive and negative energy offers messages we are invited to explore.

You are developing the courage to self-explore on levels you did not initially realize existed. Your choice is grounded in the desire to create pleasure for yourself and others. You are moving beyond seeing the world as you have been taught to see.

So, when I think of sunshine, this is like a metaphor for enlightenment. That is, I am on a path of progressive learning that is one other people can share if they choose.

Exactly. And each person is repeatedly invited to see the good. If you are not willing to step back and review, then you really have no idea about how you truly feel.

I have to ask how you know so much.

Any wisdom I have results from internal work and a lot of discipline. What you need is not a guide, but increased faith in yourself. Your journey is also my journey.

As everything is connected, then energy grows as each person works through his or her illusions. In what ways does each person benefit from this growing energy source?

Benefits are immeasurable, yet very real. To become conscious of whom you are raises your energy vibration in ways that shift your perception to details you overlooked.

What you are saying confirms that everything that has happened to me has really been on the fringes of reality. Personal revelations are reasons to be happy and feel uplifted.

You evolve to sense the truth as you learn to reflect more deeply than ever. You appreciate the wisdom shared through events you read differently. You move beyond selfishness and all those things you thought made you happy when you discover what really does. This is a process of becoming conscious of work you will do. As you allow your inner self to develop further, you make new discoveries.

Perpetual Sunshine: End of Section Exercises

1. Which lessons do you retain from this section? How would you apply them?
   - In your relationships?
   - In your work?
   - In your spiritual pursuits?
   - In other ways?

2. How would you describe your energy and enthusiasm on mental, emotional, physical,, and spiritual levels? Would you like to change any of this? How?

3. What causes does this fulfillment, sense of inner joy, and peace emerge in your mind?

4. Do you nurture a sense of inner peace and contentment? If not, why not?

5. What can you do to reframe your life experience and better appreciate your behavior?

6. How would a change of heart influence your evolving purpose and life conditions?

PERSPECTIVE

> *"In the perspective of every person lies a lens through which we may better understand ourselves."*
>
> —Ellen J. Langer

> *"The more I see the less I know for sure."*
>
> —John Lennon

As my perspective is ever-changing with my awareness, how do I ground this?

Perceived problems and hardships are catalysts for you to create perspective. You strengthen your grounding to beliefs, alter the outlook and focus of your life.

You imply it is useful to change, but you do not tell me how.

That is always your choice. Human beings resist being empowered. Choose to be healthy. Choose to be sick. Choose to be loving or not. All have consequences.

Consider a quest to acquire wealth, power, and prestige often leads to unanticipated personal and other debts, where implications may only be better understood after emotional or other disappointments. To overspend, to progress socially and technologically at the expense of worsening poverty and the environment, ultimately leaves people feeling empty and questioning their real purpose.

Start with yourself, then, look outside to reinforce reasons you have to create new perspective. You are always expanding on what you think you know, the reasons why you think you are in the situation you are in, why you stay in your state of mind.

A person does not create a sense of lasting stability if that person spends more energy working on what is not destiny than on what is. Consider Andrea Bocelli, the son of a farmer who attended law school. Anyone who has heard the voice of this magnificent tenor would not imagine him fulfilled as a farmer or a lawyer. A person needs to be fully engaged in the present and attuned to himself to make choices that are compatible with his soul.

To read your soul is to read energy. Teachers and training enter your scope.

To sniff out opportunities and act on my gut, then, is a sign I am honest with myself.

No human is without perspective. What you perceive is not always faithful to who you are. You increase a sense of fulfillment as you honor your talents, use and develop them. Your true nature is not a thing anyone can teach you. As you discover dimensions, how you relate to people and the world around you changes.

I get that. A person may get a neat job, choose a particular partner, have children or adopt, even run a marathon, set out to climb a mountain, only to learn the original choices were not truly meaningful. Results do not always make the person feel happy or successful.

A sense of failure is itself a vision of success. Initial goals do not matter as you learn to see through them to your underlying intention. Completeness comes from living by values that make you feel authentic in a given moment. Every sense that empowers you to reach conclusions is meaningful.

People seek tangible and intangible perspective. They seek goals and endure pain. Whatever the case, everything shapes perspective. What I do and do not choose to do. People struggle with problems that are grounded in their original ideas of success.

Views of success change. The acquisition of tangibles is not the root of contentment. You may desire none of these things, but still be encouraged to do so.

Many people adopt impoverished values of not wishing to be bothered with the troubles of others, and focus on a life built up of things.

As a result people sense imbalance. You are longer be confused about the meaning of life. It is not uncommon to feel successful and yet, unfulfilled at the same time. This signals that you delude yourself about aspects of your view of success.

Many people tend to lead unexamined lives. The more these kinds of people examine their lives, the more they lose perspective; dwell on what they do not feel they can change.

People will widen their perspective or narrow their perspective with intention. The process of deciphering underlying intentions leads to revealing the hidden truth.

Oh, is that all? Learning to trust myself without second-guessing has been a process.

Many people tune out from their own energy. They choose not to develop conditions that empower them to tune in again. This is to be respected. As you rediscover yourself, stages of raising self-awareness help you grasp perspective.

People work hard to earn money to buy things that make them happy. To take that positive feeling and sense of accomplishment away from them does not seem right or fair.

Perspective is not meant to belittle what you have experienced. It is meant to expand how you view understandings of commitment, devotion, and self-love.

Perspective: End of Section Exercises

1. Which lessons do you retain from this section? How would you apply them?
   - In your relationships?
   - In your work?
   - In your spiritual pursuits?
   - In other ways?

2. In what ways do you develop perspective? Do you always desire more, or a situation other than what you have? How are you realizing you do not have to be that way?

3. How has your sense of success changed over time? What has influenced the changes?

4. Recall two examples where you've drifted apart from people who were once important to you. Why? Do you wish your current feelings/conditions were different?

5. How would you like to redefine the meaning of some of your past relationships?

6. In what ways could you simplify your life?

BLESSINGS

> *"Reflect upon your present blessings of which every man has many—not on your past misfortunes, of which all men have some"*

—Charles Dickens

"Each day offers us the gift of being a special occasion if we can simply learn that as well as giving, it is blessed to receive with grace and a grateful heart."

—Sarah Ban Breathnach

I am wondering about blessings found in doing what I am doing where I am. When you explore how to stretch perception, energy is always involved, but what is the mind role?

Real spiritual development begins with character, will, and intelligence before deepening self-understanding. Later, psychic aptitudes manifest spontaneously.

So if you fear what people think, imagine these people believe what you do is a blessing. A person needs to stop believing they deserve any other treatment.

Be grateful for what is going for you. When you sense what does not resonate, turn away. It is a blessing to love yourself as you are. Then, you engage fully in life.

For me existence is a blessing. I discover things to help free myself from limitation.

As you explore within, you learn about what you value and do not value, thoughts and behaviors you outgrow, and which ones you wish to adopt. As your inner guidance strengthens, you become less vulnerable to people who would manipulate you through your fear. It is a blessing to realize the truth must be felt.

To sift through memories of challenging periods in my life has led me to perceive differently. I recognized a turning point when I stopped seeking outside myself for help, and started listening within. The information I requested presented itself. It gets to the point where items are lost, I call out for assistance and suddenly, I find them.

When your motives are pure and unselfish and you aim to serve all human beings, then requests for transcendental knowledge are always answered. Wisdom is a blessing only to those souls prepared to absorb it.

I am driven by this belief that there is more to myself that I must explore. For me, seeking to deepen my connection to higher forces is part of my sense of progress. The will to do this is a blessing. As I sense that my ego is no longer at odds with other parts of me the way it used to be, I detach naturally from struggle and drama.

You have clarity about what has become most important to you.

My choice to reorient goals is a turning point, to appreciate life and uncertainty more as I sense them. Events are what they are. My mind merely discerns energy as personality.

Energy shapes your life and always has, even if you temporarily forgot or grew apart from its power. Coming to terms with how you have lived is a blessing. It is all about discerning where and why you choose to act out of compassion or fear.

On a basic level I have come to believe analogies can be made between gut-wrenching experiences and a series of health crises like heart attacks. In each case the physical body and emotions are drawing attention to imbalance, discomfort, self-neglect, and self-sabotage. If you happen to live through trying experiences, then this is an opportunity to take steps to read yourself and your life choices differently. To share personal stories is a way to encourage and empower others who can choose to perceive their lives differently.

To sense all you have is a clue to all you are. Fear and ego are something else. You find blessings by tearing down all the emotional barriers inside yourself.

As each day passes I sense blessings in everything that happens to me and around me. As I explore possible answers to life mysteries, I realize the answers change as I evolve.

The greatest mystery is your self. It requires lifetimes to explore.

I sense a growing spiritual side is part of a process of coming to terms with the things I have disregarded or avoided. Suddenly I interact and sense energy more openly and freely.

You are the source of your own clarity. As the most far-reaching influence on your own life, you work through misunderstandings to bring yourself to the light.

Blessings are subtle, immeasurable, and beyond description when based on sensations and the unseen world. They relate to everything that evokes feelings of gratitude.

Your destiny evolves throughout your life experience based on awareness. As you evolve to realize the basis for many of your beliefs is unfounded, you release them. The process of learning who you really are is a blessing itself.

I had not realized how fortunate I was to come to terms with my own ignorance.

If you had been aware of this process from birth, then the process of raising awareness, taking tests, and learning, would lose meaning.

Blessings: End of Section Exercises

1. Which lessons do you retain from this section? How would you apply them?
   • In your relationships?
   • In your work?
   • In your spiritual pursuits?
   • In other ways?
2. Describe blessings in your life. Imagine more acceptable existence. What sort of blessings would this include that you do not experience or, have not recognized?
3. How can you create joy in your life when people you see struggle, falter, or give up?
4. At some point in your life, you have avoided help. Why? How would you react now?
5. How can feelings of inadequacy and insecurity be blessings in your life?
6. In what areas of your life do you still feel sources of meaning still remain obscure?
7. Whatever the choices, your life has potential. Which feelings are truly blessings?
8. How is the knowledge you are gaining a blessing?

SIGNIFICANCE OF DREAMS

> *"I was not looking for my dreams to interpret my life, but rather for my life to interpret my dreams."*
>
> —Susan Sontag

> *"In dreams and in love there are no impossibilities."*
>
> —Janos Arany

I have evolved to believe dreams have more significance than I initially realized.

Dreams are free-flowing images, ideas and sensations that emerge in your mind during stages of sleep. They nourish your hopes, or reinforce things you fear. Dreams are also visions you indulge in while awake. When you realize these visions, or they enlighten you, dreams trigger joy. They are a reply to your real experience. They can be seen as encoded images that will lead you back to your fullest capacity.

Dreams are clues to my desires. As I listen, really listen to my inner self, I work toward perceiving life differently. They remind me about things I overlook.

Dreams fill human beings with energy and incentive to act. If you ignore your dreams, then some goal inside of you suffers.

If deciphering dreams teaches people about themselves and offers clues to heightened joy, peace, and love, then why do people shy away from learning more?

Human beings fear they will blossom to their full potential. If they never dare act on their impulses, then they allow their dreams to wither. Faith can nurture you even when what is going on around you and within you is unclear to you.

Based on what you say, I am supposed to accept being unclear about a lot of things.

Your mind, body and spirit have different levels of awareness. Until you align your energy, part of you will always understand less than parts attuned to knowledge. Dreams point you in directions to help you align. Your decisions you are based partly on your confusion about what dreams mean.

Some people assume dreams have no significance or they do not remember any.

What you choose to remember or not about dreams reveals things about your level of awareness in waking life. Learning to interpret your dreams builds confidence and reinforces what you already sense about your destiny and responsibilities.

I encourage people to journal what they remember about dreams.

Strength develops is you as the result of your dreams. They remind you not to suppress the real you. When you dismiss dreams, you suppress part of yourself.

I have come to view it as unhealthy not to investigate possible meanings of dreams or not to pursue what you see as your underlying goals. Ignoring aspects of your true self may cause you to feel bitter, angry, and distant. Listening to yourself releases such stress.

Even when it is not initially clear, and you feel like quitting, something will still speak louder; feel right, deep inside your soul. This thing speaks inside you, invigorates, and renews you. Dreams offer clues to your path to well-being. Listen closer to inner voices. You are being invited to step outside your mental prison.

Dreams have so many connotations. They prompt me to ask whether one sense of happiness is more valuable than another. I have no definitive answer.

Louis Armstrong wrote a famous song that encourages you to do more than just "Dream a Little Dream." Your life can be inspired by happy people if you find courage to envisage your own fairytales and set out to make them real.

Belief in yourself is either reinforced or not in your psych. To begin with, Faith in something greater than your previous experience and conditioning brings you back to your inner power. Your conscious mind views only part of a bigger reality. As you gain insight into your dreams, you expand the limits of your understanding in your daily world.

I believe dreams offer clues to inspiration. They drive or enrich a person's life.

Dreams teach you to recognize meaning in all your feelings. The more you learn about yourself, the better equipped you are to live a more fulfilling life.

In my mind there is a danger that self-examination could evolve to the point that it is "over-thinking."

To reflect is a way to understand your dreams. It is empowering to recognize how you are both observer and participant in your own waking life. Fear is an illusion imagined by the participant in you who permits ego to interfere. The observer develops a more objective view. The participant is unaware of the illusions he creates.

Some people believe dreams are all fluff and interpretation is destructive to character. My own view is that dreams empower each human being to manage their own self- healing.

Different views exist on health and healing. Some people assume the antidote comes from outside you. Other people believe it is an internal process.

Which is accurate?

Your dreams reveal the power at your disposal. Go forward unafraid. The love you express will be returned in varied forms. It is a question of spirit. Dream you are cherished or healed and it is more likely to be. The universe rewards you.

Significance of Dreams: End of Section Exercises

1. Which lessons do you retain from this section? How would you apply them?
   - In your relationships?
   - In your work?
   - In your spiritual pursuits?
   - In other ways?

2. Does anyone in your life fear you may evolve into something they wouldn't like? Why? How do their feelings influence your feelings and actions?

3. What activities speak louder to you than others? How do they point to your strengths?

4. Write down three day or night dreams you remember. What might they mean to you?

5. What clues do you gain about your emotions, feelings, state of mind, hopes and fears?

6. If you don't remember your dreams from sleep, what would you like to dream about?

7. How do you feel dreams reinforce or develop your view of obstacles or life purpose?

8. Which books might you find about dreaming to learn more about dream recall?

9. How does your knowledge and understanding of dreams enhance your life path?

5

Attune to the Power of Love

WHAT REALLY MATTERS

"Anything you do not love will become a lesson."

—Ross Bishop

"Difficult times have helped me to understand better than before, how infinitely rich and beautiful life is in every way, and that so many things that one goes worrying about are of no importance whatsoever."

—Isak Dinesen

LESSONS

1. Love is so much more than you assume.
2. You constantly expand parts of yourself that you do not see.
3. Gratitude deepens through self-reflection.

Relationships enrich my life. Mind you, I did not always believe that about everyone I met. It has been a struggle to learn to see through negativity, to resist and unlearn emotional reactions. The more attuned I become, the more likely I am to act to fulfill myself.

Through relationships that did not work, I grew aware of the value of support and caring. Hearing of people's experiences is not like living my own. There was a time I sensed love in bursts for specific people. Then, I grew to feel love on levels and intensities before the power of energy everywhere. Why do people struggle to awaken to the power of love?

Human beings avoid things that would allow them to feel more love. They do not choose to examine words they utter which express the opposite of what they want.

The poet Rumi made an astute remark when he said, "Your task is not to seek for love, but to find all the barriers within yourself that you have built against it."

The presence of good feelings is enough, and yet, it is not. A big part of evolving is learning how to lose the sense of feeling "special" or vital to others. I recall how my sisters said for years I was my mom's favorite. I did not believe that was the case. Mom said she didn't either. It seemed so trivial, and yet, it echoed I resisted sources of my passion.

Disagreement is necessary to realize the person you really are. A part of you is fiercely loyal to other parts that matter more than any words could ever express.

I have not always chosen relationships that enable me to feel good about myself. Yet gaining insight into those difficult ones has empowered me to discern what is truly meaningful. You realize you are attracted to some people based on your inadequacies .

Something greater than you gets a hold of you and you start to trust. You have safety and freedom. Your expectations for relationships control you based on the power you give them. You stop questioning if your life is wrong because nothing is.

People who echo their negative experiences teach me what love can do. Just to allow myself to be happy around anyone is to invite everyone to explore a deeply profound place. I have learned it is not who you are with that matters but how you choose to feel and learn.

You start to sense reflecting is effortless. You define a brand of private reality.

Everyone can grow from situations that do not work out. One of my girlfriends had a partner for nine years before she became aware she had outgrown it. She moved on.

Love is straightforward. Human beings choose not to listen to themselves.

Some people send or receive love messages like a game. Years ago I wrote a journal to a man who led my heart along a bit before he admitted his heart was already taken. His effect on my life reawakened my passion for writing. That elicited significant energy in me, soul desired response, and a direction.

To be involved in a relationship is an opportunity just like any other. You choose to perceive what is workable, justifiable, and desirable. Compatibility and compromise are in play. As you become attuned to your changing thoughts, you realize the thrust of your creative energy orients you toward your personal fulfillment.

Somewhere along the way, I moved from a focus on myself, to wider development. At one point, I opened a Chinese fortune cookie which sent me a message from my soul. It said, "Your heart always makes itself known through your words." I still have it somewhere!

I grew to feel I needed to know more about why people felt as they did, why they imposed obligations or measures on themselves. I kept writing, but saw this act differently.

You always sense what matters most. You perform more acts than you recall.

I realize part of me works toward a greater sense of completion, and this means joy.

To grow and appreciate different parts of another person enables you to sense you intersect and interconnect at different levels of energy. You thrive in spontaneity.

It is almost like I start to listen to what is calling me inside.

Human beings use tentative words such as "like," "try," etc. to reveal fear.

The point came when my former pursuits no longer mattered. I moved from a focus on ambition to find meaning in nostalgia. Remembering love is as useful as forgetting love.

You are never unprepared for what matters, only temporarily asleep and unaware. You transcend doing and move into being. This is about how your thoughts and feelings define you. Before you realize, people enter your life and bring clarity.

Every so often my inner voice would echo that if a relationship seemed all work and no joy, it was not the right path or the right person for that moment. As I permit my instincts to guide me more, I sense I create nothing meaningful in relationships on my schedule.

Rumi says, "The breeze at dawn has secrets to tell you." You are inclined to find your own direction. As you interact with others, your soul reveals its secrets.

People have these "eureka moments." I sense energy such shifts occurring. People will give things away, parts of themselves and physical objects in forms of generosity.

For instance, it is possible to view changing jobs and conditions, as moving away from mindsets that no longer matter to me. The process of awakening seems complicated.

Without interference what matters simply unfolds. You feel it with your heart.

I did not understand I interfere with thought energy, let alone how. My identity as a being is no longer based on what I have or do, who I know, or who I aim to meet. It is how I feel. From the moment I sensed this, I shifted mindsets and made new relationship choices.

You are not what other people think of you. Imagine how much of your energy has been channeled into what does not matter. Every person can retrain their mind. You are not your job, your role in your family or, your physical body either, but more.

I detect negative energy, but it does not distract me from all unexpected development.

How quickly human beings forget their intention to just give and receive love.

I feel what I am destined to be, but I do not speak or reinforce it as often as I could.

This is one way you compromise yourself. Inside, you tell yourself you could only imagine yourself doing certain things, being with certain people, while you do not. You are interconnected with energy on different levels. You continue to awaken.

The more I share parts of my journey, the more I care about other people's journeys. Just when I believe I love people, the universe sends me someone who alienates or repels me.

Each time you disrupt your inner universe, you grow. You move from fear to curiosity, to places within where you learn to love parts of yourself you had forgotten. You are invited to examine the root of "dislike" so you work through your discomfort.

When an angry person mistreats me, I ask myself what that person is attempting to tell me. I have come to realize this is a plea for love. To show compassion to others, regardless of their behavior, is a way to love parts of myself that feel hurt or mistreated. This enables me to consciously rise above anger and grudges.

Every moment is an opportunity to consciously rise above anger and grudges.

When I worked in retail, certain people were angry if they received an incorrect photo order. They had not lost a limb. Their lives were not in danger. Yet the intensity of energy sent out implied a quest for more than a few photos. I learned to love must be patient, tolerant, and understanding.

When people focus energy helping, they expand meaning in their own lives.

You move to value levels of humility. Consciousness forms your lens of life.

Media urge people to speed things up, from meeting to creating their relationships. Early on I was conditioned to think love happened quickly. When I was actively looking, I never found it. I thought this was irony. You can work hard to find love in other people and not know you have a constant stream within. It is a kind of selective blindness. If you do not recognize the fundamental form of pure love, then you will not know when it mirrors outside.

You only had to permit your soul to love what it loved and you felt the truth. At every moment, the world offers itself to you. You choose to be a victor or a victim, a prisoner of your mind or, a soul that is set free to infinity with the power of love.

Incredible!

How so?

You can spend years accumulating information about love in books, movies, and through other popular culture. To realize I was misguided for so long is actually quite funny.

Each person does what he or she has to do to realize what really matters. This has nothing to do with what anyone tells you. Your experience defines your journey.

What Really Matters: End of Section Exercises

1. Which lessons do you retain from this section? How would you apply them?
   - In your relationships?
   - In your work?
   - In your spiritual pursuits?
   - In other ways?
2. What was meaningful about your past relationships? What did you learn about you?
3. What really matters in your current relationships? What do they teach you?
4. If you currently have no personal relationships, why do you believe that is? Do you wish to change this situation? If so, how will you proceed?

5. Describe experiences you think would be enhanced if you shared them more.

6. How do you think society or other forces in your life limit whether and how you share or don't share your life? In what ways could you create some of your own rules?

7. Which life choices enable you to feel joy? How do/could you share them differently?

SOULFULNESS

"When faith is soulful, it is always planted in the soil of wonder and questioning."

—Thomas Moore

"Nothing exists; all things are becoming."

—Reiho Masunaga

Each person owns what they know, but they do not always connect the dots. I sense a new level of conversation emerging in myself and through you, through everything. This is a kind of wisdom, new evolutionary work. And yet, I connect love back to ideas of soul mates.

Soul mates do not always recall they know each other during many lifetimes. If you cherish a compatible partner, then just believe in finding one. If you think you have met before, then choose to believe in reincarnation. Based on how you grow to know yourself, soulfulness is a feeling of connectedness to everything, everywhere.

I reflect on some of my own illusions about love. As a child I read fairytales and imagined prince charming arriving on his white horse to slay the fierce dragon and carry me away into the sunset. When that vision did not unfold in real life, I taught myself to doubt.

Rather than nurture the belief you would be rescued from your illusions, you chose to teleport your mind from your misplaced assumptions. Parts of your real self are dormant and may be accessed anytime. You grow to feel emotionally or spirituality ready to take the next step in every area of your life.

You know, I did not always act to further certain relationships, yet I recall details.

Those relationships that do not become part of your conscious experience are still fragments of your unconscious experience. Energy dissipates, but not completely.

And yet, with others when I sensed I made mistakes, I saw opportunities to make similar choices and I did not. Just when I was not looking, I felt ready for a different love.

You are always getting over some phase and becoming something. Your energy frequency is love. People come together and develop soulfulness to help each. You have richness in your soul that blossoms when you finally own yourself.

Some part of me knows everything I experience is valuable. There is never a sense of any value unless you believe you exert effort. Granted, I misled myself through some situations, assumed I had it all together. I was attracted to men not knowing what I wanted.

Each infatuation is a teacher. Love is not the same as lust or fear.

In university I was wrapped up with appearance and approval, what I was wearing and what my dates were thinking. I was surrounded by people who judged harshly, and others who had no conscience. One memory was my choice to date a good friend who later came out of the closet. That revelation was great for him, but what did it tell me about myself?

Human beings only distract themselves for so long. The memories have to arise for you to know you are willing to view your creative energy ability differently.

My early love affairs were bliss, but short-lived. I see now each one was an energy message I was initially unwilling to accept. Part of me asked, "if things were different…"

At every moment you choose what to think. What is occurring now is only occurring because of who you were, because of energy interactions you embrace at a new level of consciousness. Many more levels exist to help you.

Come to think of it, I have learned feeling closely connected does not enable you to foresee the length of your life or whether your relationship will last. Yet all connections, even those short-lived, highlight a mutual desire to grow, relish life, and trigger revelations.

One man I cared for decided our relationship would not last. He opted to refocus his love and energy on his troubled nephew. I grew to realize he and I did not share the same view of reality. His choice was soulful. He helped me equip myself for a new stage of life.

Soulfulness is also a willingness to uncover wounds and to work through them. No one can evolve for you. Each experience prepares you by triggering recognition of abilities you have always had, but in context of a new reference point. Mental strength

*evolves as you imagine pain and presume sources of fulfillment,
then discard them.*

Is that a moral imperative? This is beginning to stretch the reach of
my imagination.

*Soul work has to be on yourself. As you grow to understand
what stopped you from deepening intimacy in past relationships,
then you move to a level of awareness.*

I think back to when part of me was defensive, inflexible, and
unwilling to admit certain weaknesses. I think of waiting for that
phone call from a supposed dream date. Knowing what I do now, I am
grateful I was stood up. Many experiences helped me to clarify and
revise the beliefs that drive me. I did not always choose to be aware or
to change.

As I grow soulful exchanges reframe meaning everywhere. I sense
how I constructed and bought into standards and expectation. Reflection helps me see that my earlier beliefs about relationships explain
why they did not work. There were times when I admired other people and convinced myself "this" was love. Turned out I was actually
drawing attention to something I did or did not want. My vantage
point has shifted. Now I laugh at old yearbooks.

*Karma is not based on what you achieve, but what you are in
the process of achieving. You go on from where you are with the
wisdom you choose to gain.*

Being physically separated in distant relationships enabled me to
develop new levels of soulfulness. Friends of mine who experience
frequent military moves and work transfers know how life choices
can intensify the desire for closeness.

*This conditions the idea of wanting what you believe you do not
have.*

I notice that through repetitions of heartache, people love differently. Partners will stay together in pain even believe expressing the
truth to each other is scary or dangerous.

*Hardship gives couples reason to find strength in each other or
reason to give up on each other. To think about another person at
all is raises self-awareness.*

That reminds me of the husband of a girlfriend. He told me he slept
with a whole female college athletic team (and then some) before
meeting his now wife and changing his ways. He felt a deep connection to her that prompted him to evolve away from promiscuity.

*Intent and action are not always aligned. Increasing awareness
is a process. As people expand their sense of love, they change
priorities and feelings about others.*

Soulfulness seems to take years. I realize I hold myself back with thoughts, emotions and misunderstanding about sources of my inner power. Any sense of headway comes from those things it took me a while to learn. After I really "blow it," then I realize what it means to finally "get it." The fact it has been so hard to learn enables me to value wisdom more.

You always deserve loving relationships with reciprocity and kindness. In the early stages you have no idea what this means, no reference in conscious awareness. You have many means to distract yourself. Choices reinforce or change your values.

It makes sense to feel gratitude for all relationships, for what they teach me.

Soulful means you explore more than one energy or train of thought at once.

To sense connections between past and present teaches me to reconcile parts of the subconscious. Reflection on interactions shows me what I see is not objective as I experience it. The energy I feel from each relationship is a guide to help me become more objective.

You do not see as clearly when you have a conscious, vested interest.

Love is like heights. They scare people. Many suffer a kind of relationship vertigo.

Soulfulness is a means to overcome fear. Soul growth is a personal process.

I had to learn what it felt like to reach out to a few emotionally unavailable partners to be able to discern what the opposite was. I had been unavailable to myself and others as well.

Your thoughts are your strength. They drain your power and also reconnect soul. You shift vantage points as you realize experience and loving choices replenish you. You grow to consciously shield your mind from thinking and sending bad vibes.

I am realizing I must align thoughts and shift in ways that stray from everything I had imagined. There is no need to consciously track how I relate energetically to everyone.

Anytime you think you need a person, your core belief is that you lack. Soul is a path you rediscover beyond ego. You arrive where time and space are irrelevant.

Okay, soulfulness evolves within me as I care deeply about myself. As I separated from relationships and attitudes that were holding me back, I developed deeper love. It is only when I took responsibility for my behavior that I realized I had inner power to change.

Part of you always expects the unexpected. You selectively sense and choose.

When people truly cherish each other, you may imagine they would evolve to discuss anything on health, healing, death, and dying. Yet, people avoid writing their own obituary.

Human beings have a scope of free will. Soulfulness is an opportunity to explore and dissolve fear. Every thought creates or expands energy fields. It brings you back to cause and effect. You function based on what you accept right now. Places exist where what happens in your full lifetime is perceived in a moment.

I sense soulfulness emerges when health is threatened.

Hold fast to that which you know is true.

While based in Australia, I traveled home for my wedding. Just before my honeymoon, my mom shared with my sisters and me that us she was very ill. I listened attentively. My sisters became emotional. My mom was awakening to the storm inside her. She was realizing she could be altruistic for years with others and be unaware of her plight. She also evolved to believe we each experience results of our actions, benefit from hardship, and a healing process.

Each person decides how to feel, but does not always connect physical state to beliefs and behavior. Humans have an instinct to live and an instinct to die. As you realize every thought and action has consequences, you regain control of your present state the best you can. This is about learning to reground and reconnect core energy.

To nurture my creative energy, it is useful to review my relationships and choices. The universe prompts me to rethink my reasons for where I live and how I think. That helps to explain why I relocated and be closer to my mom during her recovery process. I believe all is well within and around me until I uncover issues I create in myself.

When human beings become conscious that love makes them who they are, they understand that peace in their heart means no obstacle is insurmountable.

Knowing people who have suffered serious illness teaches me to admit what I have been unwilling to see.

Real self-mastery is love. You do what you feel drawn to do, react or do not, wherever you desire. You are connected to everyone. Their process is also your own. You are connected to others by invisible, ethereal cords that are charged with energy.

My sense of relationships evolved in part based on transplanting myself where I could gain new perspectives. This, to me, is an example of the spirit at work within me.

Your energy vibrates even at a level of silence. You know what is going on in other people's lives is not you. Yet internal knowing is on track as you sense part of yourself in others. You learn through empathy, understanding and reasoning ability.

Something about reasoning ability invites further exploration.

Human beings have capacity to raise their awareness of relationships to a level where perceived problems fade. It is not your responsibility to teach people how to detach from their patterns and beliefs. You can choose to learn from everybody. They may not choose to learn from you. Your job is to find and release your blocks.

I encourage people to get to a place within themselves where they feel at peace, whatever it takes to get there. It is hard to convey something when others do not share in it.

People choose to evolve their way. They embrace your example, or not.

Life has taught me I define sensations for myself. As part of my soulful process, I no longer permit events to control me. I stopped listening to news with negative messages.

Each person makes their own choices and lives with the consequences.

As humbling as it is, I learn from narcissism or self-defeating trends. There was a time I was unaware I even had an ego. My life reveals how I selectively ignore body signals.

You grow differently as you realize you can trust relationships to teach you.

I have known people to feel embarrassed and alienate their loved ones during crisis. Soulfulness can be painful if you take rejection personally. Yet giving yourself space is also nurturing when it enables you to care differently for yourself, to gain insight into co-creation.

The real you surfaces as you recognize stages of eternal progress of soul.

To feel how different relationships exchange energies has led me to believe in the higher will of any relationship I am in. I experience them to learn what I can as they unfold.

Knowledge may be imparted, but wisdom manifests into form with experience. Some people give and others receive. Still others only do one or the other or neither. Soulfulness is the balance found when partners take turns loving and empowering.

I have met people who choose not to listen, not to understand, and not to share true feelings. It took me a while to realize new significance in what they were mirroring back about me. Relationships become like magnets that attract the energy of my imagination.

Imagination combined with reasoning abilities has meaning in different eras. If visions are viewed as too far outside a "norm," then they get an undesirable label.

If a person is not open to learning, he will resist evolution. My encounters with people who lie teach me deceit is energy with different levels. I have felt naive on some levels, ignorant on some, aware on others simultaneously. I had to align my energy to move on.

People do not consciously set out to harm. They do not know what they do.

Relationships strike me as tools, not a means to an end. They reveal whenever you choose to deceive others, you deceive self. Vibrations teach me to see interplay of energy.

Until you sense things do not feel right or, do not serve yourself or others, then you remain out of touch with yourself. Soulfulness is the complete opposite. It means you are attuned to how you feel. You act based on love as your primary motivation.

I recall I had the best intentions when mentioning to people smoking was not good for them. I stopped being so direct and now avoid confined areas. You can tell someone behavior does not serve them, but they choose a journey to explore life and its implications. I came to believe silence is soulful. You can look at someone with loving eyes and they know.

You care for others for who they are even if you disagree with what they do. Soulfulness motivates self-healing to inspire. The world changes one person at a time.

Relationships also reveal to me how many people are desensitized. They are taught to hide feelings, to believe self-expression is undesirable. Whatever happened to being true to yourself? I recall occasions where I did not recognize the difference between truth and lies.

For some there is no difference. As you permit yourself to express confusion or other feelings in relationships, you gain insight into soul. It is not logical or emotional. To be soulful reconnect with your creative side. Explore intuitively how you feel sources of events. They can be true and untrue at the same time. This helps explain how certain beings will sense multiple realities occurring simultaneously.

Soulfulness tells me that the quality of my relationships means more than duration.

Intensity is a phase of relatedness, rhythm, and harmony, not only intervals.

I used to ask myself why I was unable to see the significance of certain relationship choices at the time of the encounter rather than later, through a period of self-examination.

At a given moment you instinctively do what makes sense for you. Working at levels of energy impulse is done automatically. As you raise awareness, you begin to understand how you always make choices deliberately with intention from cell level.

What about how relationships are described as a way to "harden" or "soften" people? Some people send emotion in waves. It is a way to touch or latch onto another energy field.

Energy connections to others enable you to see and mesh with energy in you.

So you can be happy and sad at the same time and learn to better understand yourself. No issue of change in life seems as pivotal as the loss or gain of support and encouragement from a relationship. It is soulful to learn lessons together and go on to learn new ones.

Most people undersell themselves in relationships. They do not know what they are worth because they do not choose to define that for themselves. Instead, they decide to accept any treatment that comes their way. As you change how you view yourself, you change how you treat yourself and reactions you attract from others.

Admittedly, I find love is experienced in everything I think and do. Yet I do not specifically define the meaning of a soulful connection. Instead, I just live, feel, and learn.

How you grow to define your notion of a soulful connection orients choices.

As you grow to focus on experience itself, on the ethical principles you define, then the human means of measuring and evaluating loses meaning. The intensity of energy you feel captures your attention. How you define it in words does not matter.

I find some people search for hidden meanings in their own feelings and behavior. They query why they feel lost, inspired, revitalized, or longing, even muse over fear or regret. Soulfulness is a personal journey with no boundaries, signposts, or parameters for guides.

Invoke your imagination. Decide what it will feel like to be treated the way you desire. What kind of energy would you feel? How would you create it? The visualization process allows you to steer attention away from what people do or think.

My instinct is to retain lessons at each stage of relationships. I often recognize deeper significance after a relationship or further along. Energy vibrations show me how I move.

You have capacity to adopt or ignore traits based on listening to your soul. If treatment evokes good feelings, then you move to value or respect yourself differently. You learn from everyone, choose to model their behavior, resist or create your own. Everything you experience is soulful because it is a window into soul.

So, people learn what they want, when they want. They accept or reject parts of themselves based on what they are ready to gain from what happens to people around them.

You are paying attention.

Lots of people you meet will say that if they had the same life to live over, they would make different choices.

The life you lead gives you unlimited chances to reorient your course. Turns you take at particular moments allow you to develop naturally or not. Regardless of how aware you are of your feelings, it does not change inner knowledge you possess.

Being soulful then, is not having faith when all is well. Rather, it is nurturing faith when much of what you believe or recognize about you is called into question.

Soulfulness: End of Section Exercises

1. Which lessons do you retain from this section? How would you apply them?
   - In your relationships?
   - In your work?
   - In your spiritual pursuits?
   - In other ways?
2. How would you describe feeling connected to someone who is important to you?
3. What have you done or what could you do to enhance feelings of intimacy in life?
4. Is your idea of intimacy based on life experience or fantasy or a combination? Why?
5. Explain three situations in your life where you felt connected to other people. Why?
6. Describe three situations where your efforts led to a lack of personal connection.

7. What could you do to strengthen your soulful feelings and meaning in your life?

8. What are the most useful things you learned about yourself from this section?

9. How have close interactions helped you to work through conflict or insecurity? If you haven't yet experienced this, how could a more soulful connection help you?

10. How might your soulful thoughts lead to closer or more distant relationships?

11. Offer three examples where growing closer to friends, family, and lovers been hard.

12. Describe a situation where you lied to yourself and/or to someone about your feelings.

13. What was the result? How did you feel? How did that relationship evolve?

HEALING POWER OF RELATIONSHIPS

Honesty

> *" Our lives improve only when we take chances—and the first and most difficult risk we can take is to be honest with ourselves."*
>
> —Walter Anderson

> *"I've found if I say what I'm really thinking and feeling, people are more likely to say what they really think and feel."*
>
> —Carol Gilligan

The healing power of relationships teaches me new avenues which are useful. Certain people prefer not to question what creates interconnectedness to others and grounding in life. Of course, some people resist examining what is not working. Other people rack their brains about the things they could do to strengthen relationships and get more out of them.

Communication is the mortar that seals or crumbles relationship foundations. The absence of open exchanges strains energy flow. Shared transparency evolves as each person grows willing to open up and confide. You enter more powerful states.

It is funny you say that. Meticulous self-honesty is supposed to come first. It is one thing to say you will be honest and another to consistently do it. People will say, "honesty is the best policy," and yet they often rationalize doing something else. You think you hurt less if you lie about why you are late, who you were with or, what you were really doing...

Honesty is a choice. Not everyone is aware of deepest needs or energy levels.

Life experience has taught me people who are candid about their feelings, hopes, and desires grow closer through developing shared vulnerability. The opposite is also true. The more lies you tell the greater the rift that grows between you, as if you feed energy monsters.

When people believe they are honest, they are choosing to present energy in a certain form. This does not mean the energy is in the same form or on the same level.

That figures! When I am honest I find people are not always honest with me.

Energy reverberates. Even in silence everything you do reflects back in form.

Life experience has taught me if I lie to myself about what I desire or, about what is acceptable, then I encounter dishonesty mirrored as a teacher. People choose to stay in undesirable relationships or situations if they refuse to face why they do not wish to be there.

Your level of honesty restores and strengthens or, drains your inner power. Energy you perceive is intertwined with energy fields of others and can obscure truth.

You got that right! Now, everyone may reflect on relationships where they realize they have not been completely honest. And yet, to become aware you have done things that do not serve you is not the same as choosing to change.

Raising self-awareness is a step toward taking action. Choices you made are not always desirable for the person you sense inside now. Consciously knowing this and doing the same thing again differs from choosing to experience another result.

My own life has taught me that romantic partners do not always read my mind. At times I wanted this, yet found misunderstandings grew. As I am willing to listen to a partner's feelings and act compassionately, I take honesty and mind-reading to new level.

Honesty reminds you about natural, innate abilities you have, but do not use.

Often people clam up or walk out during conflict or confrontations rather than choose to stay, listen, and grow. I have overheard people talking "at" rather than "to" each other. In fact, on certain occasions that reflected my behavior. A desire to be honest means it can be wise to postpone a chat. Timing is vital for partners to be awake, alert, and relatively relaxed.

Mutual listening is desirable. When creating a challenge, your awareness may choose a positive or negative focus or may seek balance in a compromise.

I have learned a lot about honesty from running a business with my partner. My desire to create that business was motivated by learning from dishonest practices of a former boss. Choosing to discuss all situations openly has shown me how honesty builds faith and trust.

Many teachings come back to the same things. The truth is boldly before you.

It would be a useful experiment to design a society where only honesty was permitted or people would disappear. This scenario is an invitation for a reality program on television. I mean, how long do human beings really go between telling lies, and not even realize it?

The mind gets confused about honesty when a human does not express or trust pure thoughts. If you permit yourself to develop beliefs, you convince yourself you have choices about honesty. When people discern multiple realities and energies, they experience only parts of them, and are only honest about parts they experience.

Honesty: End of Section Exercises

1. Which lessons do you retain from this section? How would you apply them?
   - In your relationships?
   - In your work?
   - In your spiritual pursuits?
   - In other ways?

2. How have you included or excluded a partner or another person in your life choices? What does this say about this phase of your life (singlehood, parenthood, retirement)?

3. Describe three relationship situations where it was hard for you to be honest. Why?

4. How honest are you with yourself? How does this relate to your childhood?

5. Give examples where you treat people in ways that you wouldn't wish to be treated.

6. How could you behave differently to value yourself and others in new ways?

Trust

> *"Trust yourself. You know more than you think you do."*
>
> —Benjamin Spock

> *"The purpose is to provide a way in which some people will be able to find their own internal teacher."*
>
> —Helen Schucman *(A Course in Miracles)*

Life experience shows people desire time to build trust, or can quickly damage it.

When you try too hard, you block energy flow, and all that is meant for you. Trust is all about learning to transmute energies which are meant for you to know.

My sense of the truth in relationships is that it evolves based on my awareness of my own life story. There was a time when I thought I developed more from learning about other people's experiences. Then I moved to a stage where I realized I must act to forge my path.

Children grow up and forget innocence. Remember what it was like to be fearless? Remember what it was like before you were taught not to trust your feelings and perceptions? As you evolve to discount and mistrust your feelings and perception, then you begin to question what other people tell you about their own.

Granted, there was a time when I believed all people created some kind of invisible scorecard, a place where you note painful treatment, rationalize why you evolve to distrust. As I understand it now, this is a choice to fear and to allow fear to control you. I resist both.

Regardless of any relationship experience you have had, you can learn to resist turbulence and choose to go with the flow. Trust brings insight into many truths.

I felt I had to do something different to build deep trust inside myself. I desire to help people grasp what makes them behave as they do while I learn how I could extend the good inside myself. I imagine how I would share the intense power I am discovering within. I am learning to trust things I do not understand. Trusting my gut in one area of my life promotes growth in other areas of my life. I fill life with activities to please me and bring greater good.

Everything you do is on your terms. You learn power is inside. You grow to channel highly-specialized knowledge you already have in ways that expand you.

When I gave decision-making authority away, I was content for other people to shape my life. I assumed they knew what I felt. As I trust myself more, more energy flows freely.

You do not need to articulate why you trust energy or why things are working. Until you figure out why certain relationships are not working, then you are holding yourself back from harnessing energy around you. To understand trust, look into the source of your experience. Examine your level of awareness at the moment of a relationship. A connection with what you do not see leads you to create what you do.

I have come to realize when I felt betrayed in a relationship, this was a sign I was betraying myself by not listening to my inner voice. I was raising awareness about the principle of the thing. It was a learning experience to be betrayed, but it was life changing to stop betraying myself. I started to think about all the situations in my life that are like that.

When you do not trust yourself, you do not set a good example for someone to develop a trusting relationship with you. You send unconscious signals of insecurity that tell people to pull back. Frustration restricts energy flow. You push, pull, or stop.

My own self-appreciation evolves through trusting others. I move to break patterns that prevent me from expanding. I remember when I began to recognize I was conditioned to trust based on what people did. I watched what I wanted and what I did not want for myself. I learned understanding trust differs in theory and practice, but only until you know yourself well enough to trust your vibes. As I began to work on myself inside, I learned to apply ideas and to listen and trust based on greater fearlessness.

Trust determines your energy vibration and the kind of people you attract. Human abilities include layers beyond intuition. You have mental muscle. Use it.

Some people push and pull emotional buttons in a relationship. This hinders ability to trust. You imagine reasons for distrust when you think about what you do not want. Some people only trust relationships to get what they want. They do not sense unconditional trust.

What people do around you stirs your emotions. This produces action. You can choose to focus on why your subconscious mind chooses to trust unconditionally, or choose to convince yourself not to trust and rationalize with the same energy.

Relationships are a means of gathering experience and insight into trust. I respond to action around me and habits I have conditioned. I had to get out of the habit of trusting people who were not good for me and choose to connect with people who were good for me.

You nurture positive energy in trust as you attract nurturing energy vibrations.

I remind myself I was born to trust automatically. Unmet needs and tragic situations distract me from what I already know about trust. I went through phases when I decided not to trust unless someone persuaded me otherwise. Then I reverted back to my own instincts.

The desire to trust and to trust again must come from within you.

My own life taught me trust relates to self-acceptance. I moved on from relationships that did not work to gain valuable insight into myself. I became willing to trust my instincts in romance rather than what heroes did in a story. Trust redefined risk and empowered me to create a deeper, personal life. I did not just talk about true love, I trusted myself to create it.

You are always in the right place to trust. Self-awareness determines your results. Boundaries and limitations simply identify the span of your attention.

As I evolved to know what loving myself meant, I no longer aspired to put it in words. I deepened trust of my life partner and inspired him to develop trust in me. I believe anyone can learn to explore trust on new levels, and choose to learn from them. Evolving trust led me to centre myself, communicate differently and make sound business judgments.

You develop trust from understanding your trials and noting your errors. You detect the vibrations of creating and giving as well as destroying and taking. Self-confidence grows in loving yourself, with teaching how trust works through example.

To nurture faith in my ideas, I had to believe trust in relationships can to be taught. I honestly ask myself what trust can do. Deciding to strengthen my trust in relationships led me to proactively act to grow income. I borrowed $4,000 and turned it into $200,000. I went from earning virtually nothing and feeling like a victim, to taking charge and creating a company that continues to expand. As I trust myself I learn that feeling cannot be taken away. I create exciting ways to learn and relish each step. The time it takes is irrelevant.

Trusting yourself leads to more trust in relationships and trust in dreams.

I have learned you can only sense so much about trust until you learn what trust is not. Spending time with people who do not know how to trust can affect your nervous system, and it can also teach you how not to be affected. Learning how not to be affected is tricky.

As you learn trust is a transferable skill, you apply this to areas of your life.

When someone promises to meet me and repeatedly stands me up, this person is not reliable and waiting repeatedly does not serve me. I hear the lover of a friend speak of commitment, but he buys a motorcycle rather than an engagement ring. I no longer trust him. When instincts prompt me to move on from a relationship, I trust in a wider learning curve.

Interpreting trust in your ways does not deny other versions of trust exist.

To me if people complain, then they do not have the courage to create the trust they want. That became increasingly apparent in me. I grew to explore which of my actions had caused my circumstances. I evolve to teach myself to stop denying what is really happening.

Trust emerges out of a process of self-disclosure. If you continue to think the same way, then you recreate the same conditions. As you trust more you evolve.

I regularly talk aloud to myself. People around me used to laugh about it, but I still do. It is a way I choose to trust a higher self. This may explain why I evolve to hear other voices.

You learn honesty and trust and self-disclose in steps. It is a chain reaction. When you are in touch with reality, this builds positive energy and strengthens you.

An example that jumps into my mind is how I would confide to a friend about being in love. In theory that friend would feel good, move to confide her feelings to someone else.

When you focus on reasons to distrust, this also sends out distrust energy.

You are so right on that! Where people discuss why they distrust people, it is difficult for them to build trust. I resist gossip, sense its destructive energy and the harm it can do. Come to think about it, I have learned people who keep secrets often fear what they hide.

Where one person in a couple reveals his life and the partner does not, trust is not nurtured. Some people are unwilling to explore reasons why they have never learned to confide. Resisting is a choice. Trust is a choice. Ignorance is a choice.

This perspective does not alter my desire to encourage people to explore their choices. If this is meant to enlarge self-understanding, then why do people fear using their abilities?

Trust begins and ends with your beliefs. This is the spirit of your nature.

When you live in different places, people you know in one place do not see you in another place. You keep your personal life private or you share parts of your experiences. I think back to how I have spoken about relationships and what I chose to keep to myself. Why is it that we share different sides of ourselves with different people? Is it different awareness?

Each relationship shows you how trust and distrust have many levels. You trust yourself to explore certain feelings, but not others. At different life stages you relate to people on different levels. It reflects to what degree you trust your feelings. Each relationship shows you how trust and distrust have many levels. You trust yourself to explore certain feelings, but not others.

I sense people feel uncomfortable when they have experienced distrust or, never learned to trust. If so, the uneasiness you sense in the energy of a person may have little or nothing to do with you. When a person you know has experienced pain, that person may feel overwhelmed by someone else's desire for intimacy and quick trust. Ask yourself if people in your family and other relationships back off from your initiatives to develop closeness.

Trust is an exercise in creating boundaries, learning to express and explore feelings differently. Trust is the key to a doorway of forgotten wisdom. Go there.

Some people are waiting for a map. Trust can be blocked if they have never learned how or they have felt victimized. Fear distracts people from exploring deeper trust.

Events are emotionally-charged with energy. Human beings only act based on personal experience. This is conscious and unconscious, from this life and previous lifetimes. The absence and presence of reciprocal trust offers clues to the "why."

I have come to sense trust emerges and each human being has a choice whether to grasp onto it, like a helium balloon floating by. The roles and rules that have defined my life form a basis for acceptable and unacceptable behavior. What I accept reflects levels of trust.

For example, if you believe in monogamy, trust your boyfriend or girlfriend and then learn that your partner has multiple partners simultaneously, you may feel degraded, yet still believe your partner when he or she promises change. In reality the person may not. If your partner lies, then your instinct may be to forgive. Your level of trust changes with each event.

Each situation resonates its own energy and invites decisions based on truth.

When I think of myself, I have consciously trained myself to forgive. I would not be in my current relationship with the devotion I feel if I had not learned it from somewhere.

Your level of self-healing and trust-building shapes how and when you trust.

If your lover reveals another partner or, an inability to deal with anxiety, or other feelings and needs, then you are invited to explore your own feelings from where you stand.

Wisdom about trust exists for all to use. Some people hold onto memories and live based on what they are told is truth, rather than choose to alter their orientation.

I recall hearing the story of an Australian man who had a wife in Sydney and another in Melbourne. Both wives assumed he was away on frequent business trips until he was in an accident in one city with images that made the national news. His double life crumbled.

Regardless of what you do, you never escape your core self or your lies.

Distrustful patterns are as destructive to your life as a habit of trusting without cause.

If you do not trust, you are controlled by fear.

Yet fear reminds you it can be dangerous to trust. People withhold personal details and justify this as a way to protect them from something undesirable.

That which causes a person to be afraid is a test for that person alone.

If you feel you control what people know about you, then you feel reassured.

In your world humans create the illusion knowledge is power. In the spirit world, thoughts are transparent. There is no desire to hide for it serves no purpose.

I have learned you cannot change your past, but you can change how you perceive it and grow. What you do not want is based in fear or ignorance of your own intrinsic value.

Energy beings are always creating. If a relationship enables you to feel good, then you trust yourself to keep it going. Natural methods unfold to handle situations.

Some people invent criteria people must satisfy before they are willing to build trust. These people set their own rigid rules about types of people worth trusting or not.

You always have reasons for doing. These reasons tell you a lot about trust. How you relate to any perceived relationship reality is based on which levels you understand you create or contribute to events. Misunderstandings also shape trust.

Trust: End of Section Exercises

1. Which lessons do you retain from this section? How would you apply them?
   - In your relationships?
   - In your work?
   - In your spiritual pursuits?
   - In other ways?

2. How could you explore new meaning in relationships by becoming more self-reliant?

3. Recall an experience where you believed someone who lied to you. Have you become more suspicious as the result? How do you think and behave differently than before?

4. Recall a situation where someone you cared about let you down. How did you react?

5. Describe relationships where you felt investments were unbalanced. (Consider family, friendships, lovers, or other relationships.) How did this develop trust or not?

6. Which relationships in your life make you feel skeptical? Why? What could you do about these situations to enable you to feel better about yourself?

7. Describe experiences in your life and how you reacted when:
   - You trusted someone and their behavior taught you not to have trusted.
   - You distrusted someone and your judgment proved incorrect.
   - You trusted yourself and the result was like you made an error in judgment.
   - You trusted yourself and your instincts turned out to have positive results.

8. What kind of person would be a compulsive liar? What does this say about trust?

9. What did such experiences teach you about yourself?

10. What kinds of wisdom did you gain that you could benefit from in future?

11. What advice would you offer to someone who aims to build trust in a relationship?

12. How does this influence what contributes to your evolving sense of life purpose?

Love

> *"Love is trusting, accepting and believing, without guarantee. Love is patient and waits, but it's an active waiting, not a passive one. It continually offers itself in mutually- revealing, and sharing ways. Love is spontaneous and craves expression. Love lives the moment; it's neither lost in yesterday nor does it crave for tomorrow."*
>
> —Leo Buscaglia

> *"Falling in love consists merely in uncorking the imagination and bottling the common sense."*
>
> —Helen Rowland

Love teaches me I am constantly evolving myself in many forms. In this light Byron Katie urges me to, "Spare self from seeking love, approval, or appreciation—from anyone."

You need not seek to define the indefinable. Relationships teach you this.

And yet, thoughts of love are often linked to unrealistic ideals. People will say love aspirations lead to disappointment. To me love is like a mirror. People do not always look at their own reflection.

Human beings invite everything with preciseness. Love is no different.

Loving feelings can also be positive and motivate deep and fulfilling inner growth. You can believe love will help heal your past pain, assist you to reframe any situation and help you to stretch yourself. Love can instill or renew your patience and help you overcome perceived obstacles. Love makes you feel young, energetic, and renewed. I begin to sense it as the basic principle of spirituality, the crux of what nurtures a person's faith in the unseen.

Human beings desire love. You imagine its forms and effects. As you examine the history of love in your life, you learn how love can

be healthy or unhealthy. Many kinds of love exist. You recognize what you experience, intuit, or opt to expect.

For me love is a kind of constantly evolving inner thought form. I do not grow wiser just by imagining it. I do not understand love simply by reflecting, reading, or even hearing about it. Rather, I completely transform each time I explore different examples of love in real life. Love teaches me how far I am willing to go, which sacrifices I am willing to make, what feelings encourage an impulsive change of heart, and when I reorient how or when I perceive.

People who never touch your life also influence your sense of love.

Yes. Strangers evoke compassion in me. I pay tolls for the car in line behind me. I also use the term, "love" in relation to how I view myself. To love all of me is a long journey. Though my mystical nature is at odds with realities most people create for themselves, I define an effective framework for self-understanding. Like love, I switch temporal realities.

Love gives your innermost being strength to share ideas you fervently believe.

I recognize the most basic love is eternal love, a force beyond me that permeates all thought. When thoughts fill with love, your words and deeds transform to focus on acts of love. This can include engaging relationships that make you feel good. You learn to identify negative feelings within you and those expressed by others. You sense they alienate you from true love. Genuine love is not the selfish type. It is not out-of-reach, but all that we are.

Basic love is inspirational, selfless, and unwavering. You gain what you do not explain or measure. You sense a deeper journey. You do not grasp eternity, but feel it. You know love as a feeling to ground you, so you will trust spontaneous motion.

People find out soon enough that if they seek a relationship to distract them from their own unresolved issues, they will suffer disillusionment. In this way I have found learning about different kinds of love is a wake-up call to care for your inner self differently.

On invisible levels love as an internal gauge for accuracy of perception. It is a mechanism that empowers you to attune to situations of value. You imagine energy fields worthy of attention or learn to disconnect from events of undeserving concern.

Relationships are opportunities to learn what it feels like to be appreciated. I have experienced the opposite feeling as well. You learn where you feel wanted, desired or not, and choose to withdraw into yourself or continue to share all that you are. Marianne Williamson says, "Love is what we were born with. Fear is what we learned here." We each decide on the nature of our earthly backbone, whether our love is conditional or given freely.

Subjective experience offers insight into your own inner processes.

People talk about traits of real love and struggle to tell the difference from illusion.

As you evolve to love yourself, you begin to detect more subtle love energy. This affects the size and shape of things before they manifest in physical reality.

Now wait a second! You suggest love is always in reach. How do you teach this?

Love is constantly ready to be manifest in physical reality. It is your call.

And yet, so many people struggle to find and experience it or to somehow incorporate it into their lives. Why must this concept we explore seem so mysterious?

To love others is a demonstration of compassion. Some people evolve to offer it with strings attached. Your intent to love exists before birth and drives your soul journey from that moment. This intent to love creates events, prompts you to enter relationships, and accept those things that resonate with positive energy. You forget.

I thought love was meant to be simple, not unnerving. Many people grow uneasy.

The conscious mind is aware of far more about love that you discern now.

Selfless love can be spontaneous. I evolve faster as I permit love to flow naturally.

The conscious self can transcend ego and become focused on pure love. As you explore personal issues, you expand awareness of levels and intensities of love.

My own life experience teaches me about love. I progressively learn what love is not. I also realize I decide what love is for me. To me love is gentle and kind. People who express this value the individuality and freedom of others, as well as their personal freedom. You can love the spirit of a person, no matter what they do. People choose words and sensations to describe the essence of love. And yet, at times no words do this justice.

Love is in spontaneous motion. Although hard to pin down, it shapes your thoughts. It is the energy that blocks fear, triggers core impulses, and self-expression.

Regardless of my relationship choices, love is defined in part by sustaining energy of goodwill. Compassion has motivated me to build friendships and associations. I share love and care for others as individuals and groups. Love is a positive expression of consciousness that liberates me from personal concern. It expands my sense of feeling connected to others.

As you grasp the feeling, you move to communicate on levels of energy beyond words. It is about expanding space to grow. This is the next stage. Much remains.

I have found complete devotion reflects insecurity and reinforces loneliness.

You are not defined by your relationships. Part of you has insight into love outside physical realities. You may ground yourself where you are, but there is more.

When I feel love in the physical world, I feel connected to people I know and have known, even when I do not see them. Love enables people to feel connected.

You feel love in their physical presence. As you start thinking about someone, love expands. You feel the vibration. You associate specific love with specific people.

Oh yes, platonic, romantic, and other sorts.

What you discern is intensity. Each person is an energy vibration. Now energy cannot be created or destroyed. That tells you all the love does not perish. In fact, the energy you feel is not always from vibrations you recognize.

I am not sure where you are headed with this line of thought, or maybe I am. At times I sense love or healing from unknown sources. This prompts me to send positive energy out into the world. I do not always know where it goes, but it does.

Love enables you to see things you would not ordinarily see using your senses. People you love appear as if in a vision or as a form in your presence.

This happens. I sense familiar energy and energy that is not so familiar. It is like I receive information yet I do not always understand the message.

The origin is love. You undertake a shamanic journey. This includes dream work where you visit or meet with spirit. This occurs when the love connection is strong. It happens in dreams or when certain people believe they are fully awake.

Some people would suggest what you describe is a hallucination.

Every human being is entitled to believe what he or she chooses. That does not mean all beliefs are grounded in truth. When love is strong it echoes truth and you do not doubt experi-

ence. When humans fear they disrupt the energy around them. Spirit only operates in an atmosphere of calm confidence. You know what you feel.

I guess you could say different ways exist to love and be loved in return.

You decide if that is an understatement. If you arrive at a stage in your life where you desire something very strongly, then your energy vibration always guides you. Whether or not you are receptive to love in its varied forms, shapes how you feel.

That reminds me of the *Teachings of Abraham* by Esther and Jerry Hicks. They present varied perspectives on the power of emotion and perception. Love is an intricate part.

Some people are content to read. Other people prefer to manifest experiences.

Love: End of Section Exercises

1. Which lessons do you retain from this section? How would you apply them?
   - In your relationships?
   - In your work?
   - In your spiritual pursuits?
   - In other ways?

2. Describe love you feel, give, and receive. Do you think it is healthy or not?
   - Recall an experience where you imagined yourself in love. How did you feel?
   - Recall real relationship experiences. How close were they to your fantasy?

3. Describe an experience where you felt exploited in love. How do you envisage balance? How can you detach/ distance from bad experiences to love differently?

4. Explain how you express love though people or contributions to organizations.

5. Create an image of a partner in a close relationship. What behavior reflects love?

6. Describe examples of what you believe love is not.

7. Do you act out your culture's idea of romantic love? Your parents'? Yours? Others? Once you identify references for romantic love and associated social roles, do you act in parallel, opposite, or chose differently? What do you think of this?

8. What prompts you to say, "I love you"? How often do you say this? Do you wait until someone else speaks first? What causes you to speak or hold back?

9. Let's say your partner expresses love, but hesitates to do so in public. Do you question your partner's feelings? What kinds of affectionate displays are better kept private? What examples do you feel are appropriate in public? What and where?

10. If you feel you drift apart from your partner or someone else you once cared deeply about, how long do you hold it inside before you express it? What is your experience?

11. What prompts you to discuss love? How would you set about rekindling strong ties?

12. What experience do you have with memorable break-ups or separation? Do you just hope things will get better? If children exist would you stay together for them?

13. Describe some memorable experiences of love you have known (where, when, why).
    • platonic love (friendship)
    • family love (parents, relatives, children)
    • romantic love (partner/ spousal)
    • passionate love (dream/ reality)
    • self-love (acceptance)
    • spiritual love
    • basic life force (unity with nature)

14. What other kinds of relationship experiences were very memorable and special?

15. If you have no reference for what you would now describe as "love," describe positive feelings you experienced in relationships you've known.

16. If you know no positive love relationships, what love would you like to know?

17. Reflect on your understanding of love and how it influences your emotions, your personal and ethical choices, judgment, your sense of joy and fulfillment.

18. Explain love in relation to your views of attraction, friendship, sexual desire, sex, deeper intimacy. (e.g., Does it have to include some or all these?)

19. What do longstanding relationships teach you about love?

20. What connections do you notice between love and your desired life direction? How do your past experiences influence the present?

Patience

> *"Everything has its wonders, even darkness and silence, and I learn, whatever state I may be in, therein to be content."*
>
> —Helen Keller

> *"Have patience with all things, but chiefly have patience with yourself. Do not lose courage in considering and remedying your own imperfections.*
>
> —St. Francis De Sales

Relationships teach patience. In fact, I would say impatience is one of my most regular teachers. This highlights challenges I create and my confusion in temporal reality.

Impatience brings you face-to-face with core reasons for dissatisfaction. You may decide to act to change your circumstances. You decide on structure and effects.

The voice inside me says part of my destiny is revealed on a need-to-know basis and not before. I meet people without knowing why and this is something I have come to accept.

The more I think about it, the more I realize developing patience is all about seeking reassurances. I may never know the reason for certain encounters in the bigger picture, but I choose to speculate on how I am accountable for what I am ready to perceive and experience.

Restlessness invites impatience. Some people mistakenly believe intolerance is good for soul. Others move beyond persistent mental abuse to grasp hidden motives.

Patience is like a voice of comfort that reminds me I offer my own legitimate assistance in any circumstance. It tends to show itself when I feel frustrated or linger on unsettled matters. In relationships my creativity initially struggled for its own growth and value fulfillment. I have placed myself in situations where I was too patient for a partner to change when I was urging part of myself to change. Realizing this was a breakthrough.

Each revelation insures continued expansion of your abilities and natural self. Part of you is seeking redemption. You desire expression to shift your energy-field.

Whatever my circumstances I know I am meant to be where I am. That does not always make it easy to stop wishing an experience was over, that I had already learned a lesson or graduated from some relationship test. I learn my moods are not always rational.

Patience teaches you to detach from moods at different levels of awareness.

Hold on! I begin to grasp the idea of different levels of energy and multiple events occurring simultaneously. I gather this implies a person is involved in multiple relationships at the same time, but may not be consciously aware or even able to see them. That prospect is a bit weird. Yet why do parts of me accept not knowing things, while other parts do not?

That is a magical part of your reality. You have free flow of information at some levels of consciousness and you prevent it from flowing freely on others. The part of you that has patience is aware of the information you need. The part of you that is impatient is grappling with the bigger picture. This triggers mental processes.

Just by listening, by being there for people, I find that my patience flows more easily. This suggests something would be missing if I was not reaching out to create relationships.

As you wait for things to happen, your energy is constantly evolving. People evoke feelings in you, but your evolution does not depend on people. How you react in a given moment affects your level of awareness. Patience signals you stretch your perception of time, to reexamine events for the purpose of your own learning.

You know, that makes sense! I recall occasions when I struggled to be patient with people. I wished for a partner's work assignment to be over so we could spend more quality time together. I wished for children I looked after to settle so we could interact like before. Some of my friends have wished pregnancies were over to end discomfort and get on with the desirable part they imagine later. Patience is like pause or rewind. You want fast forward.

Discomfort is meant to teach human beings about themselves. Your conscious self is unaware what is next. Soul knows. Other parts recognize it when it happens. Inside your heart ideas grow. This is about perceiving energy fields more clearly.

From a spiritual view the decisions I make and the actions I take determine how time affects me. When I stopped structuring relationships around time constraints, this changed the flow of my emotions and my situation. Why do many people resist this cause and effect?

When you resist free flow of energy, this keeps you where you are, thinking and acting as before. Not everyone is willing to change their orientation completely.

As I realize my actions and beliefs create my reality, I alter my view of who I am. How I sense energy reveals I have adopted a new orientation. I create reality through a field.

Believe a new situation unfolds. The usual senses evolve to super-sensory levels.

Patience: End of Section Exercises

1. Which lessons do you retain from this section? How would you apply them?
   - In your relationships?
   - In your work?
   - In your spiritual pursuits?
   - In other ways?
2. How might you decide to make choices to help avoid your past mistakes?
3. How do you respond to relationship hardships? How could you be more patient?
4. Describe a situation where patience has been helpful to you in personal relationships.
5. Describe three situations in your personal life where it has been difficult to have patience. How did you react and deal with them? What did you learn from that?
6. What did you learn about yourself though these life experiences?
7. Explain why you feel you have changed in terms of gaining or losing patience.
8. How does your changing view of patience relate to your purpose on various levels?
   - *Personal Relationships:* Parents, Children, Friendships, Romance, Partner/Spouse, Other?
   - *Work Relationships*: Boss, Coworkers, Other?
   - *Spiritual Relationships:* With yourself, higher forces, spiritual peers, the unseen, other?

Passion

> *"We are cups, constantly and quietly being filled. The trick is, knowing how to tip ourselves over and let the beautiful stuff out."*

—Ray Bradbury

> *" I had learnt to seek intensity and more of life, a concentrated sense of life."*

—Nina Berberova

Not everyone feels relationships are exciting. Some people even think, why bother? This invites a closer examination of passion. It has got to be more than compelling intensity.

How you view passion depends on how familiar you are with intense feelings. They become the medium through which you may reach levels of your deepest being.

For me passion is the source of enthusiasm. It orients me to my most creative side. It explains why I am driven to express myself. Sources of my passion become clearer to me as I am honest with myself and trust my intuition about choices. What about people who are not openly creative? Does that stifle their discovery of inner passion?

Everyone has a catalyst for action. Since awareness is a choice, each person decides on a level of awareness at a given moment, turn it on and off at will. To hide or divulge sources of passion reveals how comfortable you are with your enthusiasm.

Okay, so a person could have a job, relationship, or be on the brink of discovering what they need and still not connect with passion. I know what it feels like to lack a sense of fulfillment. To disregard or overlook interests blocks passion. How do you attune to passion?

Passion is awakened with the courage and initiative to explore the inner self. This is not about what you do now or how much, but how you feel about your choices.

Yet people justify why they do not listen to their impulses or inner drive. I went through a period where everything was more important than a relationship because I was not ready to accept what I desired. When I finally did I had to go through stages of getting-to-know myself before I was able to make choices to listen to my passion frequency.

Your passion is a bridge to soul. The process of fulfillment unfolds as you gradually listen. You detect energy of something external, like a relationship or work. You learn the difference between inner and outer energy sources. Passion connects.

Come to think of it, I met my partner about when I attuned to my writing passion.

To attune to passion at one level enables you to align with other passions. Many humans only physically see what is right in front of them and believe results only arise from conscious action. In fact, energy is discerned on many levels with many senses. You attract people and conditions; the invisible in everything resonates.

This almost suggests one person completes another based on compatibility of energy.

People do not complete you. Relationships complement self-acceptance. You encounter people based on your energy and attitude. External vibrations stabilize or destabilize you at the core. How you connect to your passion can even be seen to define the scope of your health, well-being, and desired stages of growth and healing.

Friendships are relationships that develop from exchanges of positive energy, a sense of compatibility, and shared values. I had forgotten passion is a side of friendships, too.

Human beings are masters of creation. They rarely know their own strength.

What about the voices that urge people to make practical choices or predictable ones? Energy emitted does not seem intense. Where energy is stable, it suggests passion is absent.

Thoughts affect energy fields, how you relate to your body and your health. You create your limits, decide how you will explore the energy of your imagination.

That reminds me how distance romance has inspired me to co-write electronic books as a way to nurture positive energy. My sense of a choose-your-own adventure evolved as I wrote a chapter, forwarded it, and received the next chapter back. We invented characters, mindsets, moods, and evolved in real life to create the sorts of adventures we wrote about.

Passion shapes your state of the mind, sense of romance and much more.

I have known people easily influenced by certain energy that can make them more sensitive, attuned, or uncontrollably excited with intense emotion like love or anger.

Passion can be destructive. Humans are susceptible to passions of jealously, wrath, ambition, greed, conflict, winning, or

*even addictions. Passion can also come from deep suffering or
irritation. Reasons for losing self-control are also connected.*

From my view passion is energy linked to everything. I sense it differently already.

*This phenomenon brings you closer to grasping the field of your
life. We will expand on traits and meanings of these colorful energy
fields at a later stage.*

Gee, you know, passion also reminds me of yet another force I
sense but do not see.

Passion: End of Section Exercises

1. Which lessons do you retain from this section? How would you
   apply them?
   - In your relationships?
   - In your work?
   - In your spiritual pursuits?
   - In other ways?
2. Reflect on passion. How did you view it before and after reading
   this section?
3. Describe a situation when your passion got out of control. What
   did you learn?
4. What causes you to feel a sense of passion? How has it changed
   over time?
5. How do you imagine a passionate evening? Are romance and passion always related? Describe examples where they are and are
   not. Would your partner feel the same?
6. Do you think a romantic evening planned by your partner that
   always finishes with sex started with that motive in mind? How
   would your partner deal with you refusing?
7. How often would you like to be romanced? If it is not often, does
   love lose magic or impact? If you're romanced infrequently, do
   you question strength or depth of love?
8. What are the most romantic things your partner has done? What
   is the most romantic thing you did for someone? What other sug-
   gestions would you make?
9. How would you like to be appreciated in your relationships? (Are
   you already?)
10. How might your sexual passion relate to your spiritual passion
    (or lack thereof)?

11. What are the different sides you recognize in your own passions? What kind of influences do you associate with each of the above passions? (These could be human, related to real-life experiences, dreams or other inspirations.)

12. In what ways has learning more about your passions helped you to better understand your sense of life direction? Do you wish to take a different turn?

Intimacy

> *"Intimacy is being seen and known as the person you truly are."*
>
> —Amy Bloom

> *"Touch is the magic wand of intimacy. Love is keeping in touch."*
>
> —Denis Waitley

Life experience has taught me intimacy is defined by different levels of closeness. It defines all aspects to enriching a sense of completeness. This is a kind of uplifting revelation.

Intimacy is a process, an evolution toward deeper self-understanding.

There was a time when I only viewed intimacy as the physical side to a relationship. I thought the more intimate you were the more sex you had. I came to realize intimacy evolves as you grow to know belief systems beneath the surface, to read subtle nuances in energy, gestures, things that enable you to finish someone's sentences even if you choose not to.

To know yourself or anyone intimately is to sense reasons behind actions. You anticipate, foresee what has not yet happened, but could happen. Intimacy shared by two people defines a couple experience however they define it, in thought or behavior.

For me exploring love and devotion for someone has always been a learning exercise. I gradually grew to feel more comfortable with openness, to express how I feel when I feel it, to share personal thoughts, fears, and desires, and to be able to laugh at myself. It is a sign of self-acceptance to be able to divulge elements of your past, without scaring, intimidating, or frightening others or yourself. Intimacy is about sharing energy and using inner power well.

Intimacy is a choice. As you uncover fears and face them within yourself, you become intimately acquainted with soul and connect differently with yourself, others.

I used to think that how well you know a person was directly related to how much time you spent with them. Then I evolved to realize it is not the quantity but quality of time.

Feelings evolve through shared experience and the mutual desire to grow together. Levels of energy and cords that interconnect define the depth of intimacy.

So we are back to the relevance of the unseen.

It has always been. Reasons exist why you gradually choose to see the unseen.

I find the desire to create intimacy grows as you explore self-expression in words, sounds, gestures, and dreams. When people do things together and desire to do more for and with each other, this affects intimacy, whether it goes stale or continues to evolve.

Inner power grows as you gain self-knowledge. You know things about your behavior, but you often know less about your impetus. Secrets to human interactions relate to past and present relationships. Energy is invisible, but you always sense it.

It comes back to fear again. Some people cannot get enough intimacy. I have known people who want to know everything about me, but refuse to divulge about themselves. Such behavior sends conflicting messages. Couples break up because of too much or too little sex, too much or too little dialogue. Each action offers insight about intimacy and comfort zones.

Energy expands when each person is on a similar wavelength. Imagine an energy grid with crisscrossing lines. Intimacy is like elastic. It stretches in many different directions throughout that energy grid. How energy intersects and at which intensities, determines the nature of relationships. What levels of energy you detect influences when you are prompted to act, how, and what you will share with whom.

To feel good about intimacy implies I behave in ways that promote mental and physical health and well-being. I have known situations where self-assurance and mutual support evolve naturally, but I also know fear reminds you of relationships that did not work. When people manipulate or emit dense energy, you feel uncomfortable with their vibrations.

Intimacy teaches you the power to be found in shared vulnerability. Honesty, trust, love, and patience are key building blocks for creating an environment where intimacy will grow. To sense the energy of these feelings creates safety and security.

So people with dense energies invite me to react positively to uplift them. That is opposite to conditioned fear of being drained. Before I reframed risk as fear in relations, I sensed urges to act, yet held back. As each person has power, he or she decides how to use it.

Your sense of connection to energy vibration is what prompts you to act. Energy vibrates constantly in everything. It reflects beliefs you admit or repress. You are not intimately aware of energy vibrating everywhere. You selectively attune.

It seems my choice to attune to certain energy reflects my willingness to evolve, to learn new things. This desire, when shared, can expand and connect superficially or deeply.

The complexity of inter-connectedness is always open to be explored.

My instinct is to turn to the nature of intimacy that can grow in distance relationships. My own life taught me when partners are physically separated they choose to explore the drawbacks or the benefits of their conditions. They choose to creatively strengthen bonds or give up and decide it is not worth the effort.

More choices always exist than you imagine. You only speak from experience.

My notion of intimacy evolves as I take steps to listen to my intuition and express my true self. I recall when I decided to send questionnaires and request responses from a man I had just met. When we exchanged our answers simultaneously via e-mail, we discovered how many of our responses were identical or very close. That relationship has grown since then.

Human beings need not enter a distance relationship to expand creative abilities and gain insight into the self. As you savor perceived imaginary and real experiences, you realize you create both and expand your sense of what is possible.

To develop intimacy we spoke by phone, wrote handwritten letters, sent photos electronically, and even interacted during night dreams before meeting again in person.

Intimacy grows as you explore the unknown with joy and excitement. It is about harnessing energy. It even permits you to travel through time and space.

I would not believe you if I had not experienced this kind of time travel myself. One incredible example was when I was recording and sharing night time dreams as part of my developing distance romance. In one instance I typed out a scenario about being in an

Asian rice field at lunchtime. I turned to observe a man with a camera on the back of a motorcycle driven by a local man. They drove over pot holes behind a slow truck. When I awoke I e-mailed a detailed dream recollection before my boyfriend phoned to share details of his day. At the time he had no e-mail in Vietnam. He had in fact, been taken on tour by a local man to photograph the area. His shared experience mirrored my dream. This told me my mind was observing him on the other side of the world while my physical body slept somewhere else.

You relate to people on levels that defy human logic. The truth of energy is experienced. You sense when you are with someone even if not in a physical sense.

That kind of repeated experience took my understanding of energy to a new level.

Breakdowns in faith precede any breakthroughs in self-mastery. On basic levels intimacy is experienced as you use senses to detect gestures, tears, and sensations. The external journey unfolds so you give yourself permission to take an inner journey. In spite of where you have been, or how you felt, you relearn energy.

I believe this helps explain why I have powerful urges to contact people. On three separate occasions, I dreams where I felt a pull to phone my grandfather. At the time, he was located 18,000 kilometers away. Each time he needed to hear a voice and I responded

Human beings align with energy flow to balance and strengthen the whole energy field. Healing energy is directed beyond usual ranges of human senses. You do not question reflexes if your physician hits your knee and you kick forward. This is a visible action—reaction. Similarly you have no reason to question your impulses that are attuned to higher energy vibrations, the origin of which you do not see.

I find that my level of inner growth and sense of planes of reality relate to how open I am with my feelings. How comfortable I feel determines how well I adapt to unexpected events in my life. When I choose to disclose intimate aspects of myself to others, I begin to sense feelings differently. I grow to recognize what prevented me from doing so before.

To get to know yourself intimately reveals you have levels of defenses. The simplest form of guidance speaks as discomfort at a particular level. Attuning to energy levels you go through stages of character—building and deconstructing.

Yet I sense different guides. I read signals that tell me to be diligent with certain situations. The pull is so strong inside me to take action or observe that I do not question it.

The process of becoming more attuned to yourself is training for other things.

I would gather that. When I began to experience dreams that involved past lives, I was drawn to seminars that enabled me to learn about past-life regression. They led me to other teachers and deeper exploration of a concept to prepare me for new facets of life work.

Information that flows through a clear channel is often beyond the frequency of a rational mind. Logic sends out its own energy vibrations. As you gain insight into intimacy, you receive information in a non-linear way. You trust what comes.

Intimacy: End of Section Exercises

1. Which lessons do you retain from this section? How would you apply them?
   - In your relationships?
   - In your work?
   - In your spiritual pursuits?
   - In other ways?

2. How in your life have you developed vulnerability or do you shy away from it? Why?

3. How could you be creative with your partner to develop new kinds of intimacy?

4. What kinds of feelings could you develop from sharing such creative experiences?

5. Relate a real or imagined distance relationship story where intimacy was/is nurtured.

6. How has building confidence in one area of your life influenced your journey to know intimacy? If you lack confidence, how might you develop it to strengthen intimacy?

7. Describe your expectations for intimacy in relation to what you've experienced. What has influenced your evolving view?

8. Do you wish to change your real points of reference for intimacy? Why or why not?

9. How do your hopes for developing or changing your experience of real life intimacy relate to your personal relationship patterns and your overall life purpose?

10. How do feelings or experiences of intimacy in some aspects of your life affect your desire and progress to develop intimacy in other areas of your life?

Respect

> *"I feel sometimes as if I am expected to justify life's conditions, when of course they do not need any such justification."*

—Jane Roberts, from Session 896 with Seth, January 16, 1980

> *"I am aware that the deepest inner need any person has is to find his or her way home, to the real self, the divine within."*

—Barbara Ann Brennan

As special consideration for my authentic self grows, I sense shared responsibilities with people I know and do not know. Can you place that? It is like I respect soul differently.

All energy contains consciousness. As you attune to your energy, or anyone else's energy, you actually attune to everything. You express a respect for everything.

I have this growing feeling that to honor one another is a principle of life. You can develop esteem or reverence for a person, based on what they create or how they set an example. Yet what I feel is unrelated. This pertains to relationship bonds on a deeper level.

Respect implies interacting with ease and recognizing the good qualities in each other. This is perceived as fair treatment. It reflects you recognize another person's interests count as much as your own. Respect is to assume individual responsibility for your actions and how they might affect the other person.

I would also say to respect someone is to recognize when sharing certain information is appropriate or inappropriate. It is a feeling. You become willing to respect their wishes if they do not desire you to be around. You choose not to take their mood swings personally.

Respect has energy vibrations. Each has a frequency. You assign meaning.

Okay, so respect develops in the mind in so far as two people wish to communicate and work to be understood. You may choose to listen to another person's views and feelings. Whether or not you and/or your partner support and encourage each other is another example. It is when you feel treated in ways that enable you to feel safe to express yourself.

Whenever two people interact, their energy fields are affected or unaffected.

Right! I think of examples where it is instinctive to refrain from interfering or intruding on someone. In that case respect is like giving someone space, privacy, and time.

To give other human beings what they need is also a way to respect yourself.

Respect: End of Section Exercises

1. Which lessons do you retain from this section? How would you apply them?
   - In your relationships?
   - In your work?
   - In your spiritual pursuits?
   - In other ways?

2. How do you respect or not respect people in your personal relationships?

3. How do you define respect in your personal, work, and spiritual relationships?

4. Describe three experiences where you feel you weren't respected by another person.

5. How did you react? Were you respecting yourself? If not, why not?

6. What did you learn about yourself from these experiences?

7. Recall three situations when a person respected you/your wishes. Were you happy?

8. How do these experiences bring you closer/further from living by your purpose?

Understanding

"A successful life is one that is lived through understanding and pursuing one's own path, not chasing after the dreams of others."

—Chin-Ning Chu

"All truths are easy to understand once they are discovered; the point is to discover them."

—Galileo Galilei

To get a message someone aims to convey is to grasp their intended message.

Each effort to dialogue is an initiative to strengthen or replenish energy.

Two people can appreciate each other's views without having harmony in opinion. Yet understanding does imply willingness to listen, to be tolerant, even agree to disagree.

Acting independently, as in discussing or debating opinions, enables partners to explore and enlighten themselves about the worlds they know. These are as limited or as infinite as they are willing to create. You may believe you understand, yet not.

In my mind this is part of a process where people learn new reasons, attributes, and aspects they value in each other. There exists the mutual desire to connect and exchange energy. As I evolve to perceive as a process, this brings a different motivation to learn.

Teachers speak to you in your thoughts and dreams, echo in self-expression and every choice you ever make. This is a realignment process with your deepest self.

Growth occurs not only through the exchange of energy, but also through reflexive listening and realigning. This means listening and also feeling like one is being heard. The nature of energy exchange is based on a level of involvement.

I do not know how many times I can recall my own experience or hearing from others how someone just did not seem to get an idea or intention. This is a feeling of being situated on a plane of energy. Sometimes you feel incredibly connected. Other times you do not. When you sense you are not heard, you clarify misunderstandings, and/or change the subject.

Your primary models for love and understanding go back to your parents, guardians and other early caregivers. This said, you may find yourself with no functional model or dependable memory for understanding. You connect or do not.

In my mind as understanding evolves to become more widespread, mutual respect will shift energy vibrations. Love teaches people energy exchange requires involvement.

Each experience you choose expands you in ways you do not yet recognize.

Understanding: End of Section Exercises

1. Which lessons do you retain from this section? How would you apply them?
   - In your relationships?

- In your work?
- In your spiritual pursuits?
- In other ways?

2. Reflect on a situation when you felt emotional or confused. What did you do to build new understanding? How is this useful to your quest for deeper life meaning?

3. Who or what are your models for emotional reactions and coping mechanisms?

4. How would you characterize your understanding in relationships?

5. Describe sample situations when you could have been more understanding:

6. Describe situations when someone could have been more understanding.

7. What does this teach you? How does this further your sense of life purpose?

Flexibility

> *"When you cling, life is destroyed; when you hold on to anything, you cease to live."*
>
> ——Anthony de Mello

> *"It's easier to bend the body than the will."*
>
> —Chinese Proverb

Relationships that nurture me deeply teach me the usefulness of being flexible and open-minded. People grow together when they evolve and adapt to changing circumstances. When people do not choose to adapt to each other, then for me, a situation is not as flexible as it could be. People evolve in separate ways. That is good, too.

Much like energy has levels of flow, relationships have levels of growth.

Conditions affect an individual and the couple. People may be willing or unwilling to make changes for each other. My life shows me nurturing relations evolve to stay together.

Reluctance also reflects how much you value another in relation to yourself.

One partner may receive a job offer that requires a move or increased work hours in exchange for higher salary. Both partners may discuss consequences of this potential change. Only they determine if the changes are worth the new salary. So many factors come into play.

If you bring love to conscious awareness, then you adapt automatically with your heart. You make decisions to enable you to feel lighter, in this world and beyond.

Well, not everyone will be so flexible as to adapt to relationships that continue beyond the physical world. Some people grapple with that. They detach or cannot disconnect.

Energy teaches you that bonds remain between human beings in the physical world and human beings who have released the physical. Leave that for a future meditation. To be flexible on many levels does include dimensions beyond yours now.

Through experience people can recognize that ineffective dialogue reduces a partner's understanding and flexibility. If your partner does not seem to listen to you or make shared decisions that take your views into account, then you may rethink impact of job loss, change, or transfer. Practical issues are naturally discussed when couple energy is in sync.

Feelings are an inner psychological force that invites new levels of awareness. Mental and physical flexibility change based on the nature of your consciousness. You may be more flexible during dreams or meditation states than during other mental states. Increased flexibility in one state can carry over to affect other areas.

Flexibility: End of Section Exercises

1. Which lessons do you retain from this section? How would you apply them?
   - In your relationships?
   - In your work?
   - In your spiritual pursuits?
   - In other ways?
2. What would you be willing to adapt in your habits and lifestyle for a relationship? How might you be compelled to reevaluate your priorities, health concerns, etc.?
3. Write qualities or traits in another person that help to give you a sense of balance.
   - How might your partner answer this question?
   - How might a good friend answer this question?
   - How might a relative who knows you/ doesn't know you answer this question?

- How might your children (if you have any) answer this question?
- How compatible would the above answers be? Explain any differences.
- How do your answers compare to what you know of your traits? What does this tell you about how to reinforce and strengthen sources of meaning in your life?

4. Do you think "absence makes a heart grow fonder"? Write about how flexibility helps you deal or could help you better deal with people you miss, grieve for, or have known in the past but are no longer part of your life.

Commitment

> *"Unless commitment is made, there are only promises and hopes; but no plans."*
>
> —Peter Drucker

> *"Passion is the quickest to develop and the quickest to fade. Intimacy develops more slowly, and commitment more gradually still."*
>
> —Robert Sternberg

Commitment is something that I have come to reexamine within myself. How I feel about my commitments reflects how honest I am with myself and others.

When you engage your attention, you are involved without saying.

In terms of relationships this is a pledge or an open promise to share life experiences, and to devote self to the health and well-being of your partner. Theory differs from practice.

Different sides and hidden levels exist to every perception of commitment.

To me the desire to exert effort reveals a level of commitment. The desire to communicate and understand reveals additional levels. People may also share principles, choose to be creative and resourceful. They do what they feel is required to keep the relationship evolving, irrespective of various perceived obstacles. I lose track of levels.

There is no need to measure or define all levels. Simply notice them.

Commitment includes your desire and action to restrict or limit your own freedoms. It is behavior of devotion that would help circumvent harm done to your partner.

Ever-present concern does not have to evolve through outright fear.

As you get to know yourself and each other, you gain insight into how you define your limits and boundaries, what it is safe to say or not, safe to do or not. The parameters of your relationship shape what you will accept or not accept in your partner's behavior.

Increasing personal and external acceptance is always within your grasp.

Commitment assumes both partners have some desire to look after each other.

Energy connection evokes mutual concern and support with ramifications. Psychological patterns completely escape your radar. You are surrounded by clues about your character traits, levels of co-dependence and attraction of energy fields.

Many people desire to be in a committed, intimate relationship, but they do not necessarily know what this is. Through life experience, you can grow to define what feels good and what does not feel good. Commitment is reflected in the choices you make in your life that value yourself and the influence of a partner who's supposed to feel the same way about you and reflect choices accordingly.

Human beings do well in relationships with shared views about the value of commitment. A mutual understanding of where lines are drawn comes with dialogue.

Commitment to relationships can vary. You hear different stories. Some couples are together almost forever and other relationships do not last. My maternal grandparents were married for seventy-two years. I have not known any couples who were married longer.

Regardless of examples that appeal or not, you define your personal context.

Some committed relationships have been prearranged by family, or undertaken by partners for purely social, economic, or other reasons. I know a man who resisted his family's wish for an arranged marriage. He initially knew only pain in partners he chose for himself. Later, he relented and married according to his family's wishes. He was initially surprised how compatible and happy he became in that committed relationship. It worked for him.

Individuals may convince themselves they are in love when they are not. Lying to oneself can be acceptable. Some people do not admit this.

The absence of love expressed by you or for you or your partner defines another kind of commitment. To what or to whom do you commit? Shared interests and desires do not always seal a relationship. Diverging principles and desires do not always break it up either.

Commitment evolves based on love and love expands insight into commitment.

I have known people who are under the impression all their needs will be met by another person without making any efforts themselves. Couples may stay together out of a sense of duty or obligation. Such reasons may reflect loyalty or commitment without love.

Commitment does not require love, yet evolving love requires commitment.

Even with negative images in history and literature, shared intention has been known to motivate two people to stay together. Each person has a responsibility to create a nourishing environment for a relationship to grow.

It is a choice to accept or encourage people to evolve together and alone.

I know people who fear commitment. People can be in relationships for ages and choose not to evolve to the next stage of "going steady," getting engaged and married, or deciding to make shared decisions. They may prefer to change partners frequently.

Your wounds are revealed by reactions. The healing path is echoed by soul. Commitment can be viewed as conscious reunification of your past with your present.

A previous or current partner may have hurt you or appeared to sabotage the relationship. You may have otherwise considered it to be working well. Were you scared of causing a commotion, being noticed differently, or assume your partner might desire to leave? Some people reject each new partner because that is conditioning. This draws attention to how people can choose to learn commitment based on what it is not.

Commitment is learning to connect with people in the moment in ways that draw them out of a mindset of fear. It is about respecting boundaries and behaving in ways that promote balanced energy exchanges. You attune on levels to promote calm.

I have known people who crave attention in relationships, but do not know what to do with it once they have it. They desire and fear commitment at the same time in different settings, even at the prospect of a longer-term physical relationship. They do not admit what they want or why they prevent themselves from getting it.

Words, body language, and vibrations all send messages out on commitment. Anyone can learn to read their own signs. It is a choice to learn to love parts of yourself. It is also a choice to com-mit to learn more about yourself and accept all.

There was a time I desired a long-term partner, but I had unrealistic and unhealthy ideas about suitors. I convinced myself I fell in love with partners who were uninterested in intimacy or commitment. Yet I attracted partners who feared commitment and did not see it.

Any relationship that does not feel right is inviting you to explore energy.

Commitment: End of Section Exercises

1. Which lessons do you retain from this section? How would you apply them?
   - In your relationships?
   - In your work?
   - In your spiritual pursuits?
   - In other ways?
2. What is your notion of commitment to family, friends, and inti-mate relationships?
3. Have you developed a commitment phobia? Or do you know someone who has?
4. What has life taught you about yourself, your patience, and goals for commitment?
5. What kind of relationship commitment interests you?
6. How do you reciprocate this in practice?
7. If you have a partner, how do you think this person would describe commitment?
8. How would you like your ideal partner to demonstrate commit-ment to you?
9. How does your experience compare to your expectations? What have you learned about yourself and others in the past that you can offer as wisdom to a different situation?
10. Describe the characteristics of the intimate partnerships you know (and have known). Include examples of anger, love as you perceive it, why you feel peaceful, valued and/or demoralized (Table 1).
11. What do you learn about your relationship patterns?
12. Which characteristics do you not desire in an intimate partner? Why?

Table 1

Anger	Love	Peaceful	Valued	Demoralized

13. How does your use of time enable you to better know your partner?

14. How would you describe your commitment (or desired commitment) to a partner?

15. What do you (or do you not) do to clarify your understanding of commitment?

16. Describe an experience where you did not feel comfortable with your own commitment and/or someone else's commitment to you. How did you feel? What did you learn?

17. Recall when you felt you were in love then knew you were not. How did you know?

18. What kind of images and life examples around you shape your idea of commitment?

19. Imagine you are a critical partner. How do you feel? What would your behavior tell you about your past relationships? Do you desire closeness with someone destructive?

Values

"When men and women agree, it is only in their conclusions; their reasons are always different."

—George Santayana

"The less you talk, the more you're listened to."

—Abigail Van Buren

As I sense value in all relationships I also sense that when I am ready, the right opportunity will appear to stretch me. Value is what makes choices pertinent, worthwhile.

Value is how you sense something that enriches the overall quality of your life. It draws attention to your capacities and increases understanding of who you are.

So value is like a gauge of my ability to recognize people and situations as helpful opportunities. It is not limited to what I can explain, but opens my evolution and expands my wisdom. A sense of value also motivates me to build trust in unpredictability and uncertainty.

This is what causes you to believe advantages outweigh disadvantages.

Further, it is reason to detect something that comes naturally in me. I think of relationships with people who encourage me to discern, strengthen, and develop innate talents. It compels me to express deep feelings of self-acceptance that I had not expressed as openly before. As a child I recall engaging in ice skating and joining groups empowered some of my skills. This kind of nurturing led me to sense benefits in different choices as I grew up.

Participating in certain activities draws your attention to different areas of the psyche. Stimulation you get helps you to sense meaning in new kinds of energies. The meaning you get out of life any moment stems from your innate value, or core being.

It becomes more apparent how value evolves in relationships as I sense it clearer within myself. Couples develop confidence in each other and develop a notion of a shared purpose. People ask themselves why they stay with someone. The answer is that situation has value for you. In other words, you get something good out of it that prompts you to stay.

Value is first and foremost internal. It manifests those things that enable you to feel more engaged in life. It is that unwritten incentive to engage in things at all.

Revelations about relationship values transform into forms of judgment, too.

Value implies a sense of feeling appreciated and respected. This raises esteem and self-worth issues. Shifting awareness, beliefs ,and priorities help to explain distancing relationships. Yet each relationship is very personal. You define yours.

This reminds me how we can value people on different levels. I think back to a high school party I hosted six months after graduation. Although peers had gone their separate ways, about one hundred reunited to catch up. A year later I hosted another gathering and under ten people showed. This did not mean the rest did not value each other. We had less in common and the value evolved to become a different sort. It also highlights levels of energy.

This teaches you more about the psychology of experience and energy flow.

Values: End of Section Exercises

1. Which lessons do you retain from this section? How would you apply them?
   - In your relationships?
   - In your work?
   - In your spiritual pursuits?
   - In other ways?
2. Recall early in life things you enjoyed but no longer do. Which of these things would you like to engage in again? What do they teach you about what activities you value?
3. What kinds of values have you learned from your various relationships?
4. How would you relate courage and trust to spiritual and intimate relationships?
5. What qualities of your partner do you value? What behaviors do you not value?
6. How do you express to your partner what bothers you? If not, why not?
7. How does your perspective contribute to your sense of purposeful life choices?
8. What do you notice about your choice of partners from each experience (Table 2)?

Table 2

	Positive	Negative	My view of why
Partner #1			
Partner #2			
Partner #3			
Partner #4			

9. Explain how relationships contribute to or take away from your sense of completeness.
10. Do your partner choices draw attention to repeated themes? Key voids in your life?
11. How does such reflection strengthen your sense of life purpose?

Lasting Romance

" Is this not the true romantic feeling; not to desire to escape
life, but to prevent life from escaping you."

—Thomas Wolfe

"To love one's self is the beginning of a life-long romance."

—Oscar Wilde

Another kind of value relates to romance energy. People sense reasons to love others.

Understand the real reasons why you wish to feel closer to another person. You sense part of the person that reflects what you accept and value in yourself.

Each of my romantic experiences has required I slowly realize certain of my illusions. I sensed different kinds of value in each romance. The good feelings remained my focus unless reasons for that sense of value faded. In some cases, I evolved to believe romance was an illusion I created to compensate for things missing in my life. When I arrived at such a conclusion, the romance no longer had the same appeal, but retained intrinsic teaching value.

Each time you experience romance, you grow and evolve as an individual.

Romance gains intangible value based on how I feel I satisfy needs for affection and companionship I sense within. Romance grows from taking time to develop trust. You also grow by knowledge you gain about each other and through each other.

Value is feeling appreciated on your terms. It begins and ends within.

A desire to prolong romance implies you are on a quest toward deeper love and meaning in relations. Writing a romantic book with a partner enabled me to bring this to life.

Romance takes different forms at different life stages. Partners share a desire to develop it and expend mutual effort. You know it when you feel it. This makes effort seem valuable.

Your instinct to reach out to sources of love is rooted in your unconscious. Your unconscious visions evolve based on your childhood and relationship conditioning, how your needs were recognized, satisfied, or not.

Through my journey I grow to value and apply senses I had overlooked. To love and feel loved in return brings unspoken validation. You can do, be, or feel anything you choose.

Lasting Romance: End of Section Exercises

1. Which lessons do you retain from this section? How would you apply them?
   - In your relationships?
   - In your work?
   - In your spiritual pursuits?
   - In other ways?

2. How did your parents express romance? What did they discuss, but rarely/never do?

3. How did your grandparents express their romance? How did they discuss romance?

4. Recall situations where romance has/ hasn't lasted. What issues/ feelings do you see?

5. What would you take away as useful knowledge to apply to your own relationships?

6. In what ways do romantic feelings or actions make you feel self-conscious?

7. How could you nurture chronic excitement, adventure, and change to your love life?

8. Where does romance (or invisible forms of love) fit into your life purpose?

9. What have romantic relationships enabled you to learn about yourself (Table 3)?

Table 3

Partner # (name/ initials)	Examples of romance	What you appreciated	What you didn't like	Patterns (relations/ family)

10. What have you learned about falling in love? How has your notion of romance? What qualities would lasting romance have for you? Do you nurture one? If so, based on your track record, what makes you think it will last? Is this within your control?

11. What things do you think weaken the intensity or vitality of romance?

12. What kinds of struggles have you encountered during romance? How did you deal with them? If you've been discouraged by romance, what did you learn about you?

13. How can your spiritual views and pursuits contribute to your idea of lasting romance?

14. Out of all the available options, why have you chosen your current romantic partner?

15. Describe a romantic experience you would like. List the steps required to create it. Visualize each step. What else will you do to influence this happening?

Reasons You Know

> *"Uncertainty is the only certainty there is, and knowing how to live with insecurity is the only security."*

—John Allen Paulos

> *"Only fools can be certain; it takes wisdom to be confused."*

—Anonymous

Certainty is a myth. The more I learn what gives my life meaning, the more I realize every choice teaches me about energy and a process of reconnecting to love. This feeling expands as I explore relationships, yet my knowledge of love is not limited to that.

Persuasion is an internal exercise. Every possible reality disperses itself in energy. You pick and choose your concerns and blocks, just like health and vitality. You choose conditions that are suitable for the lessons you are ready to learn.

Developing closeness in human relationships is a way to gauge how you feel and whether or not you are where you are meant to be right now. I know like I know just because. Every question I ask helps or complicates. Why do only some people learn how to ask why?

People only ever focus on what they believe matters. You have gained wisdom to proceed further on your path. Being human means you exist on levels where you are unable to sense the true nature of your awareness or state of evolution. What matters to you is to be comfortable with who you sense are and how you live.

In my own mind relationships symbolize a commitment to grow on psychological, emotional, spiritual, and other levels. Beliefs, desires, values, are not all easily reconciled.

Every choice is a step. You feel energy, but register only what you accept.

Each person knows inside if he or she connects to someone or makes another choice for the right reasons. Those which make you feel good also enable other people to feel good.

Devotion to self-growth develops esteem, confidence, and energy awareness.

My love deepens. I travel an unfathomable distance on spiritual planes in order to grasp earthly revelations about this life. Attuning to love involves everything I encounter.

Part of you feels stunned, as if you have just begun to live. You discover a source of inner strength to help you to see clearer, to celebrate the joys and better master your reasons for perceiving challenges. To be you redefines your existence. For now what is unseen in some ways is discerned in others. Your senses are expanding. How you feel, how you attune and create them, shapes what evolves next.

I ask myself what I know. To recognize the presence of higher forces in some form enables me to reframe obstacles and expand healing and growth. This is like soul power.

Discomfort is how the universe reminds you of where you should be and how you are meant to feel. Be more conscious of where you are. Feelings shake you up.

Some people choose conditions based on a false sense of security or ignorance. They choose relationships based on age, assumed compatibility, physical or other motives, without exerting effort to get-to-know themselves. I have learned my own misunderstandings are reason to raise my self-awareness. To feel grounded I do the best I can with gifts I possess.

As you choose to get to know, develop, love, explore, and respect yourself, you begin to explore realities unseen and unrecognized. This is a creative process.

In my own life exploring conditions nurtures a peace and serenity that reassures me. Certain connections will compel you to seek more as impulse, not because people tell you.

Each human being is invited to experience emotional levels to reach a destination of expansion where these experiences take on new significance. Movement is inward and then in numerous directions which defy explanation.

How I connect with people and the world around me has gone through a complete transformation. I sense things I did not even notice before, choices I make and did not know.

You begin to sense more than one of you exists. I do not mean physical clones. Each feeling you choose to experience fragments your sense of self. You are joy and sadness, anger, and pain. You are all the experiences you choose, and far more.

What about you? I feel connected to you, what you say, share, and draw out of me. It is as if you have guided me in ways I am just beginning to discover. When will it end?

Brace yourself. I am yet another reflection of you. As a guide, you can view me as a facet of yourself, all you may yet become and all that you are at this moment. You exist in multiple realms and in multiple energy forms simultaneously. I am but one.

Yet I am not invisible. You help me see that I still have infinite lessons to learn.

The part of you that has incarnated as a physical being forgets more than you realize. When you show me gratitude, you express gratitude for your own existence.

Whoa! You encourage me to experience new levels of the power of synchronicity.

That is a piece of the truth. Self-disclosure is the path to infinity.

Reasons You Know: End of Section Exercises

1. Which lessons do you retain from this section? How would you apply them?
   - In your relationships?
   - In your work?
   - In your spiritual pursuits?
   - In other ways?

2. Reflect on reasons why you do/don't find someone who makes you feel complete.

3. How do you create boundaries and share responsibilities in relationships? How does your behavior compare to your expectations for yourself, friends and/or your partner?

4. How do differences in socioeconomic, political, and religious views influence how you perceive your partner? How do such issues affect your reality and past partners?

5. What are the reasons you are content or not about your family relationships (Table 4)?

6. What does your life experience teach you about connection and compatibility?

7. How do opposing opinions within yourself obscure your sense of self-confidence?

Table 4

Partner/ family	Why this person enriches you	What leads you to feel more complete	Why worry or not?

8. What could you change about you to get more satisfaction out of your relationships?
9. Which perspectives or beliefs do you hold about death and the afterlife?
10. How does this section further your sense of life purpose or direction?
11. How connected do you feel to forces beyond what you know in this world?
12. Have you ever had a supernatural experience? If so, describe it. If not, would you?

Chapter Lessons

SUMMARY

Chapter 1: Lessons:

1. Take responsibility for where you are and how you feel.
2. When you focus on something, you decide that it matters.
3. Find the courage to detach from what you do not need.

Chapter 2: Lessons:

1. The dividends from your efforts arise later than you think.
2. Places of emptiness bring us closer to grasping the imperceptible.
3. To better understand yourself, listen closer to your words.

Chapter 3: Lessons:

1. To dream of the person you would like to be is to waste the person you are.
2. It is always possible to reframe your conditions.
3. What you think is reality differs greatly from the truth.

Chapter 4: Lessons:

1. Your senses empower you to master your visible and hidden self.
2. The soul seeks evolution and experience beyond the physical.
3. The process of raising awareness teaches you learn forever.

Chapter 5: Lessons:

1. Love is so much more than you assume.
2. You constantly expand parts of yourself that you do not see.
3. Gratitude deepens through self-reflection.

Investigative Questionnaire #1

If time was not an issue, what would you wish to study, practice, master, or research on a

- Personal Level: _____
  _____

- Professional level: _____
  _____

- Spiritual level: _____
  _____

- What someone who knows me well might say: _____
  _____

- What someone who knows me superficially might say:_____
  _____

What particular skills or qualities have brought you the compliments on a

- Personal Level: _____
  _____

- Professional level: _____
  _____

- Spiritual level: _____
  _____

- What someone who knows me well might say: _____
  _____

- What someone who knows me superficially might say:_____
  _____

If money wasn't a concern, what would you be willing to do for free on a

- Personal Level: _____
  _____

- Professional level: _____
  _____

- Spiritual level: _____
  _____

- What someone who knows me well might say: _____

- What someone who knows me superficially might say: _____
  _____

What talents, skills and abilities do you have the most confidence in on a

- Personal level: _____
  _____

- Professional level: _____
  _____

- Spiritual level: _____
  _____

- What someone who knows me well might say: _____

- What someone who knows me superficially might say: _____
  _____

Which **THREE** things would you attempt to do if you would not fail on a

- Personal Level: _____
  _____

- Professional level: _____
  _____

- Spiritual level: _____
  _____

- What someone who knows me well might say: _____

- What someone who knows me superficially might say: _____
  _____
  _____

If you only had six months to live (in perfect health), what activities would you do on a

- Personal Level: _____

  _____
- Professional level: _____

  _____
- Spiritual level: _____

  _____
- What someone who knows me well might say: _____

  _____
- What someone who knows me superficially might say:_____

  _____

Describe the "perfect job" (not life) in terms of duties, activities, and responsibilities on a

- Personal Level: _____
- Professional level: _____

  _____
- Spiritual level: _____

  _____
- What someone who knows me well might say: _____
- What someone who knows me superficially might say:_____

  _____

What activities give you the greatest pleasure, make you feel the happiest, give you the most fulfillment and peace of mind on a

- Personal Level: _____

  _____
- Professional level: _____

  _____
- Spiritual level: _____

  _____
- What someone who knows me well might say: _____

  _____
- What someone who knows me superficially might say:_____

  _____

  _____

Which skills/ activities/ themes are apparent in your above answers on a

- Personal Level: _____
  _____

- Professional level: _____
  _____

- Spiritual level: _____
  _____

- What someone who knows me well might say: _____
  _____

- What someone who knows me superficially might say: _____
  _____

Do you think the personal reward would be worth the commitment to this dream on a

- Personal level: _____
- Professional level: _____
- Spiritual level: _____
- What someone who knows me well might say: _____
- What someone who knows me superficially might say: _____

What would you be willing to sacrifice (change habits, decisions) to realize a goal on a

- Personal level: _____
  _____

- Professional level: _____
  _____

- Spiritual level: _____
  _____

- What someone who knows me well might say: _____
  _____

- What someone who knows me superficially might say: _____
  _____

Have you envisioned yourself doing this? How would it affect your current life on a

- Personal level: _____
  _____
  _____

- Professional level: _____

- Spiritual level: _____

- What someone who knows me well might say: _____

- What someone who knows me superficially might say:_____

- If your conditions changed would you still pursue this dream?__

Is this goal/dream you've isolated something you FEEL you MUST do on a
- Personal Level:_____

- Professional level: _____

- Spiritual level: _____

- What someone who knows me well might say: _____

- What someone who knows me superficially might say:_____

If higher forces (God) were to tell you right now that it would be possible to accomplish something during this lifetime on earth, what would you wish it to be on a
- Personal level: _____

- Professional level: _____

- Spiritual level: _____

- What someone who knows me well might say: _____

- What someone who knows me superficially might say:_____

What could God do with you, for you, through you, in you, for the
rest of your life on a
- Personal level: _____
  _____
- Professional level: _____
  _____
- Spiritual level: _____
  _____
- What someone who knows me well might say: _____
  _____
- What someone who knows me superficially might say: _____
  _____

What are you confident in doing now that you knew nothing of a few
years ago? _____

What do your view as your greatest opportunities at this moment
on a
- Personal level: _____
  _____
- Professional level: _____
  _____
- Spiritual level: _____
  _____
- What someone who knows me well might say: _____
  _____
- What someone who knows me superficially might say: _____
  _____

Which ideas have you dismissed lately? Why? on a
- Personal level: _____
  _____
- Professional level: _____
  _____
- Spiritual level: _____
  _____
- What someone who knows me well might say: _____
  _____
- What someone who knows me superficially might say: _____
  _____

Which talents and/or abilities seem to naturally flow out of you on a

- Personal level: _____

  _____

- Professional level: _____

  _____

- Spiritual level: _____

  _____

- What someone who knows me well might say: _____

  _____

- What someone who knows me superficially might say:_____

  _____

In which areas or endeavors do you normally produce appealing results? _____

What do you think about when you lie awake at night just staring at the ceiling on a

- Personal level: _____

  _____

- Professional level: _____

  _____

- Spiritual level: _____

  _____

- What someone who knows me well might say: _____

  _____

- What someone who knows me superficially might say:_____

  _____

What kinds of needs, opportunities, activities and ideas really motivate you on a

- Personal level: _____

  _____

- Professional level: _____

  _____

- Spiritual level: _____

  _____

- What someone who knows me well might say: _____

  _____

- What someone who knows me superficially might say: _____
  _____

What issues or things deeply concern you on a
- Personal level: _____
  _____

- Professional level: _____
  _____

- Spiritual level: _____
  _____

- What someone who knows me well might say: _____
  _____

- What someone who knows me superficially might say: _____
  _____

What dreams are almost impossible to put out of your head?_____
  _____
  _____
  _____

Which activities, skills, or ideas keep repeating on a
- Personal level: _____
  _____

- Professional level: _____
  _____

- Spiritual level: _____
  _____

- What someone who knows me well might say: _____
  _____

- What someone who knows me superficially might say: _____
  _____

Why do I really wish to pursue the goal(s) I've isolated in the previous question on a
- Personal level: _____
  _____

- Professional level: _____
  _____

- Spiritual level: _____
  _____

- What someone who knows me well might say: _____
_____
- What someone who knows me superficially might say:_____
_____

Am I aspiring to these goals for my own selfish desires on a
- Personal level: _____
_____
- Professional level: _____
_____
- Spiritual level: _____
_____
- What someone who knows me well might say: _____
_____
- What someone who knows me superficially might say:_____
_____

What kinds of things will I prioritize if I undertake the goals I've isolated?_____
_____

Would I feel as though I could use my discerned gifts if I pursue such goals on a
- Personal level: _____
_____
- Professional level: _____
_____
- Spiritual level: _____
_____
- What someone who knows me well might say: _____
_____
- What someone who knows me superficially might say:_____
_____

Would pursuing these goals bring out the best in me as a person on a
- Personal level: _____
_____
- Professional level: _____
_____

- Spiritual level: _____

- What someone who knows me well might say: _____

- What someone who knows me superficially might say: _____
  _____
  _____

List five changes that you are observing in your life on a
- Personal level: _____

- Professional level: _____

- Spiritual level: _____

- What someone who knows me well might say: _____

- What someone who knows me superficially might say: _____
  _____
  _____

What would you like the world to be like? _____
_____
_____
_____
_____

What are your greatest fears on a
- Personal level: _____

- Professional level: _____

- Spiritual level: _____

- What someone who knows me well might say: _____

- What someone who knows me superficially might say: _____
  _____
  _____

When I was a child, the hobbies, interests, ideals, and mentors that were most important to me at various ages were (take opportunity to refer back to photos or other material if desired):

- Before age nine
Hobbies-Interests-Ideals-Music-Mentor

_____

_____

- Between age nine and twelve years old
Hobbies-Interests-Ideals-Music-Mentor

_____

_____

- From age thirteen to fifteen years old
Hobbies-Interests-Ideals-Music-Mentor

_____

_____

- From age fifteen to eighteen years old
Hobbies-Interests-Ideals-Music-Mentor

_____

_____

- From age nineteen to twenty-one years old
Hobbies-Interests-Ideals-Music-Mentor

_____

_____

- From age twenty-one to twenty-five- years old
Hobbies-Interests-Ideals-Music-Mentor/inspiration

_____

_____

- From age twenty-five to twenty-nine years old
Hobbies-Interests-Ideals-Music-Mentor

_____

_____

- From age twenty-nine to thirty-two years old
Hobbies-Interests-Ideals-Music-Mentor

_____

_____

- Beyond age thirty-two years old
Hobbies-Interests-Ideals-Music-Mentor

_____

_____

If you had to give three messages to the people of the world which for you were the most important guidelines for them to live by they would be?_____

_____

_____

If you had three wishes from a genie, what would you ask for? _____

_____

_____

If your children asked you why we live, why we are on this planet, what is the purpose of life, what their goals should be in this life, how would you answer them? _____

_____

_____

_____

What would you describe as your talents and abilities which come naturally to you? _____

_____

_____

In which situations have you felt the greatest satisfaction, fulfillment or sense of comfort with yourself and the world around you? _____

_____

_____

What kinds of activities or situations bring you joy? _____

_____

_____

What is it that you think you are best equipped to offer to your fellow man? _____

_____

_____

What talents, abilities, or character traits would you like to develop
further? _____

_____

_____

If stranded on an island, what ten things would you choose to have
with you and why? _____

_____

_____

If stranded on another planet, what would you take or wish to have
with you and why? _____

_____

_____

Investigative Questionnaire #2

(TO BE COMPLETED AFTER #1 ANSWERS EXCHANGED)

Y___ N___ Were my answers what you expected?

Y___ N___ Was there any answer that was totally unexpected (pleasantly)?

Y___ N___ Was there any answer that was totally unexpected (unpleasantly)?

Y___ N___ Do you feel my responses were in sync with your expectations?

Y___ N___ Do you feel my responses were in sync with yours?

Y___ N___ Do you feel I answered the questions with enough detail?

Y___ N___ Do any of my answers disappoint you?

Y___ N___ Do you have any regrets about sending me the questionnaire?

Y___ N___ Has your perception of me changed?

What do you perceive my reaction to your answers was (1) very positive (2) positive (3) no reaction (4) negative (5) very negative _____

Y___ N___ Do you think anything in your answers disappointed me?

Y___ N___ Did you have second thoughts about any of your answers but sent them anyway?

Y___ N___ Did you have second thoughts about any answer and withheld it?

New questions separate from last questionnaire.

If higher forces offered you a chance to achieve personal goals of love, romance, marriage with a partner who meets your expectations, and having children but to do so you would leave earth twenty years early. Not knowing when you would die, what would you choose? __

_____

_____

_____

If the same choice was given but on about work fulfillment, which option would you choose?_____

_____

_____

If you could choose between totally fulfilling your personal OR professional goals, or partially fulfilling both with major compromises, which would you choose and why? _____

_____

_____

If you achieve your goal of romance and a loving marriage but did not have triplets but instead had three children over a period of six years. This would make any chance of fulfilling your professional goals difficult as it would have you out of the system for up to twelve years. Would you stop after the first child to allow you to combine both family life and work or pour your energy into home life? _____

_____

_____

If higher forces gave you a "shopping list for life" with a strict condition that once filled out it is unchangeable and must be followed in order one item per year. What ten items would you add one (first) to ten. This list can include emotions, career path, personal needs, and global needs, but no material items. _____

_____

_____

How would you assign priority (1-10) to career advancement, recognition in field, spiritual fulfillment, children, marriage, romance, travel, time alone, family time, and other._____

_____

_____

From what you currently know of me, what three things would you change? _____

_____

_____

From what you currently know of me, what things would you never want to change?_____

_____

_____

What do you think I may want to change in you?_____

_____

_____

If you could ask me one question that I must answer what would it be?_____

_____

_____

If you wished upon a shooting star tonight, where would you wish to be and doing what? _____

_____

_____

Why did you decide to pick up this book, answer questions and exchange them?_____

_____

_____

Do you find the exercises helpful? Do the answers you read meet your own expectations?_____

_____

_____

How have the answers you've read about yourself and your partner increased or decreased your faith in your instincts? _____

_____

_____

Are you deterred from moving to the last questionnaire or do you feel excited about what you may learn about yourself, your partner, and others as the result? _____

_____

_____

What is the most memorable group of answers you read about your partner from the initial questionnaire and why? Feel free to refer to more than one question and how it strengthens or weakens your sense of connection. _____

_____

_____

_____

_____

Investigative Questionnaire #3

This questionnaire explores how you would like to remember your partner in life or another specific loved one when this person passes on. How you perceive this person, how well you actually know him/her, as well as what you'd like to get to know more about will likely reveal itself in comparing and discussing your answers later on.

1. a: If money isn't a concern, and you were responsible for commemorating your loved one's death, what kind of marker would you choose and why? What about for yourself?
   b: What would you write on your loved one's marker? What do you desire on yours?

2. a: If you wouldn't choose a marker, explain what you would do as an alternative.
   b: If you didn't wish to have a marker, explain what you'd prefer as an alternative.

3. a: Write your an obituary/ celebratory piece for your partner meant to be published in a newspaper.
   b: Write the kinds of things you'd like to have mentioned in your obituary/ celebratory piece about a life achievement.

4. a: Write your partner's eulogy.
   b: Write the kinds of things you'd like people to remember about you in a eulogy.

5. a: Describe where you think your partner would like to be buried, (ashes stored/sent) or where you'd choose to bury the remains. Why? If you're unsure, what would you do?

b: Describe where you'd like to be buried (or ashes stored/sent) and why.

6. a: What gesture, ceremony or event might you consider to commemorate your loved one's passing/celebratory event (marriage/retirement)? Who would you wish to involve? Where would it take place?b: Answer the same questions with yourself in mind and your own wishes.

7. a: What would you choose to do for your partner apart from typical cemetery rituals?
   b: What would you like to have done in honor of your passing outside typical rituals?

8. a: Do you think your partner believes in reincarnation? How does this influence his or her view on life and death?
   b: Do you believe in reincarnation? How does this impact your view of life and death?

9. a: If you're partner died unexpectedly, what would you wish you'd said to that person while they were still alive?
   b: If you died unexpectedly, what might you liked to have said, but didn't?

10. Go back and answer all questions 1-9, but imagine you do it for yourself.

When you have finished, share answers with your partner or another person concerned. Consider what your answers reveal about how you perceive one another, as well as what kind of assumptions you both have. Consider this in light of how you wish to be perceived by this person and what kind of identity you wish to portray outside yourself. What does this tell you about your energy fields? What do you notice? Are you aligned? Aligning? Out-of-sync? What are you prompted to do about this?

Printed in the United Kingdom by
Lightning Source UK Ltd., Milton Keynes
138972UK00001B/138/P